FC NG
UR

THE Hillier GARDENER'S GUIDES

PLANTING FOR COLOUR

Susan Chivers

David and Charles

A DAVID & CHARLES BOOK
David & Charles is a subsidiary of F+W (UK) Ltd.,
an F+W Publications Inc. company
First published in the UK in 2005

A catalogue record for this book is available from the British Library.
ISBN: 0 7153 2025 4

Printed in Singapore by KHL Printing Co Pte Ltd
for David & Charles
Brunel House Newton Abbot Devon

Produced for David & Charles by
OutHouse Publishing, Winchester, Hampshire SO22 5DS

Series Consultant Andrew McIndoe

For OutHouse Publishing:
Series Editor Sue Gordon
Art Editor Robin Whitecross
Editor Polly Boyd
Design Assistant Caroline Wollen
Proofreader Audrey Horne
Indexer June Wilkins

For David & Charles:
Commissioning Editor Mic Cady
Art Editor Sue Cleave
Production Beverley Richardson

Visit our website at www.davidandcharles.co.uk

David & Charles books are available from all good bookshops; alternatively you can contact our Orderline on (0)1626 334555 or write to us at FREEPOST EX2 110, David & Charles Direct, Newton Abbot, TQ12 4ZZ (no stamp required UK mainland).

ORNAMENTAL PLANT OR PERNICIOUS WEED?

In certain circumstances ornamental garden plants can be undesirable when introduced into natural habitats, either because they compete with native flora, or because they act as hosts to fungal and insect pests. Plants that are popular in one part of the world may be considered undesirable in another. Horticulturists have learned to be wary of the effect that cultivated plants may have on native habitats and, as a rule, any plant likely to be a problem in a particular area if it escapes from cultivation is restricted and therefore is not offered for sale.

Contents

INTRODUCTION 6

INTRODUCING COLOUR IN THE GARDEN

Garden design through the ages 10
Colour theory 18
Speaking botanically 22
The impact of light 24
Colour in the past and present 26
Scale and distance 32

COLOURS

Black 38
Blue 40
Green 42
Yellow 44
Orange 46
Red 48
Pink 50
Violet 52
White 54
Grey and silver 56

MOODS

Calming 60
Exciting, vibrant 64
Dramatic 68
Subtle 72
Sophisticated 76

SITUATIONS

Town gardens 82
Country gardens 86
Seaside gardens 92
Woodland gardens 94
Water gardens 98
Hard landscaping 102
Containers 106

SEASONS

Early spring 112
Late spring 122
Early summer 134
Late summer 148
Autumn 160
Winter 172

AUTHOR'S CHOICE: favourite colour planting groups 182

Index 184

Introduction

I became a gardener because I had to. Faced with an old cottage garden that had been neglected for years, I started gardening over 30 years ago with a distinct lack of enthusiasm and scant knowledge. Much to my amazement, my enforced labour proved to be the most satisfying of pastimes and it wasn't long before I experienced a sort of Damascene conversion that opened my eyes to the wonderful world of plants.

With unbridled enthusiasm I set about filling my patch with small trees, shrubs, perennials, bulbs, fruit trees and vegetables – anything that took my fancy. Luckily, this random, untutored approach did not result in too awful a picture; I ended up with an archetypal cottage garden with its own higgledy-piggledy kind of charm, but, no doubt, it would have been a much more exciting and satisfying one had I known even a little about colour theory and how to use plants to create specific colour effects. In those days I was happy simply growing anything, and the terms colour harmonies, contrasts, shades, tones, saturation and intensity had yet to enter my lexicon. It was only later, when I began to read the works of great gardening writers such as Gertrude Jekyll, Russell Page, Penelope Hobhouse, Rosemary Verey and Christopher Lloyd, and started visiting gardens of all kinds, that I began to appreciate that there is much more to making a good garden than simply building up a collection of plants.

Today, as a writer and lecturer on garden-related subjects, I am often asked about colour, and it strikes me that there are many amateur gardeners who are somewhat intimidated by the thought of working with colour. Some people are at a loss as to how to make their garden colourful throughout the year, while others simply find putting colour schemes together difficult. Moreover, I find that many gardeners have definite colour preferences, and they want me to suggest plants to fit into their particular schemes. Others, often urban gardeners, have problems finding colourful plants for shade, and there are some country gardeners who are perplexed about how they can blend their gardens into the landscape beyond. With the emphasis now on gardens used as outside rooms, there are also people keen to know how to use colour to create specific moods.

In writing *Planting for Colour* I have tried to address some of these questions, but principally my aim has been to illuminate this somewhat complex subject and encourage readers to cast aside their prejudices and be more willing to experiment with colour. Researching and writing this book has certainly made me re-examine my own garden.

Susan Chivers

CHOOSING PLANTS FOR COLOUR

Plants are seductive and it is all too easy to buy them on impulse without giving thought as to whether they are suited to their soil. In the same way, it is all too easy to be so intent on creating a colour scheme and including certain plants that you fail to take into consideration their specific cultivation requirements. The secret of good gardening is providing a plant with ideal growing conditions. There is little point selecting a plant for a scheme if your soil is alkaline and the plant is an acid-lover as it will never thrive. A poor performer will ruin your carefully thought-out effect. Also, make sure that you are not including sun-loving plants for shady areas or shade-loving plants for hot, dry sites. Plants whose native habitats are scrub or grassland where fertility levels are low, such as prairie-type perennials and grasses, should not be planted in fertile soils, as this will encourage them to make leaves at the expense of flowers, and a colour scheme dependent on their flowers will be spoiled. On the other hand, those plants that need fertile, humus-rich soil should always be grown in soil that is in peak condition. Flowering times must be taken into consideration too. Some plants flower over a long period, while others are over in a week and their decline will change the look of a scheme. For this reason it is worth including plants with attractive leaves that will fill the gaps left by short-lived flowers.

In choosing the plants for this book I have selected some of my favourites but have also borne in mind the plants' 'garden worthiness'. Many of them have a ♀ symbol after their names. This denotes that they have been awarded the Royal Horticultural Society's Award of Garden Merit (AGM). Plants awarded this have proved to be easy to grow, resilient, and relatively resistant to pests and diseases. While an AGM denotes quality, a lack of it should not deter you from growing other plants.

LEFT: *Papaver somniferum* 'Black Paeony'.

INTRODUCING COLOUR IN THE GARDEN

To use colour successfully in a garden, it is necessary not only to grasp something of colour theory but also to have an awareness of the importance that colour has played in gardens of the past and how its use differed from today. Gardeners also need to be aware of how changing light affects colour, and how best it can be utilized to enhance a garden's size and shape, as well as its mood.

RIGHT: *Cirsium rivulare* 'Atropurpureum' backed by *Hesperis matronalis*.

Frescoes like this one in Pompeii, Italy, dating from the 1st century CE, give us an idea of the kind of formal and predominantly green gardens that were made in ancient Roman times.

Garden design through the ages

We take colour in our gardens very much for granted, not always appreciating that only comparatively recently has it assumed such a high level of importance. Plant breeders today are constantly producing new cultivars in an amazing diversity of colours, which means that modern-day gardeners can devise planting schemes in a variety of styles and moods. This wide choice was not available to the majority of our gardening ancestors.

From the writings of Pliny the Younger (*c.*62–113 CE) we know that the ancient Romans were accomplished gardeners, yet they tended to regard plants as raw materials – like stone or marble – to be trained, trimmed and clipped to fit into the formal designs that were characteristic of their gardens. Green was the principal colour at this time.

In the medieval era the most resourceful gardeners were monks and nuns, but they grew plants for food and for medicinal purposes rather than for their decorative qualities. Tapestries of the period reveal that flowers such as roses, lilies, violets, irises, hollyhocks, peonies, lavender, periwinkles and columbines were grown at the time, although sometimes it seems they were valued more for their symbolism than their beauty. Colour certainly didn't feature in the first gardening book written in English – *The Feate of Gardening*, by Jon Gardener, written in 1440 – in which the writer instructs his readers on how best to grow wild herbs and a few vegetables, plants that are hardly likely to make a garden a riot of colour.

Some flowers, including roses, have been cultivated since antiquity, but for centuries they were grown principally for their symbolic meaning, or for medicinal or culinary purposes, rather than for their aesthetic qualities. In the Middle Ages, for example, roses were cooked and served with honey.

TUDOR AND ELIZABETHAN GARDENS

Flamboyant colour was a feature of the gardens at Hampton Court and Nonsuch near Ewell, in Surrey, created for Henry VIII. However, it was the brightly coloured artefacts such as banqueting pavilions, painted seats, arbours, fences and gilded heraldic beasts on long

This baroque fountain at Het Loo Palace in Holland illustrates how elaborate gardens had become by the 17th century, but colour was often in artefacts rather than plants. Tulips, which arrived in Europe from Turkey in the 1500s, began to be grown solely for their beauty, making gardens more colourful.

posts, rather than the plants, that would have dazzled visitors. The gardens of the Tudor monarch were designed to reflect his brilliance, but there was no such splendour for the more humble of his subjects, whose gardens would have been used primarily for growing food.

All this was to change, however, when Elizabethan navigators and explorers returned home with plants and seeds from all over the known world. This influx of new plant material began to transform British gardens and, in the process, made them much more colourful. For the first time, individual plants became the focus of interest

Green was the principal colour in the large parterres of beds lined with box (*Buxus sempervirens*) that were made, often in complex patterns, in grand gardens in France, Holland and England in the 17th century.

and a new breed of plant connoisseurs, notably John Gerard and the John Tradescants, father and son, created gardens full of rarities. By the time James I became king in 1603, a keen English gardener was able to acquire and grow an array of colourful flowering plants, including tulips, bearded irises, dog's tooth violets, hyacinths, anemones and bulbs such as narcissi.

17TH-CENTURY FORMALITY

During the 17th century, people with money and power were, for the most part, preoccupied with making grand gardens as a mark of their status; although good plantsmanship was not lost, the interest in growing unusual and interesting plants was kept alive by only a minority of gardeners. With the Restoration of King Charles II in England in 1660, French gardens became the vogue. The Frenchman André Mollet began transforming the gardens at the London palaces of Whitehall and St James's Park for Charles II. At nearby Hampton Court he began the canal, the Long Water. Later, after the accession of William and Mary in 1688, Dutch gardens (which were strongly influenced by the French) came into favour.

Both French and Dutch styles were formal and, as in all formal gardens, the predominant colour was green. Some colour was provided by flowering shrubs and

Many 18th-century artistocrats in Britain created landscapes, complete with grand buildings and artefacts like this Palladian bridge in Prior Park, in Bath. Older gardens were frequently destroyed in the process.

RARE PLANTSMAN

The London apothecary John Parkinson was a connoisseur of plants. In 1629, he published *Paradisi in Sole, Paradisus Terrestris* – a rich source of knowledge about 17th-century garden design and the plants grown at the time. What makes it unique for its day is that Parkinson demonstrates a love of flowers for their own sake and argues that they are worthy of growing solely for their beauty.

Left: *Alcea rosea*, the original hollyhock, is mentioned by Parkinson.

choice flowers, but it was the greens of hedges, topiary and trees that contributed most. We can see a late 17th-century, Dutch-inspired garden at Hampton Court today, as the King's Privy Garden has been restored to its original splendour.

18TH-CENTURY LANDSCAPES

The famous landscapers of the mid-18th century – Charles Bridgeman, William Kent and Lancelot (Capability) Brown – were commissioned to produce harmonious settings for the grand houses of their patrons. Each in his own way produced schemes where there was an interplay between landscape, water, buildings and trees, and so once again green was the predominant colour of their creations. (At Rousham in

Oxfordshire, perhaps William Kent's finest garden, there is a range of greens provided by evergreens and deciduous trees, but virtually no other colours.) However, it is a misconception to believe that 18th-century English landscape gardens always lacked flowers and shrubs. It is true that they were often confined to walled gardens away from public view, but by the 1750s the word shrubbery had become commonplace and shrubberies began to appear in even the grandest of gardens. In some they played a pivotal role, for example at Painshill Park, the Hon. Charles Hamilton's garden in Surrey.

Hamilton planted vast numbers of 'new' plants from America to create colourful shrubberies for his many visitors to admire – it was a style much ahead of its time. Thomas Whateley, in his *Observations on Modern Gardening*, published in 1770, described Painshill as 'a park happily united with the capital beauties of a garden', and it is now generally agreed that at Painshill, Hamilton successfully melded landscape with colourful shrubberies, setting in train the fashions of the 19th-century English garden.

Colour certainly played a part in the gardens created by Humphry Repton, the last of the great 18th-century landscapers. Recognizing that tastes were moving away from the pure landscape of the mid-18th century, Repton remodelled his clients' parks and made them more 'gardenesque'. He achieved this by introducing flower gardens and shrubberies near the main house and by having less structured planting farther away, blending these more natural plantings seamlessly into the landscape.

INSTANT TRANSFORMATIONS

Humphry Repton (1752–1818), who described himself as a 'landscape gardener', was a marketing genius. In his famous 'Red Books', he invented a way of demonstrating his design ideas to prospective patrons. The books contained watercolour sketches of the existing grounds, which could be altered by the turning of flaps or the pulling of tabs to show how they would look after his suggestions had been carried out. Such was the success of his practice that during his career he designed 330 gardens throughout Britain, some of which survive, for example Endsleigh in Devon.

19TH-CENTURY FLAMBOYANCE

England at the start of the 19th century was becoming increasingly affluent as industrialization of the country grew apace. While, for the most part, the working class lived in appalling conditions, the upper and emerging middle classes had money to spend and were keen to improve their properties and gardens. The age of ostentation had arrived and, with it, a desire for colour in the home and the garden. Rich patrons commissioned the building of grand terraces and parterres around their

Affluent landowners in the 19th century often displayed their wealth by commissioning architects to make them grand gardens with elaborate terraces and parterres, like this one at Bowood House, in Wiltshire.

country houses from architects such as Sir Charles Barry and William Andrews Nesfield, and it became the fashion for the beds in parterres to be bedded out with annuals twice or three times a year. 'Carpet bedding', as it was called, relied on the skill of head gardeners who, armed with improving technology – it was now possible to heat glasshouses reliably – could produce vast numbers of plants as and when they were needed to create the sensationally colourful displays.

The most colourful and popular plants used for bedding schemes were from South America and included zinnias, calceolarias, petunias, verbenas and *Salvia splendens*. To start with, the displays were mixtures of plants, but gradually it became the fashion to group similar plants together in large, single-colour masses. The schemes were usually planned with contrasting colours, and to our eyes many would have seemed garish or daring in the extreme. Their colouring zenith was reached in the 1840s and 1850s, for by the end of the 1860s bedding schemes were more restrained and the colours more muted. Foliage rather than flowers became the vogue, with succulents such as echeverias, sempervivums and sedums used to create the patterns, some of which were as intricate as the designs on oriental carpets. George Thomson, the superintendent of the park at Crystal Palace, in London, once created a design, using succulents, featuring six species of butterfly.

A MORE NATURAL APPROACH

While large, prestigious gardens and parks were still full of vast bedding schemes in the 1860s, there were some gardeners advocating more naturalistic styles of planting. Gardening writer the Reverend Shirley Hibberd led the field, and he had very definite views about the use of colour. He suggested that his readers should try growing plants with neutral colours and eschew those with primary ones; he dismissed repetitive plantings of vividly coloured plants, such as scarlet pelargoniums with yellow calceolarias, as tasteless; and he declared that bedding schemes were vastly overrated.

Hibberd's ideas led the way for William Robinson, the high prophet of naturalistic planting, who published his ground-breaking book *The Wild Garden* in 1870. Robinson loathed the artificiality of the bedding system and, with missionary zeal, set himself the task of changing the way the world gardened. Robinson's premise was that plants grown in a garden should be given the same conditions they would have enjoyed in the wild, and that native and exotic plants should be planted together in woods, on the edge of woodland and in meadows, as well as in the more conventional setting of a bed or a border. This ecological approach seems utterly sensible to us today, but at the time Robinson was writing it was considered radical. However, Robinson, who tried out many of his ideas in his own garden at Gravetye Manor, in West Sussex, soon had an army of followers who began to change and develop gardens following his principles.

The trend towards more naturalistic gardens began in the late 1800s, especially after William Robinson's *The Wild Garden* appeared in 1870.

While Robinson was not primarily a colourist, his ideas were adopted by those who were, and they in turn had a significant influence on the way that gardens developed during the 20th century.

THE 20TH-CENTURY COLOURISTS

In the latter years of the 19th century the Arts & Crafts Movement was gaining ground in Britain, and Robinson's ideas were very much in accord with their beliefs. However, the gardens made by members of the movement harked back to medieval times, when clipped hedges, trellis-covered rose bowers and beds full of simple flowers such as hollyhocks and columbines provided the perfect setting for a troubadour to woo his maiden. This was the style taken up by perhaps the greatest English colourist gardener, Gertrude Jekyll, who modified and expanded it to embrace her views on the use of colour and planting.

Miss Jekyll trained as an artist when young, and this gave her great insights into how to use colour. In the gardens she designed she planted reds, yellows and oranges together, and used blues and yellows as contrasts. In the long herbaceous borders for which she was renowned she advocated planting hotter colours at

After 1889 Edwin Lutyens and Gertrude Jekyll collaborated in designing over 100 gardens in which Lutyens, an architect, designed the hard landscaping and artefacts, like this seat at Hestercombe, Somerset.

the centre and cooler colours at the ends, so that as one walked along them the colours rose in a crescendo and then tailed off to a muted ending. As a friend and disciple of Robinson, she was in accord with his ideas about plants and the wild garden.

Gertrude Jekyll was already well known in gardening circles when she met the architect Edwin Lutyens in 1889. They began working together straightaway, designing houses and gardens in a partnership that lasted 20 years and during which they completed over 100 commissions. Such was their brilliance that their collaborations came to be recognized as the epitome of good taste and set the standard for many years to come. Lutyens designed the houses and the layout of the gardens, including their structural elements such as paths, pergolas, pools, terraces and steps, while Miss Jekyll designed the planting that owed much to the romantic ideal of the cottage garden, with masses of plants spilling out of borders and draping pergolas and walls. Today, their work can be seen in restored gardens such as those at Hestercombe, in Somerset, and at The Manor House, Upton Grey, in Hampshire.

In 1907, Lawrence Johnston bought the land for the garden at Hidcote, Gloucestershire, and in the 1920s and 1930s Vita Sackville West and Harold Nicolson designed their gardens in Long Barn and Sissinghurst Castle, in Kent. When they began making their famous gardens, they followed the precepts for planting and for the use of colour fostered by Robinson and Jekyll. Hidcote's Red Borders and the Sissinghurst White Garden have become world-famous, and paved the way for the fashion for single-coloured, themed borders and for colourist gardens.

Today, there are numerous examples of gardeners demonstrating the art of using colour in the garden. Nori and Sandra Pope's garden at Hadspen, in Somerset, started in the 1980s, features monochrome plantings; Marylyn Abbott's historic garden at the National Trust's West Green House, in Hampshire, which she began restoring in the mid-1990s, is renowned for its flamboyant and exciting use of colour; and Pam Lewis's garden at Sticky Wicket, in Dorset, is admired for its colourist naturalistic plantings.

Miss Jekyll was an accomplished gardener by the time she met Lutyens. Since she had trained as an artist in her youth, she had a particular interest in colour theory. Her planting schemes, many of which were on a grand scale, reflected this.

Colour theory

It goes without saying that colour is a vital ingredient of all gardens, and learning how to use it to best advantage adds another string to a gardener's bow. Colour not only makes gardens more interesting, it creates their mood. A skilful gardener can use colour to manipulate space, for example by making small gardens seem larger or large gardens more intimate.

If a light beam is passed through a prism the beam is split into separate and distinct colours, the colours we see in a rainbow. These colours are red, orange, yellow, green, blue and violet, and they are known as the 'spectrum'.

While we can see all the colours of the rainbow, in fact our eyes' retinas contain light-sensitive cells, called cones, that can distinguish only three colours: red, yellow and blue. These are known as the primary colours of the spectrum. The other colours that we see in a rainbow – orange, green and violet – we see because they are mixtures of the three primary colours. These are called secondary colours. Anyone who has mixed paints knows that mixing red with yellow produces orange, while yellow and blue produces green, and mixing red and blue makes violet. By altering the amounts of red to yellow when trying to produce an orange colour, blue and yellow when making green, and red and blue making violet, it is possible to produce an enormous number of different oranges, greens and violets. Likewise, the spectrum is really composed of an infinite number of colours, although at a glance we can pick out only a few.

COLOUR WHEEL

If the colours of the spectrum are painted side by side to produce a coloured band, and the band is then bent to make a circle, the resulting structure is called a colour wheel. Half the wheel is composed of hot or warm colours, such as red, orange and yellow, and the other half consists of cold or cool colours, including blues, greens, violets and indigos. The colour wheel's main use for gardeners is to demonstrate the differences between harmonies and contrasts.

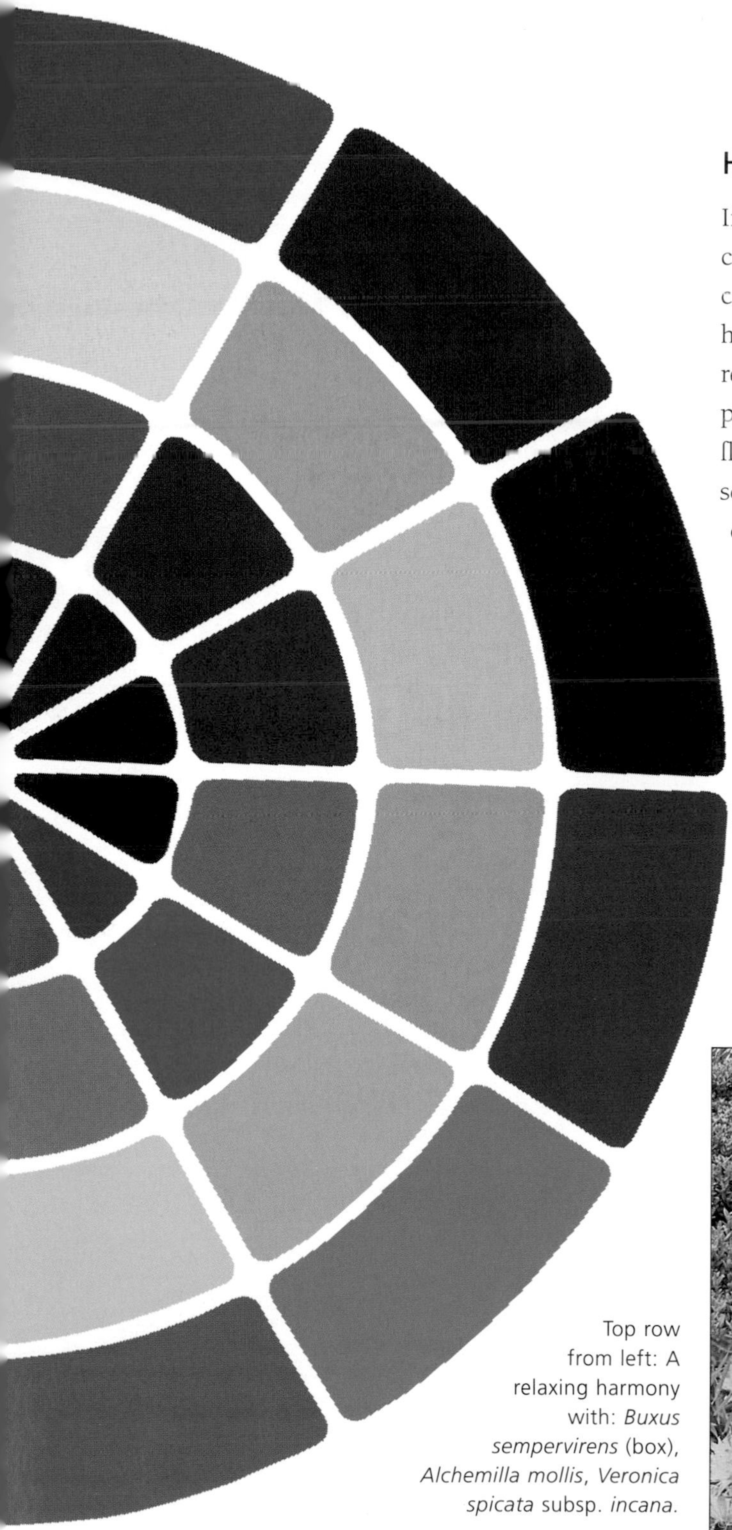

HARMONIES

If, when planting a border or bed, we use plants with colours that are adjacent or near each other in the colour wheel, a harmony is produced. However, not all harmonies have the same character. There are soothing, relaxing harmonies, and exciting, vibrant harmonies. A planting scheme incorporating blue- and yellow-flowering plants and evergreen foliage produces a soothing, calming harmony, for example a parterre edged with *Buxus sempervirens*♀ (box), bedded out with the cream- and green-flowered *Veronica spicata* subsp. *incana* and the pale blue-flowered *Muscari armeniacum* 'Valerie Finnis'. On the other hand, a harmony produced by planting orange-flowered plants with yellow and red ones, such as the orange-flowered *Alstroemeria aurea* grown in proximity to red crocosmias, such as *Crocosmia* 'Lucifer'♀, and the yellow grass *Carex elata* 'Aurea'♀, results in an effect that seems vibrant and filled with energy. Christopher Lloyd, in his Great Dixter garden, in East Sussex, has magnificent plantings of hot, vibrant harmonies.

Top row from left: A relaxing harmony with: *Buxus sempervirens* (box), *Alchemilla mollis*, *Veronica spicata* subsp. *incana*.

Bottom row from left: An exciting harmony with: *Alstroemeria aurea*, *Crocosmia* × *crocosmiiflora* 'Jackanapes', *Carex elata* 'Aurea'.

COLOUR INTENSITY

The intense contrasts produced by putting together opposites in the colour wheel are best managed by ensuring that the saturation levels of the colours are approximately equal. For example, a muted violet will contrast most happily with a yellow if it is a dull yellow. The same applies to harmonies, as seen above: the silver and purple combination would not work so well if the purple was a more intense colour. When using single colours, however, choose plants that display differing degrees of saturation, or intensity, as this makes them more interesting. This technique is used by the Popes at their garden at Hadspen, Somerset, in their colour-themed borders.

CONTRASTING AND COMPLEMENTARY COLOURS

A planting scheme with flowers or leaf colours that are not close to each other on the colour wheel is known as a 'contrast'. Contrasts always involve a hot colour being matched by a cold colour. Contrasting colours placed together do not soothe but shock and even disturb. For example, the pale purple flowers of *Campanula glomerata* 'Superba'🏆 would make a sharp contrast to the yellow of *Aquilegia chrysantha* 'Yellow Queen', because purple and yellow are not near each other on the colour wheel. (See 'Contrasting and Complementary Schemes', below.)

Colours that are opposites on the colour wheel are known as 'complementary' colours, because each makes up for everything that its opposite in the wheel lacks. Complementary colours are red and green, orange and blue, and yellow and violet. Planting combinations of these colours will always result in the most shocking of vibrant colour schemes as the most intense contrasts are between colours that are opposite in the wheel. (See 'Contrasting and Complementary Schemes', below.)

CONTRASTING AND COMPLEMENTARY SCHEMES

The clear yellow *Hemerocallis lilioasphodelus*🏆 (1) grown in front of *Ceanothus* 'Blue Mound'🏆 (2) produces a sharp contrast to and highlights the mauve-blue.

The contrast produced by growing bright blue *Agapanthus* 'Blue Giant' (3) in a sea of orange flowers of *Heliopsis helianthoides* var. *scabra* (4) is a complementary scheme designed to stimulate, and perhaps shock.

In the picture that is created when the deep red climber *Tropaeolum speciosum*🏆 scrambles up a dark, rich green yew hedge (5), the colour saturation levels are approximately equal.

SATURATION AND TONE

A saturated colour is a colour at its most intense and pure. So, the more saturated a colour is, the stronger it is and the more it will stand out from its surroundings. Obviously this has to be considered when devising planting schemes, especially those that incorporate saturated reds, oranges and yellows. Saturated colours can be useful when a dash of rich, strong colour is needed. Pots of bright red pelargoniums on a dark balcony never fail to attract attention, for example, and the orange berries of *Pyracantha* 'Orange Glow'♡ show up brilliantly against the dark green of its evergreen leaves. Many late-flowering daisy-flowered perennials, such as heleniums and rudbeckias, have vivid yellow flowers, whose colour will dominate a planting. The less saturated a colour, the less intense it is, so the more it will blend and recede into its surroundings, particularly if they are shades of blue. *Salvia patens*♡ has saturated blue flowers that instantly capture the attention, whereas those of *Veronica gentianoides*♡ are less noticeable as they are a pale, unsaturated blue.

These alliums have a lighter tone than that of the purple foliage behind, so they stand out. The dark-toned leaves of the smoke bush (*Cotinus*) are much less dominant and they recede into the background.

In this well-composed grouping, the strong lime-green colour of the euphorbia's flowers is perfectly balanced by the rich orange of the leaves of the heuchera planted beside it.

Whereas saturation is a measure of a colour's intensity, tone is a measure of its lightness or darkness. All colours have an intrinsic tone, which may be light or dark. Yellow has a light tone and violet has a dark tone. The rod cells in the human eye can detect differences of tone and they function better in dim light than the cones, the other light-sensitive cells in the eye. This makes it possible to pick out tonal differences in a garden even when their colours are lost in darkness. In a garden, distinct tonal differences can be exploited to produce dramatic effects, for example the black-stemmed bamboo *Phyllostachys nigra*♡ can be grown in front of a pale-coloured wall, or the silver-leaved *Cynara cardunculus* (cardoon) in front of a yew hedge.

Speaking botanically

Many people ask why it is necessary to use Latin names for plants rather than common names, which are often better known. The reason is that Latin is an international language, so it allows us to communicate accurately with other gardeners, wherever they are in the world. Just a basic knowledge of botanical Latin can give us a lot of information about plants.

The oak tree, *Quercus robur* (left), provides us with an excellent example of why Latin botanical names are so useful. In Britain this tree is often known as the English oak, yet it has several alternative names (including the common oak and the pedunculate oak). To add to the confusion, it grows not just in Britain but throughout Europe, and no doubt it has colloquial names wherever it is found. However, by referring to it by its Latin name, *Quercus robur*, confusion is avoided because any gardener with knowledge of botanical names can identify the plant exactly.

GENERA AND SPECIES All botanical names have at least two words to describe them. The first always has a capital letter and is the name of the genus, or plant group, to which the plant belongs. For example, all oak trees belong to the genus *Quercus* (Latin for oak). Within each genus, plants can vary enormously but they all share some characteristics. In the genus *Quercus*, for instance, there are 600 kinds of oaks – they all produce acorns, but they are highly variable: some are evergreen, some are semi-evergreen and others are deciduous. Each kind of oak is known as a species. To differentiate one from another, an adjective is placed after the word *Quercus* that defines all members of one particular species. So *Quercus robur* is one species, while *Quercus rubra* (above) is another.

The species component of a plant's name may refer to its origins or its native habitat, for example *Quercus georgiana* is an oak that is a native of Georgia in the USA. Alternatively, it may give a clue to size and shape, as in the case of *Quercus rotundifolia*, which is an oak with round leaves (*rotundifolia* means round leaves in Latin). The species part of the name may also refer to a botanist or plant hunter, for example *Quercus douglasii* is an oak that commemorates David Douglas, the Scottish plant hunter who discovered many plant treasures in the north-western USA. Alternatively, it may describe a colour exhibited by the plant. For example, the Latin name of the water oak is *Quercus nigra* and that of the American red oak is *Quercus rubra*. *Nigra* is the Latin for black, while *rubra* is an adjective meaning red.

CULTIVARS AND HYBRIDS Nurserymen or plant breeders often select species that manifest slightly different or interesting qualities to propagate from

COLOUR CHARTS FOR GARDENERS

Throughout the plant world there are species with names that give a clue to their colour. We understand what this means as we have an expectation of what a colour will look like. However, the standardization of colour has only happened comparatively recently. John Parkinson in his *Paradisi* of 1629 (see page 13) talks of an orange tree as having red fruits because the word orange was unheard of at the time. It wasn't until the early 1900s that the first colour charts, such as the *Code des Couleurs*, were created. This was originally intended for mycologists, who studied fungi, but it was taken up by British gardeners. The Royal Horticultural Society only became involved between 1939 and 1941, when it collaborated with the British Colour Council to produce its own colour chart for gardeners.

COLOUR DESCRIPTIONS USED IN BOTANICAL NAMES

Below is a chart listing some of the many Latin colour adjectives found in plant names. As with nouns, Latin adjectives have male, female and neuter versions, and their gender generally matches that of the noun they describe. For example, *Quercus* is a female noun, so the adjectives accompanying it are also in the female form, for instance *Quercus nigra* or *Quercus rubra*. (The male forms are *niger, ruber* and the neuter are *nigrum* and *rubrum*.) Alternative gender endings of the adjectives are given in brackets.

Colour in Latin	Translation	Example
argenteus, -a, -um	silvery	*Salvia argentea*
armeniacus, -a, -um	apricot	*Muscari armeniacum*
aurantiacus, -a, -um aurantius, -a, -um	orange	*Primula aurantiaca*
aureus, -a, -um auratus, -a, -um	golden yellow	*Lilium auratum*
azureus, -a, -um	sky blue	*Penstemon azureus*
caeruleus, -a, -um	blue	*Polemonium caeruleum*
candidus, -a, -um	pure white	*Lilium candidum*
canus, -a, -um or incanus, -a, -um	greyish white (caused by hairs)	*Philadelphus incanus*
coccineus, -a, -um	scarlet	*Schizostylis coccinea*
dealbatus, -a, -um	whitened, e.g. by hairs	*Acacia dealbata*
flavus, -a, -um or lutescens	pale yellow	*Crocus flavus* subsp. *flavus*
glaucus, -a, -um glaucescens	glaucous	*Rosa glauca*
griseus, -a, -um	pearly grey	*Acer griseum*
lacteus, -a, -um	milky white	*Cotoneaster lacteus*
lividus, -a, -um	greyish brown/blue	*Helleborus lividus*
luteus, -a, -um	yellow	*Asphodelus luteus*
niger, -nigra, -um nigrescens	black	*Sambucus nigra*
purpureus, -a, -um	purple	*Euphorbia amygdaloides* 'Purpurea'
roseus, -a, -um	rosy pink	*Hyssopus officinalis* 'Roseus'
ruber, -rubra, -um rubescens, rubellus, -a, -um	red	*Centranthus ruber*
sanguineus, -a, -um	blood red	*Geranium sanguineum*
violaceus, -a, -um	violet	*Passiflora × violacea*
viridis, -is, -e	green	*Santolina viridis (now called Santolina rosmarinifolia* subsp. *rosmarinifolia)*

The fascinating subject of plant names and their meanings is fully explored in Hillier's *Plant Names Explained.*

cuttings. These plants are known as cultivars (from culti-vated var-iety). Cultivars may have the standard two names with another name added or simply a generic name, for example *Quercus* 'Pondaim'. This part of a cultivar's name is always enclosed in single quotation marks. *Quercus rubra* 'Aurea' (left) has young leaves that are golden (*aurea* is the Latin word for gold) rather than green.

If two species cross-pollinate the result is a hybrid. A hybrid's name always contains an ×, for example in *Quercus × sargentii*, which is a hybrid of *Quercus prinus* and *Quercus robur*.

NAME CHANGES

In the ancient world it was difficult to have precise names for colours as they varied depending on the way the pigments were extracted and then handled. Also the ancients' perceptions of colours often differed from ours. Tyrian purple, known to the Greeks as *porphyra* and the Romans as *purpurea*, was reserved for imperial robes and aristocrats' togas as it was a highly expensive dye. It was extracted from small glands found in a particular sea snail (*Murex brandaris*), with 8,000 snails being needed to produce one gram of dye. Today, we would describe the colour as crimson not purple.

THE ORIGIN OF *COCCINEUS* (SCARLET)

The colour adjectives in plant names have come down to us from the ancient Greeks' and Romans' dyestuff and pigment industries. The ancients extracted a red dye from an insect that lives in certain oaks, including *Quercus suber* (cork oak). However, initially they mistook the female insects swollen with eggs for berries growing on the trees. In Latin, the word for berry is *coccus*, so *coccineus* became the adjective used to describe the scarlet dye extracted from the insects. In botanical names, this is the adjective used to describe something that is scarlet, and is applied to berries or flowers when appropriate. *Schizostylis coccinea* has scarlet flowers in late summer and early autumn.

The impact of light

Light changes according to the time of day, the season and the climate; in the process, it alters our perception of colour. Knowledgeable and creative gardeners take the variable nature of light into account when planning their plantings, and make use of this phenomenon to make their gardens more beautiful and atmospheric.

Planting red, yellow or orange flowers, such as these poppies (*Papaver rupifragum*), where they are touched by low, golden sunlight in the evening or early morning emphasizes their colours.

One of the great pleasures of owning a garden is being able to stroll around it in the early morning or evening, when the rising or setting sun appears to bathe everything in a beatific light. This soft glow occurs because the sun is at its lowest point in the sky, so light passes through the atmosphere at a low angle. As this happens, it tends to pick up dust, much more than when the sun is high in the sky at midday. The dust particles have the effect of diffusing the light and emphasizing the warm end of the spectrum, making it appear red and giving it a familiar glow. When creating a colour scheme, we can make use of this by planting reds, oranges and yellows in places where they will pick up the morning and evening sun. There is no point in doing the same for schemes featuring blue, violet or white as these colours look dark and lifeless when the sun is rising and setting.

After the sun has set, everything changes. The light ceases to have a reddish glow and becomes bluer. As the light fades, warm hues are lost and the only colours discernible are blue and white. Again, one can exploit this by selecting plants that feature these colours for terraces, patios and other areas used for evening entertaining in summer. A simple idea would be to plant some pots with white annuals such as petunias and others containing blue agapanthus.

A walk around the garden at midday reveals that at this point the light appears to be colourless. In fact,

A table in a shady seating area has been painted blue and a planter is filled with blue-flowered grape hyacinths. This is effective because blue shows up well in shade or when the sun has set in the evening.

Some colours are more prevalent in one season than another. In spring many trees and shrubs – like this *Amelanchier lamarckii* – have white blossom, so make the most of this in your spring planting schemes.

sunlight has a yellow tinge but it is not apparent because the blue of the sky cancels it out. The sky's ability to reflect blue light is most powerful in shade, which is why shadows appear bluer at midday. Again, we can make use of what nature offers by planting blues, white and purples in areas that receive no midday sun, because these colours make their most telling impression in blue light.

SEASONAL CHANGE

Many of us who live in northern temperate climates enjoy the fact that each season has its own character. In winter, when the sun is something of a rarity, our northern light seems grey and muted; if the sun does appear, it creates long shadows. This is the time to revel in subtle nuances of colour that are best observed in this light, for example the varying browns of bark, the russet of beech leaves, and the pearly white of flowers such as snowdrops (*Galanthus*) and *Helleborus niger*♡.

In spring and autumn, the sun is more evident than in winter; the sun slants across the sky and its light appears to be cool and soft. In spring this has the beneficial effect of lessening the impact of some of the bright yellows we associate with the season. The misty light of autumn has a similar effect on that season's brilliant leaf colour. When planning colour schemes for spring and autumn, again it is wise to follow nature's example and base them on their characteristic colours. So, plantings featuring blues, yellows, cream and white would be appropriate for spring, as these are the colours we most associate with the season, while yellows, oranges and reds would be right for autumn.

In the same way, gardens in temperate climates in summer look best if they reflect the colours of indigenous plants, which tend to be more muted than those found in hotter and tropical climates. They should, therefore, have a predominance of pinks, mauves, blues, purples and dark reds, as well as pale yellows and greens, while gardens designed to look sub-tropical should feature hot, exciting primary colours. It is also worth noting that in high summer, when the sun is at its highest and strongest, even in temperate climates, colours seem more washed out in the middle of the day and the best time to see them is in early morning and evening.

WINTER STRUCTURE

If a garden has 'good bones', in the form of evergreen and deciduous trees and shrubs and elements of hard landscaping, it will manifest all kinds of subtle but immensely satisfying colour associations in winter. Examples of winter colour include the whiteness of silver-birch bark against a yew hedge, silhouettes of deciduous trees and shrubs against a leaden or a clear blue sky, stone paving after a bout of rain, crystals of hoar frost on brown earth, or cobwebs strung between the beige remains of herbaceous foliage.

Colour in the past and present

When we consider traditional use of colour in the garden, we must look to British landscape gardener Gertrude Jekyll (1843–1932), who was arguably the most influential gardener of her generation. Although the subject of colour was much discussed in gardening magazines from the 1820s onwards, it was Miss Jekyll – with her prodigious knowledge of plants, their cultivation needs and flowering times, combined with her insights about colours – who became the supreme garden colourist. She continues to be an inspiration to gardeners today.

Miss Jekyll trained as an artist and learned colour theory – invaluable knowledge when, in middle age and with failing eyesight, she began to design planting schemes. Today, many people imagine that Gertrude Jekyll began the trend for planting schemes of subtle pastel shades that have become so familiar and are often seen as epitomizing traditional English-style gardens. In fact, consciously tasteful, muted plantings owe much more to Miss Jekyll's disciples, notably Vita Sackville-West, than to Miss Jekyll herself. It is true that, for the most part, Jekyll created harmonies rather than contrasts, and preferred using subtle shades rather than pure spectral colours, but it is not the case that all of her schemes were muted or featured restrained colours. Sometimes she chose hues that were decidedly bright – garish even – as she admired all colours and believed that all had their uses.

Generally, it was Miss Jekyll's practice to arrange plants in irregularly shaped drifts. This meant that the colours of individual plants wove together to produce 'kaleidoscopes', whose impact depended on the colour juxtapositions of neighbouring plants. Her skill lay in devising schemes where the flowers appeared at just the right moment to provide the subtle gradations of tone she was aiming for. Sometimes she created hot harmonies, with reds merging into oranges and then into yellows; in other situations she chose the cooler combinations of blues, violets and greyish greens. She added depth and balance to her compositions by the careful use of foliage as well as flowers, contrasting rounded and upright shapes and, when necessary, using arresting bright colours as focal points.

Hot harmonies using reds, oranges and yellows featured in many of Gertrude Jekyll's planting plans.

Miss Jekyll studied the paintings of J.M.W. Turner, and it was his use of colour she most admired. He believed that the substance of the visible world could be represented by the spectrum's three primary colours, red, blue and yellow. In his impressionistic painting, *The Fighting Temeraire*, the picture's blood-red sunset and its reflection dominate the canvas, while the ship, surrounded by blue, seems to recede into the distance. The sky is a blaze of colour that gradually changes from rich red above the sun to golden yellow and then into a pale yellow; the pale yellow then progresses to the white of the moon, and this transmutes finally into the pale blue of the sky. This colour sequence was often employed by Turner and, in turn, by Miss Jekyll. Indeed, this was the basis of the planting for the famous long herbaceous border in her own garden at Munstead Wood, near Goldalming, in Surrey. Vibrant reds dominated the middle of the border, while on either side the colours gradually cooled from the hotter oranges and yellows to the whites and blues at either end.

BARRINGTON COURT

Examples of Gertrude Jekyll's use of colour may be seen at Barrington Court in Somerset, where she designed the planting for a group of gardens in the early 1900s. The National Trust has restored the gardens, basing the planting schemes on Miss Jekyll's designs.

In the USA, there is only one garden designed by Gertrude Jekyll, namely the small area surrounding the Glebe House Museum at Roxbury, in Connecticut. This garden has been skilfully restored using Miss Jekyll's original planting plans, but without the delphiniums, which do not fare well in the New England climate.

Cool, calm harmonious plantings of blues, mauves, and greys, like this one, were favoured for the ends of the long, colour-themed borders designed by Gertrude Jekyll.

As a painter, Miss Jekyll was greatly influenced by Turner's use of colour and often her plantings reflected this. In the long borders for which she became famous, her practice was to grade the colours from cool to hot, with the hottest hues in the centre and the cooler, recessive ones at both ends. To create these spectacular effects she had to know a great deal about the flowering times and the needs of the many plants she used.

FROM JEKYLL TO THE PRESENT DAY

The subject of colour in the garden is discussed as much today as in the 19th century, and Gertrude Jekyll still continues to inspire many gardeners in this respect. Penelope Hobhouse, whose classic book *Colour in Your Garden* was published in 1984, describes how reading Miss Jekyll's books and the theories of the French Impressionists inspired her to stop being what she calls 'a good taste gardener', and transformed her into someone who was excited by the 'infinite possibilities of weaving colour pictures with plants'. Moreover, Miss Jekyll opened her eyes to the fact that it was just as rewarding to create contrasts as harmonies, and that colour can be used to evoke different moods and to manipulate perspectives.

While everyone would agree that Miss Jekyll's contribution to our understanding of colour and how to use it has been enormous, there are significant differences in the way colour is used in gardens today. Thanks to plant hunters, breeders and nurserymen, today's gardeners have a much greater range of plants to choose from, many of which feature tones that Miss Jekyll could only have dreamed of (see 'Modern cultivars, below). Newer cultivars of trees, shrubs, herbaceous perennials and bulbs now offer us the possibility of using colour in exciting and very different ways from gardeners in the past.

SINGLE-COLOUR BORDERS

While harmonies rather than clashing or vibrant contrasts have traditionally held sway in English gardens, one-colour borders have also been ingredients of many gardens; indeed, several of these – for example the White Garden at Sissinghurst, in Kent – are renowned all over the gardening world. Single-colour borders first became popular at the end of the 19th century, after the Reverend Shirley Hibberd (see

MODERN CULTIVARS

It is interesting to speculate about the look of plantings Gertrude Jekyll would have created had she been able to use some modern herbaceous cultivars. For example, the greyish-plum-coloured oriental poppy *Papaver orientale* 'Patty's Plum' (1), the mid- to pale pink *Verbascum* 'Jackie in Pink' (2), the burnt-orange daisy *Helenium* 'Waldtraut'♀ (3), the muted red *Astrantia* 'Hadspen Blood' (4), the bluish-grey leaves and purple flowers of the annual *Cerinthe major* 'Purpurascens' (5) and the almost black-leaved cow parsley, *Anthriscus sylvestris* 'Ravenswing' (6).

The Red Border at Hadspen Garden in Somerset is a fine example of a monochrome border. Monochrome borders create their own mood and rhythm and allow an onlooker to enjoy the plants' textures and shapes without being too distracted by their colour.

page 16) had written about creating schemes using plants exhibiting varying tones of a single colour. Contrary to popular belief, Gertrude Jekyll did not care for monochrome borders, and advised her readers to include small amounts of other colours in them to provide 'punctuation marks'.

Today, there are still many gardeners who prefer to plant in monochromes, taking the view that single-colour schemes create mood, provide rhythm, and highlight the textures, shapes and nuances of plants. Nori and Sandra Pope, creators of the monochromatic colourist garden at Hadspen, near Castle Cary, in Somerset, prefer one-colour schemes because, as they say in their book, *Colour by Design*, it allows them to 'control the colour shift, the saturation of colour and the tonal change from dark to light'. Moreover, they feel that by separating colours the full impact of each can be appreciated. Like the majority of today's gardeners who want their gardens to look enticing for as long as possible, the Popes design their plantings to look good for about seven months of the year. This is in stark contrast to Gertrude Jekyll, who could plan schemes that would look their best at a certain time of year and then be closed off when another scheme came into its own.

Many gardeners prefer to create plantings of mixed colours rather than monochromes. The one shown here was designed by plantswoman Carol Klein and has yellows, purples and silvers in close proximity.

Large naturalistic plantings of perennials and grasses, like this one designed by Piet Oudolf at RHS Garden Wisley, have been made in recent years for public spaces and parks in Britain, Europe and the USA. Domestic gardeners are increasingly adapting this idea for their own gardens.

NATURALISTIC PLANTINGS

A major factor that has contributed to the changing use of colour has been the burgeoning interest in gardens that look 'natural'. This has manifested itself in the widespread creation of wildflower meadows and in large perennial plantings featuring plants whose natural habitats are the prairies of North America. For this reason, grasses have become increasingly popular, and their neutral shades – browns, straws and parchments – have come to play an increasing role in modern gardens. Added to this, there are now many small, urban gardens whose owners want simple, stylish, low-maintenance, minimalist schemes, where hard landscaping takes precedence over plants. In these situations, a restricted palette featuring the greens of evergreens, blacks, whites and neutrals is often the theme of choice. When a colour is included, it is often provided by plantings in containers or by a few choice plants, selected as much for their foliage as their flowers. The concept is one of 'furnishing' the space.

EXOTIC PLANTINGS

The availability of inexpensive air travel and the popularity of garden-makeover programmes on television have also affected the way many people garden and use colour today. In particular, there is

As the interest in creating jungle-style gardens has grown, so has a desire to grow more unusual plants, such as the tree fern, *Dicksonia antarctica*.

increasing interest in creating exotic gardens or, at least, in growing some subtropical plants in among more traditional plantings. These days it is not unusual to find gardens given over to yuccas, cordylines, tree ferns and palms, not to mention bananas, as owners attempt to capture the exoticism of a favourite holiday destination or emulate designs featured on television. The strong architectural forms of many subtropical plants, allied to the desire to create a 'jungle' effect, call for bold use of colour with the result that there are now many gardens featuring vibrant, exciting harmonies and contrasts quite unlike those commonly associated with traditional English gardens.

Moreover, there are now more garden writers and commentators urging readers to be more imaginative and brave with their colours, especially when trying out contrasts. Christopher Lloyd, one of England's most respected gardeners and gardening writers, urges readers of his book *Colour for Adventurous Gardeners* not to be 'too precious' or to 'play it too safe'. In his garden at Great Dixter, in Kent, Lloyd practises what he preaches: dazzling, flamboyant plantings consist of daring colour combinations worthy of Henri Matisse and Les Fauves (a group of painters in France in the early 1900s who, bored with the conventional use of colours of their predecessors, chose to paint with 'barbaric' colours to create vivid harmonies and clashing contrasts). In late summer, Lloyd's Exotic Garden vibrates with reds, oranges, greens, purples, whites and yellows, a spectacle that has all the senses tingling – just the sensation Mr Lloyd wants his visitors to experience, for he considers gardens should be exciting as well as calming places. He also believes that everyone should try putting even the most clashing colours together because, as he says, 'Violent contrasts will sometimes work against all the odds, depending on the light and the time of day, on the time of year and on our own mood'.

In general, however, there seems to be a consensus among today's colourist gardeners and designers that the way we use colour in the garden is entirely up to us, to our own personal tastes, and that there is no right or wrong when it comes to using colour. Of course we can learn from the past, but it does not always pay to be bound by convention.

Gardener and gardening writer Christopher Lloyd has an exotic garden at Great Dixter, in East Sussex, full of stark contrasts (left) and hot harmonies (right). He believes we should all be braver when choosing colour schemes for our gardens.

Scale and distance

Colour has a vital role to play in establishing a garden's atmosphere, and can also alter the viewer's perception of scale and distance. Careful use of colour in a small garden can create a feeling of spaciousness and light, while in a larger garden it can act as a link, melding the garden into the surrounding landscape and providing cohesion within.

It is possible to create illusions of space and depth by the placing of pale and dark colours together in a planting scheme. In this border at White Windows, in Longparish, Hampshire, an illusion of depth has been created by placing plants with yellow foliage and flowers, including *Euonymus fortunei* 'Emerald 'n' Gold', *Potentilla fruticosa* 'Elizabeth' and *Achillea* 'Moonshine', in front of the dark-leaved *Physocarpus opulifolius* 'Diabolo'.

The important thing to remember when using colour to deceive the eye with regard to space is that pale and warm, bright colours will appear closer, while cool colours, such as dark green and blues, will appear farther away. This is important when planning the hard landscaping of a garden as well as its plantings. A small walled garden, for instance, will appear smaller if it is surrounded by brightly coloured walls but will feel larger if the walls are dark and merge into the undergrowth. Also, a planting of white or pale pastel shades in front of a dark hedge at the far end of a long garden will appear closer and make the garden seem shorter. If rich blue flowers were planted in front of the hedge instead, the garden would not appear foreshortened in the same way.

COLOUR IN SMALL GARDENS

Every small garden, whether it is a front garden on view to the world or a private back garden, has to be attractive throughout the year. For this reason, foliage plants are the most important constituents, and form the backdrop against which more colourful flowers can be introduced. In temperate climates, these background plants should be subtle – dark greens, reds, browns, blacks and silvery greys – as they will not clash with the brighter flower colours and, being dark, will make a garden seem larger. Small trees, evergreen and deciduous shrubs with dark leaves, for example black-leaved *Sambucus nigra* f. *porphyrophylla* 'Gerda'♀('Black Beauty'), and ferns and leafy perennials are all suitable foliage plants for a small garden, and it is a good idea to include some that will provide interest in more than one season; for example, the small tree *Amelanchier* × *grandiflora* 'Ballerina'♀ has pretty, fluffy white blossom in spring, followed by pinkish-green fresh young leaves that turn dramatic shades of crimson in autumn.

The choice of more ephemeral colour for a small garden will depend on the mood one wishes to create. If the aim is to have a tranquil space for relaxing, then calming colours – blues, pinks with touches of violet, silver and white – will obviously work best. On the other hand, gardens designed for activity could include vibrant, lively colours such as bright oranges, reds and yellows. Whatever the colour scheme, the rule of thumb is to place the strongest colours nearest the house and the most muted colours nearest the boundaries, as this will help to make the space seem larger. When reds, oranges and yellows are being used, the brightest should be planted close to the house and darker tones, such as ochre and brown, farther away. Deeper blues, pinks and mauves should also be in the foreground, with greyer, more discreet tones graduating towards the perimeter of the garden. Reds may be used at the boundaries, provided they are sufficiently dark and on the blue side of the spectrum rather than the orange. Mixing crimson with violets, purples and mauves in boundary plantings works well too.

A garden seems larger if the strongest colours are placed nearest the house and muted ones are on the garden's perimeters. Here, purple alliums form a belt of strong colour in the foreground while the subtle colours beyond increase the sense of distance to the garden's boundaries.

RESTRICTING COLOUR

It is always wise to restrict the number of colours used in a small garden, perhaps to three or four. However, avoid limiting a small garden to one colour only: it demands great skill not to produce something very dull indeed. One-colour gardens work best when they are constituents of larger gardens where, as Sir Roy Strong says in his book *Creating Small Gardens*, 'there is room for indulgences'.

LIGHTENING SMALL GARDENS

Small gardens tend to have dark areas that can be lightened using light-reflecting plants. Those with variegated or light-reflecting leaves, such as epimediums, asarums, hellebores and silver-leaved plants are best, while plants sporting white or yellow flowers are

Compositions featuring silver and golden leaves, yellow-flowered plants and light-reflecting foliage are guaranteed to bring light and cheer to any part of the garden. This grouping includes *Thalictrum flavum* 'Illuminator', *Milium effusum* 'Aureum', *Euphorbia schillingii* and golden forms of feverfew and origanum.

invaluable in these situations too. Shrubs with silver or variegated foliage and those with shiny, light-reflecting leaves, such as skimmias and *Viburnum davidii* ♕, should be placed in the foreground, as they will make the space seem smaller if planted on the boundaries. When a small garden doesn't have a view, the perimeter walls or fences assume much more importance, so care needs to be taken to select climbers and wall shrubs that will not close in the space even more. Dark-leaved shrubs and plants with small and unobtrusive, pale yellow, cream, apricot, blue or turquoise flowers fool the eye into believing the space is larger than it is.

PLANTING FOR A DARK CORNER

A small dark corner can be enlivened by underplanting a *Fatsia japonica* 'Variegata' ♕ (1) with snowdrops interspersed with *Corydalis lutea* or *Epimedium* × *versicolor* 'Sulphureum' ♕ (2) for spring interest. White-flowering tobacco plants such as *Nicotiana sylvestris* ♕ (3) would give height in summer, while at ground level *Cyclamen hederifolium* ♕ (4) would provide attractively mottled leaves and pink flowers in autumn.

In larger gardens, where extensive plantings do not look out of place, there is the opportunity to experiment with interesting and unusual colour combinations. However, colours should always be repeated throughout a planting to provide a sense of unity. In a predominantly red border at White Windows, in Longparish, Hampshire, the planting is pulled together by the repetition of bronze and silver foliage.

COLOUR IN LARGE GARDENS

By their very nature, large gardens tend to be found in rural settings and often have a view of the landscape beyond. Boundaries of such gardens are vitally important. The best solution is to keep them muted in a variety of greens. Mixed plantings of shrubs, such as willows, species roses with subtle-coloured flowers, and elders, will not jar and will act as a link between garden and landscape. For more dense living boundaries, through which, perhaps, a view can be glimpsed, the choice should always be a hedge of indigenous species. These will vary, depending on the situation of the garden – it is a good idea to look at established hedges in the area and replicate them. In Britain, a hedge may include plants such as blackthorn, hawthorn, holly, yew, spindle, field maple and dog roses. Hedges help to place a garden in its context; they also provide a haven for wildlife.

Large gardens offer the opportunity to create a number of smaller gardens within them, each with its own mood; they also enable the gardener to make large plantings, with great swathes of colour that would be overwhelming in a small space. Colours should always be repeated throughout a large planting, as this will lead the eye around it, giving it character and a sense of unity, and there should always be a focal point to draw the eye. Large plantings of gentle, harmonious colours will be given a touch of excitement if deliberate contrasts are added here and there.

COLOURS

There are plants with flowers in every colour of the rainbow, giving gardeners the richest of palettes to play with. In order to make the most of this diversity, it is a good idea to get to know something of each colour's individual character and potential and develop an understanding of how colours behave when placed alongside each other – information that is of the utmost importance when constructing planting schemes for a garden.

RIGHT: *Rubus cockburnianus* 'Goldenvale' underplanted with *Ophiopogon planiscapus* 'Nigrescens'.

Black

Coco Chanel, the high priestess of Parisian chic, always wore black and white as she thought they were the most elegant of colours. Plants with black flowers have the same aura of glamour and sophistication and, perhaps because they do not occur in nature, plant breeders have been trying to produce them for centuries.

The novel *The Black Tulip* by Alexandre Dumas, written in 1850, may be a fictionalized account of the Dutch craze for tulips (known as Tulipomania) in the early 17th century, but it gives us an insight into the passion that black has always ignited in some horticulturists – a passion that is still as intense today. Luckily for those caught up in the black mystique, there are now more plants sporting black flowers than when previous generations sought them out. In addition, there are perennials and shrubs displaying striking black leaves and stems.

It should not be forgotten that true black does not exist in nature. Flowers, leaves and stems that we think of as black always contain an element of red or purple. So, the popular 'black' tulip ***Tulipa* 'Queen of Night'** is, in fact, a deep purple, and the leaves of the lesser celandine ***Ranunculus ficaria* 'Brazen Hussy'** are a very dark bronze.

Black plants certainly give a planting scheme drama. Since the strength of their colour tends to draw the eye away from the paler items, they should be repeated at regular intervals throughout the scheme.

When plants exhibiting a black quality are planted with whites, they accentuate each other in the way that complementary colours do. The drama of the composition is heightened by the shadows and silhouettes created by the dark tones, as in a chiaroscuro drawing. So, a combination of the black-flowered hollyhocks ***Alcea rosea* 'Nigra'** and ***Alcea rosea* 'Black Beauty'** with white-flowered perennials, for example *Eupatorium rugosum* or *Lysimachia*

BLACK FLOWERS

Today's gardeners are fortunate to have black to plant in a variety of situations. *Iris chrysographes* 'Black Knight' is a beardless iris with dark violet to almost black flowers; it will grow happily in sun or shade but prefers a dampish soil. *Veratrum nigrum* 🏆 is an imposing perennial that will bring a touch of class to a shady corner

but needs a cool, deep, humus-rich soil. It has pleated leaves and plumes of very dark reddish-brown flowers, which may appear black in some situations, on stems up to 1.2m (4ft) tall. Shown left is a *Helleborus × hybridus*, one of a very variable group whose flowers may be white, yellow, green, pink or purple. The purple blooms are sometimes so dark they appear almost black, as here. (See also pages 42, 114, 173, 180.)

clethroides♀, will make the flower colours of each seem considerably more intense. The dark leaves of ***Actaea simplex*** **Atropurpurea Group 'James Compton'** will appear in silhouette, especially if combined with large white flowers, for example those of the statuesque *Galtonia candicans*♀.

Minimalist gardens can look very elegant when given a black and white colour scheme. The black-stemmed bamboo ***Phyllostachys nigra***♀, grown in large white or silvery pots, would be eye-catching in a small urban courtyard. On a smaller scale, stone pots planted with the black, grass-like ***Ophiopogon planiscapus*** **'Nigrescens'**♀ and white snapdragons or marguerites would be chic in summer; add white crocuses or snowdrops for winter decoration.

Occasionally, black and white are both found in a single plant. The Oriental poppy ***Papaver orientale*** **'Black and White'**♀ has flowers with papery white petals with a black blotch at their bases. ***Physocarpus opulifolius*** **'Diabolo'** and the cow parsley ***Anthriscus sylvestris*** **'Ravenswing'** also have dark purple, almost black leaves and white or pinkish-white flowerheads. ***Sambucus nigra***, the common elder, has some highly attractive black-leaved cultivars, such as ***Sambucus nigra*** **f.** ***porphyrophylla*** **'Gerda'**♀ (formerly *Sambucus nigra* 'Black Beauty'), which has fern-like, rich purple-black leaves and pretty pale pink flowers, and ***Sambucus nigra*** **f.** ***porphyrophylla*** **'Eva'** (formerly *Sambucus nigra* 'Black Lace'), with black-purple leaves and deep pink flowers. These shrubs will tolerate most soils, and will grow in sun or shade, although they are best in sun. Both look good against a white wall.

Silver or grey foliage (see pages 56–57) also enhances black-flowered plants. The tiny ***Viola*** **'Bowles' Black'**, interspersed with the finely silver-leaved *Artemisia schmidtiana* 'Nana'♀, would make an eye-catching edging for a stone path, while the silvery foliage of *Cynara cardunculus*♀ (cardoon, see page 57) would make a dramatic backdrop for the striking black flowers of ***Iris*** **'Study in Black'**.

Ophiopogon planiscapus 'Nigrescens' with cyclamen and snowdrops.

Above, left to right: *Tulipa* 'Queen of Night', *Sambucus nigra* f. *porphyrophylla* 'Eva', *Cornus alba* 'Kesselringii', *Pittosporum tenuifolium* 'Tom Thumb', *Alcea rosea* 'Nigra', *Iris* 'Study in Black'.

OTHER BLACK PLANTS

Aeonium 'Zwartkop'♀ – Succulent with shiny black, purple-tinged leaves.

Aquilegia vulgaris var. *stellata* 'Black Barlow' – Perennial with double black flowers in late spring.

Cornus alba 'Kesselringii' – Deciduous shrub with blackish-purple winter shoots.

Geranium phaeum var. *phaeum* 'Samobor' – Perennial with mauve, almost black flowers.

Hedera helix – Ivy with black berries.

Hermodactylus tuberosus – Perennial with black, iris-like flowers in spring.

Hyacinthus orientalis 'Midnight Mystique' – Almost black hyacinth.

Lysimachia ciliata 'Purpurea' – Perennial with dark purple, almost black leaves.

Pittosporum tenuifolium 'Tom Thumb'♀ – Evergreen shrub with dark purple or bronze foliage and a compact habit.

Rhodochiton atrosanguineus♀ – Climber with deep purple and black flowers from summer to autumn.

Trifolium repens 'Purpurascens Quadrifolium' – Four-leaved clover with purple or maroon, green-edged leaves.

Blue

Gardeners are beguiled by blue perhaps more than any other colour. Who has not been moved by a sea of bluebells (*Hyacinthoides non-scripta*) in a beech wood in England in spring, or marvelled at billowing *Mertensia virginica* in the woods of Pennsylvania in May? We all want to include blue in our gardens, for it is one of the most soothing colours and combines beautifully with a wide variety of other plants.

Plants with true blue flowers are rare in nature and, despite the best efforts of plant breeders, in cultivation too. Many of the plants described as having blue flowers or leaves are actually tinged with other colours, for example the cottage-garden favourite ***Centaurea montana*** (see page 140) has flowers with reddish-blue petals, and the leaves of ***Hosta* 'Halcyon'**♀, known for their blueness, are in fact more green than blue.

The prize for the truest of blue flowers probably goes to **delphiniums** and **salvias**. Towering delphiniums in a border are, for many, a defining image of an English garden in summer, and the fact that they have names such as ***Delphinium* 'Blue Nile'**♀ and ***Delphinium* 'Blue Jay'** leaves no doubt about the colour. However, delphiniums are found in a range of tones that illustrates just how varied blues can be. ***Delphinium tatsienense*** is cornflower-blue, ***Delphinium grandiflorum* 'Blue Butterfly'** is a much deeper colour, while the flowers of ***Delphinium* 'Cliveden Beauty'**, a Belladonna Group hybrid, are sky-blue. Among salvias, ***Salvia patens***♀ has the clearest, purest blue flowers, followed closely by ***Salvia uliginosa***♀. These natives of South America make splendid additions to a gardener's palette, because they flower in late summer and autumn, at a time when blue in the garden is a rare sight.

All-blue plantings create an aura of calm, but there are fewer blues found in perennials than any other colour, so when trying to create such a planting it may be necessary to add some annuals, such as **forget-me-nots** (*Myosotis*) and **love-in-a-mist** (*Nigella*). The beauty of these simple cottage-garden plants is that they will self-seed and so reappear year after year. On light, well-drained soil one could also sow the flax ***Linum grandiflorum***♀, and the larkspur ***Consolida ajacis*** (formerly *Consolida ambigua*), removing stems that produce white or pink flowers rather than blue.

While all-blue plantings are cool and restful to the eye, they can be enhanced and lightened by the introduction of greens and whites. In early spring, the mottled dark green and cream leaves of *Arum italicum* subsp. *italicum* 'Marmoratum'♀ (see page 124) provide a perfect foil for blue-flowered bulbs and perennials. A striking effect can also be achieved by planting the pretty white tulip *Tulipa* 'White Triumphator'♀ (see page 54) with pale blue ***Brunnera macrophylla* 'Hadspen Cream'**♀.

The sharpest of all contrasts are achieved by planting blue with orange, because the two are complementary

colours. Planting a bugle, such as ***Ajuga reptans***, and allowing the orange tulip *Tulipa* 'Prinses Irene' ♔ (see page 46) to grow through it produces this kind of strident, sizzling contrast in a spring planting. Late in summer, one could achieve a similar effect by planting orange cannas, such as *Canna indica* (see page 148), interwoven with the tall, intensely blue ***Salvia uliginosa*** ♔.

Planting blue in combination with yellow also produces a contrast, but a less intense one than in the case of orange and blue. We have all seen blue and yellow combinations in spring gardens, for at this time of year there are so many yellow- and blue-flowering bulbs: ***Scilla siberica*** ♔ or ***Chionodoxa forbesii*** ♔ (also known as *luciliae*) planted among drifts of daffodils for instance; or the bright yellow-flowered *Epimedium × perralchicum* ♔ combined with the intense blue of the evergreen perennial ***Omphalodes cappadocica*** ♔ (see page 127). These combinations accentuate both colours, with the yellows appearing more prominent and the blues seeming to recede.

BLUES IN SHADE AND SUN

Blues show up best and look their most stylish in shade. In a garden there may not be space to grow drifts of bluebells or mertensias, but planting blue-flowered bulbs such as *Anemone blanda* ♔, or low-growing perennials such as *Omphalodes cappadocica* ♔ (1) under a specimen tree – perhaps a white-stemmed birch, for instance *Betula utilis* var. *jacquemontii* (2) – can create similar effects on a small scale.

Blues in sunshine appear pinkish, so in a sunny site they look best teamed with pinks and mauves to produce subtle harmonies. Pale blue veronicas, such as *Veronica gentianoides* ♔ (3), pink geraniums and *Allium hollandicum* ♔ (4) spilling into each other at the front of a border combine to create a simple but harmonious planting.

Above, left to right: *Iris sibirica* 'Ego', *Delphinium grandiflorum* 'Blue Butterfly', *Anemone blanda*, *Hosta* 'Fragrant Blue', *Agapanthus* Headbourne hybrids, *Nigella damascena* 'Miss Jekyll'.

BLUES FOR THE GARDEN

Pale blue flowers
Allium caeruleum ♔
Amsonia tabernaemontana
Camassia cusickii
Campanula cochlearifolia ♔

Mid-blue flowers
Agapanthus Headbourne hybrids
Ceratostigma willmottianum ♔ (see page 165)
Echium pininana ♔
Iris sibirica 'Ego'
Meconopsis × sheldonii

Deep blue flowers
Aconitum carmichaelii 'Arendsii' ♔
Anchusa azurea 'Loddon Royalist' ♔ (see pages 134, 135)
Baptisia australis ♔ (see pages 140, 141)
Gentiana verna
Pulmonaria 'Blue Ensign' (see pages 62, 115, 116)

Glaucous-blue leaves
Echeveria elegans ♔
Eryngium × oliverianum ♔
Festuca glauca 'Blaufuchs' ♔
Helictotrichon sempervirens ♔
Hosta sieboldiana var. *elegans* ♔ (see page 127)

Green

To be a gardener in a temperate climate is to be immersed in a world of greens – the rich dark green of yew, the yellowish green of young euphorbias, the soft green of young beech leaves, the glistening blackish green of laurel, the brownish green of unfurling ferns, and the intense bright green of springy new turf. Green soothes and calms, and acts as a foil for every other colour in the garden. It also provides a vital, seamless link between garden and landscape.

Dark greens in the garden recede into the distance, while yellowish greens advance into the foreground. However, since the leaves of most perennials are mid-green they neither stand out from nor disappear into a planting; instead, as they interweave among the colours, they tend to bring an element of unity to the whole.

Mid-greens are neither on the warm side of the colour wheel with the reds, oranges and yellows, nor on the cool side with the blues and violets. This explains why they perform so well as buffers, soothing contrasting colours that, if placed side by side, would give too much of a jolt to the senses. The brightest reds, magentas and oranges may all be planted together provided there is plenty of green mixed among them; for example, the bright red Oriental poppy *Papaver orientale*

GREEN FLOWERS

We associate green with leaves and shoots, but there are also plants that produce green flowers; these have cast a spell over gardeners from John Parkinson (see page 13) onwards. They may not be rare, but their colour makes them seem so. The many-petalled rose *Rosa × odorata* 'Viridiflora' (1) is far from being the showiest, but it has an avid following of growers who love its quirkiness. The early flowers of *Viburnum opulus* 'Roseum' 🏆 (2) are a soft lime-green before the flowerheads develop into creamy white snowballs. Later in the year, the prize for sheer class must go to the unusual pale green racemes of the bulb *Eucomis bicolor* 🏆 (3) and to *Allium* 'Mount Everest' (4), whose creamy white, green-eyed flowers quickly change to attractive green seedheads. (For more green flowers, see box, opposite.)

REJUVENATE A BORDER

Deciduous leaves of trees, shrubs and perennials start to look jaded as summer progresses, but by cutting back some perennials – geraniums, columbines and nepetas – after flowering, it is possible to spur the plants into producing fresh green leaves. This crop of leaves can help rejuvenate a tired-looking border and provides a backdrop for later-flowering perennials, such as Michaelmas daisies and phlox. Sometimes the plants even produce a second crop of flowers.

'Allegro' may be planted close to the magenta *Geranium psilostemon*♀ and the brick-red *Geum coccineum* because all have masses of mid-green foliage, enabling the colours to work together.

Gardens with a predominantly green theme can be extremely striking, and the colour has assumed a new importance in the perennial plantings of landscapers such as Piet Oudolf, Wolfgang Oehme and James van Sweden, who make much use of grasses, arranging them in subtle gradations of green. On a smaller scale, a green herbaceous planting consisting of interesting variations of texture and colour could include green-flowered hellebores, for example ***Helleborus orientalis* 'Hillier Hybrid Green'** or ***Helleborus* × *hybridus***, and heucheras such as ***Heuchera* 'Key Lime Pie'**. These are good interspersed with hostas, for example the large, bluish-green leaves of ***Hosta sieboldiana* var. *elegans***♀ (see page 127), and grasses, for example the green and creamy margined leaves of ***Calamagrostis* × *acutiflora* 'Overdam'** (see page 171) and ***Stipa tenuissima***, with erect, bright green leaves and soft, feathery panicles in summer (see also page 171).

Green-themed gardens need to exploit plants' textures, shapes and tones. They should include pale and dark greens, as well as those veering towards blue and with a hint of yellow. A simple but satisfying green garden can be made by planting walls of yew (***Taxus baccata***♀) and laying out a pattern of box-lined beds (***Buxus sempervirens* 'Suffruticosa'**♀) inside the yew walls, with standard green hollies such as ***Ilex aquifolium* 'J.C. van Tol'**♀ as centrepieces for the beds. The additions of ***Tulipa* 'Spring Green'**♀ and white forget-me-nots will provide spring interest and, later, the annuals ***Zinnia* 'Envy'** or the tobacco plant ***Nicotiana* 'Lime Green'**♀ may be planted in the beds for summer colour. Large pots of the handsome foliage plant ***Melianthus major***♀ will add glaucous green.

Above, left to right: *Helleborus* × *hybridus*, *Heuchera* 'Key Lime Pie', *Cornus controversa* 'Variegata', *Stipa tenuissima*, *Nicotiana* 'Lime Green', *Matteuccia struthiopteris*.

OTHER GREEN PLANTS

Green flowers
Alchemilla mollis♀ (see page 154)
Astrantia major
Euphorbia palustris♀
Euphorbia schillingii♀ (see page 127)
Galtonia viridiflora
Garrya elliptica
Helleborus argutifolius♀
Kniphofia 'Green Jade'
Paris polyphylla
Tulipa 'Spring Green'♀

Shiny green foliage plants
Asarum europaeum (see page 178)
Fatsia japonica♀ (see page 78)
Ilex latifolia and other hollies
Prunus lusitanica♀ (see page 82)

Dramatic green foliage plants
Acanthus spinosus♀
Darmera peltata♀
Gunnera manicata♀
Rodgersia podophylla♀ (see pages 65, 101)

Green ferns
Athyrium filix-femina♀
Matteuccia struthiopteris♀ (see also page 73)
Polypodium interjectum 'Cornubiense'♀
Polystichum setiferum♀

Yellow

After green, yellow is the colour most easily manufactured by plants, which explains why in spring and summer there are so many yellow flowers in hedgerows, beside roads, on hillsides and in gardens. We all feel happier for seeing primroses on a mossy bank shyly lifting their heads to the sun. However, while there are some gardeners who love yellow for its brightness and cheerfulness, there are others who shun it, fearing its overpowering brilliance.

In temperate gardens, pure yellow looks best in spring and autumn; this is because the sun, which is relatively low in the sky, produces a soft light that dilutes its intensity. In contrast, the summer sun, being higher in the sky, casts dark shadows that intensify the impact of yellow and may make it seem too harsh. This is not the case in Mediterranean gardens, where the sun is so strong that all colours are leached and no yellow seems too intense.

As yellow is such an intense primary colour, it can dominate more subtle colours and make strident contrasts with stronger ones if not used carefully. The skill lies in choosing the best shade for a particular planting, remembering that yellow harmonizes with oranges and reds and its complementary colour is blue. The contrast between intense blues and yellows can appear too sharp, so when combining blue and yellow it is a good idea to add paler and darker shades of both colours.

YELLOW PLANTS

Today we have an *embarras de richesses* of yellow-flowering bulbs, perennials and shrubs to choose from. In addition, there are plants with yellow stems, as well as trees whose leaves turn yellow in autumn and those that have variegated foliage. Many plants have leaves that are yellow from the moment they appear, for example the false acacia ***Robinia pseudoacacia*** 'Frisia'♕, the bright yellow Mexican orange blossom ***Choisya ternata*** SUNDANCE ('Lich')♕ and ***Dicentra spectabilis*** 'Gold Heart'.

Primrose-yellow is the easiest shade to accommodate in a garden, as it harmonizes with fresh young leaves and makes pleasing contrasts with lots of blue-flowering bulbs and perennials, for example *Brunnera macrophylla*♕ (see page 62). The dangling flower clusters of the upright shrub ***Corylopsis sinensis*** are lemon-yellow, making it one of the most attractive shrubs for acid or neutral soil in mid-spring. Another beautiful yellow flower is found on the primrose-yellow Caucasian peony, ***Paeonia mlokosewitschii***♕, whose single, bowl-shaped flowers, the texture of tissue paper, appear in late spring. In summer, another Caucasian plant, ***Cephalaria gigantea*** (giant scabious) produces primrose-coloured flowers. Carried aloft on stems 2.5m (8ft) tall, they add lustre to the back of any border. The prize for the prettiest primrose-yellow, daisy-like perennial surely goes to the chamomile ***Anthemis tinctoria*** 'E.C. Buxton'.

Some of the earliest flowers to appear in the year are those of the winter aconite ***Eranthis hyemalis***♀. Naturalized in grass under deciduous trees, its cheery, buttercup-like flowers, with their ruffs of shiny leaves, are especially welcome in the depth of winter. (See Good Companions, pages 115 and 178.) Winter is also the time for the sweetly scented flowers of witch hazel to make an appearance. Among the most desirable of these is the sulphur-flowered ***Hamamelis × intermedia* 'Pallida'**♀ (see page 177), a beautiful specimen shrub for a winter garden.

Sunflowers and daisies, such as **rudbeckias** and **heleniums**, provide rich yellows for late-summer borders. While they make an impact on their own, interspersing them with paler yellow flowers enriches plantings, providing interesting gradations of tone and helping to emphasize individual flower shapes and textures. For more dramatic, exotic borders, intermingle the yellow flowers with reds and oranges.

Above, left to right: *Kniphofia* 'Little Maid', *Corylopsis sinensis, Robinia pseudoacacia* 'Frisia', *Paeonia mlokosewitschii, Clematis cirrhosa* var. *balearica, Magnolia × brooklynensis* 'Yellow Bird'.

BRIGHTENING DARK AREAS

Plants with yellow flowers and/or leaves are invaluable for lightening dark corners, shady walls or the shade cast by trees beside ponds. The captivating, pale yellow-flowered *Erythronium* 'Pagoda'♀ (1) fares well under trees and makes a lovely companion for the mottled leaves of the variegated *Arum italicum* subsp. *italicum* 'Marmoratum'♀ (see page 124).

Beside pools, *Caltha palustris*♀ (marsh marigold) planted with *Carex elata* 'Aurea'♀ (2) and the water iris *Iris pseudacorus*♀ (yellow flag) will produce a shimmering spectacle.

Yellow-variegated ivies, such as *Hedera colchica* 'Sulphur Heart'♀ (3) and *Hedera helix* 'Goldchild'♀, will give a glow to walls that are partially shady. However, their variegations are more pronounced if they are grown in full sun.

YELLOW-FLOWERED PLANTS

Spring

Corydalis lutea
Doronicum × excelsum 'Harpur Crewe' (see page 126)
Fritillaria imperialis 'Maxima Lutea'♀
Kerria japonica 'Golden Guinea'♀
Lysichiton americanus♀
Magnolia × brooklynensis 'Yellow Bird'
Uvularia grandiflora♀ (see page 126)

Summer and autumn

Allium moly
Clematis 'Bill MacKenzie'♀
Clematis rehderiana♀
Helenium 'Butterpat'♀
Helianthus annuus
Inula magnifica
Kniphofia 'Little Maid'
Meconopsis cambrica
Phlomis russeliana♀
Rosa GRAHAM THOMAS ('Ausmas')♀
Rudbeckia fulgida var. *sullivantii* 'Goldsturm'♀
Sternbergia lutea
Verbascum olympicum

Winter

Clematis cirrhosa var. *balearica*
Crocus × luteus 'Golden Yellow'♀

Orange

Orange is not a colour for the faint-hearted. It demands attention like a lively, spoilt child. 'Look at me', it seems to say, and so has a reputation for not sitting easily with other colours. For this reason, perhaps, it is the colour that arouses most passion among gardeners. There are those who think it a 'must' for its glowing warmth and intensity, while others wouldn't consider using it because of its relentless attention-grabbing qualities.

Orange is found across the plant world, from the flowers of tiny bulbs to the bark, stems and autumn leaves of trees. Numerous annuals and perennials sport orange flowers, and some shrubs make orange berries that are magnets for birds in autumn. Moreover, the glowing vivacity of orange may be enjoyed in every season.

In spring there are the eye-catching bracts of ***Euphorbia griffithii*** **'Dixter'**♀ and the majesty of the crown imperial ***Fritillaria imperialis*** **'Rubra Maxima'** (see also page 66). There are also plenty of early-flowering **tulips** (see box, right). Nothing will banish the post-winter blues better than orange tulips planted in blue pots, conjuring visions of terracotta tiles on a sun-drenched Mediterranean terrace. Summer brings the cheery deep orange of ***Geum*** **'Borisii'** at the front of a border and, later in the season, the elegant ***Canna*** **'Wyoming'** ♀ and the burnt orange ***Helenium*** **'Moerheim Beauty'**♀. In autumn the rich orange-red leaves of ***Sorbus sargentiana***♀ emerge (see page 163), as well as the striking, papery orange lanterns of ***Physalis alkekengi***♀ (Chinese lantern, see page 163), while in winter the impressive orange stems of the lime ***Tilia cordata*** **'Winter Orange'** and the burnt orange-copper bark of ***Acer griseum***♀ are a spectacular sight.

PARTNERS FOR ORANGE

The pure, saturated colour of orange calls for boldness when combining it with other plants. Using orange in combination with those colours nearest to it on the colour wheel, namely orange-red and golden yellow, yields vibrant, energized harmonies, like the flames of fire from which a devil might

EARLY-FLOWERING TULIPS

Tulipa 'Ballerina'♀ – Lily-flowered tulip in orange, red and yellow.

Tulipa 'Daydream'♀ (opposite) – Yellow-orange flowers.

Tulipa 'Generaal de Wet' – Early tulip with fragrant orange blooms.

Tulipa linifolia Batalinii Group 'Bronze Charm' – Orange and bronze flowers.

Tulipa 'Orange Emperor'♀ – Tangerine, bowl-shaped flowers.

Tulipa 'Orange Favourite' – Parrot tulip with green blotches on orange tepals.

Tulipa 'Oranje Nassau'♀ – Double, orange-red tepals flushed with rich red.

Tulipa 'Prinses Irene'♀ (right) – Pale orange flowers flushed with purple tones.

leap – a planting of yellow, orange and red tulips, for example, gives a lively, harmonious display with orange at its centre. However, a planting of orange and blue, as in the case of marigolds growing through a sea of annual blue lobelia, creates a 'shock' effect, because both colours are complementary and therefore intensified.

For those who prefer colours to have less shock value, the impact of pure orange may be lessened by placing it in proximity to bronze or ivory, which are darker or paler, unsaturated versions of itself. Bronze-coloured flowers are hard to find, but there are plenty of plants that have bronze-coloured leaves, for example the bronze-leaved fennel and heucheras such as *Heuchera* EBONY AND IVORY ('E and I'), which has dark bronze leaves and ivory flowers. Bronze phormiums and cordylines also make effective foils for orange flowers.

Reddish browns and earthy colours also associate very well with orange. Many grasses have yellow, brown and beige stems and flowering spikes, and dramatic results can be achieved by adding architectural grasses, such as the stately *Stipa gigantea*♀ (see pages 67 and Good Companions, page 151) and the elegant *Calamagrostis* × *acutiflora* 'Karl Foerster' (see page 75), with its attractive, pink-bronze inflorescences, to plantings featuring orange. (See also pages 170–71.)

Above, left to right: *Fritillaria imperialis* 'Rubra Maxima', *Physalis alkekengi*, *Alstroemeria aurea* with *Kniphofia* 'Royal Standard', *Acer griseum*, *Achillea* 'Terracotta', *Tulipa* 'Daydream'.

Pale orange and apricot, and other unsaturated forms of orange, make happy partnerships with cream, pale yellow and yellowish pink. The flowers of ***Rosa* 'Gloire de Dijon'** demonstrate how well these colours work together, as they are pinkish apricot in bud, deeper apricot when they open and they then fade to cream. As its flowers appear over a period, all these colours are sometimes present together, and the overall impression is harmonious.

LATE-SUMMER COMBINATION

A vibrant planting for late summer of oranges, reds and browns could be made with the soft orange-flowered *Crocosmia* × *crocosmiiflora* 'Solfatare'♀, which has bronze-tipped leaves, and *Kniphofia uvaria* 'Nobilis'♀, with its erect, rich orange and yellow pokers. *Dahlia* 'Bishop of Llandaff'♀ (1) would add scarlet flowers and dark purple foliage. *Helenium* 'Moerheim Beauty'♀, which has dark copper-red flowerheads with brown centres, and *Helenium* 'Waldtraut' (2), with its golden brown flowerheads with brown centres, would also be attractive elements in this planting.

ORANGE-FLOWERED PLANTS

Achillea 'Terracotta'
Achillea 'Walther Funcke' (see page 153)
Alstroemeria aurea
Canna 'Striata'♀
Colutea × *media*
Crocus flavus subsp. *flavus*♀
Dahlia 'Ellen Huston'♀
Hedychium coccineum 'Tara'♀
Helianthemum 'Henfield Brilliant'♀
Hemerocallis 'Indian Paintbrush'
Kniphofia 'Royal Standard'♀
Lilium 'Fire King'
Meconopsis cambrica
Potentilla 'William Rollison'♀

Red

Red is the most volatile of colours. Our language is peppered with 'red' metaphors to express our most violent emotions: we speak of 'a red rag to a bull', 'red-hot passion' and 'seeing red'. Red never fails to ignite a response in us, and we can't take our eyes off it – so much so that in a garden red needs skilful handling. However, more than any other colour, it has a power that can enliven, enrich and add a sense of theatre.

While we talk of red as a single entity, there are, in fact, two distinct kinds of red: the warm reds that veer towards orange, such as scarlet and vermilion; and the cool reds that veer towards violet, such as crimson, cerise and magenta. Mixing the two types in a planting makes a stimulating composition, although it can create a discordant effect, for example when pinks are combined with scarlet and vermilion.

RED FLOWERS FOR SPRING

Red flowers are something of a rarity in spring. However, there are several flowering quinces – among the first shrubs to flower – that sport red flowers. *Chaenomeles* × *superba* 'Crimson and Gold'♡ (left) has dark red flowers with yellow anthers and *Chaenomeles* × *superba* 'Nicoline'♡ bears scarlet flowers. In addition, tulip breeders are producing ever-increasing numbers of varieties of red tulips, but perhaps there is none to beat the elegance of the species *Tulipa sprengeri*♡.

RED PLANTINGS

Red and green are complementary colours, which means that seeing intense reds and green together, as in a red border, produces a sensation of tension and excitement. On the other hand, combining pure red with darker reds and bronze or coppery foliage makes a less showy effect – one with deeper and richer resonances. Some red-flowered plants have dark foliage, such as ***Dahlia* 'Bishop of Llandaff'**♡ (see page 47) and ***Dianthus barbatus* 'Nigrescens Group'**♡, so they are doubly welcome in such plantings.

Pure red is best seen at close range because, on the whole, it absorbs rather than reflects light. To make a border of bold reds that continues to radiate colour over a long period requires an assortment of both hardy and tender perennials and annuals. For example, ***Papaver orientale* 'Türkenlouis'** and ***Papaver orientale* (Goliath Group) 'Beauty of Livermere'** are scarlet Oriental poppies that can be relied upon to provide vivid early summer colour, and ***Potentilla* 'Gibson's Scarlet'**♡ flowers over a long period from early to late summer. ***Lychnis chalcedonica***♡ has clusters of star-shaped flowers that appear in midsummer, and ***Kniphofia***

'Prince Igor' produces highly dramatic orange-red pokers that are present from early to mid-autumn. Other red plants that flower from midsummer into autumn include dahlias such as ***Dahlia* 'Zorro'**♀ and ***Dahlia* 'Scarlet Comet'**, as well as cannas such as ***Canna* 'Rosemond Coles'** and ***Canna* 'Endeavour'**, and tender salvias such as ***Salvia fulgens***♀ and ***Salvia* × *jamensis***. ***Salix alba* subsp. *vitellina* 'Britzensis'**♀ has bright orange-red winter shoots.

RED WITH OTHER PLANTS

In a mixed colour planting, large patches of saturated or intense red will draw the eye like a magnet and so upset the balance and rhythm of the scene. In these circumstances it is a good idea to dot the red throughout the planting, like dabs of paint in one of Monet's paintings of poppies in a cornfield. ***Geum* 'Mrs J. Bradshaw'**♀ and certain potentillas, for example ***Potentilla atrosanguinea***, ***Potentilla* 'Gibson's Scarlet'**♀ or ***Potentilla fruticosa* 'Red Ace'** are ideal for this purpose.

Combining scarlet and vermilions with oranges and yellows results in bright, invigorating effects. Mixing bluish reds with deeper colours, such as rich dark blues, violets, purples and indigos or gold, copper, bronze and browns, produces plantings whose richness wouldn't look out of place in a Baroque Venetian palazzo. In these dark, sultry plantings in which the aim is to meld colours into an overall picture, it is best to avoid pastels, white, yellow or orange, all of which would stand out too much. Such a planting might include the crimson roses ***Rosa* 'William Lobb'**♀ and ***Rosa* 'Charles de Mills'**♀, ***Berberis thunbergii* 'Atropurpurea Nana'**♀, with red-purple leaves, the dark red ***Astrantia* 'Hadspen Blood'**, *Aconitum carmichaelii* 'Arendsii'♀, with its deep indigo flowers, and – to give a stately presence – the dark blue *Delphinium* 'Blue Nile'♀.

Above, left to right: *Tulipa* 'World's Favorite', *Potentilla* 'Gibson's Scarlet', *Salix alba* subsp. *vitellina* 'Britzensis', *Acer palmatum* 'Fireglow', *Papaver orientale* (Goliath Group) 'Beauty of Livermere', *Penstemon* 'Port Wine'.

RED FOLIAGE

Bright red leaves are not common, although *Acer palmatum* 'Fireglow' and *Acer palmatum* 'Bloodgood'♀ (see page 161) have dark red foliage, and some pieris, photinias and *Leucothoe* SCARLETTA ('Zeblid') (right) have new growth that emerges scarlet. However, there are numerous shrubs and trees whose autumn colour comes within the red palette. Among the most brilliant are the crimson foliage of *Euonymus alatus,* and *Acer rubrum* cultivars (see page 160).

PLANTS WITH RED FLOWERS

Warm reds
Canna 'Assaut'
Crocosmia 'Lucifer'♀ (see page 148)
Lobelia 'Cherry Ripe'
Papaver orientale 'Ladybird'
Rosa 'Frensham'
Salvia fulgens♀
Tulipa 'World's Favorite'
Watsonia 'Stanford Scarlet'

Cool reds
Achillea millefolium 'Cerise Queen'
Anemone blanda 'Radar'♀
Angelica gigas (see page 70)
Centranthus ruber var. *coccineus*
Clematis 'Abundance'♀
Geranium psilostemon♀
Penstemon 'Port Wine'♀
Weigela 'Bristol Ruby'

Pink

We tend to think of pink as either being fluffy, frivolous and fun, like candy floss, or gentle and comforting – a baby colour. However, pinks are much more varied than that. While the palest pinks suggest innocence and purity, one could not say the same for the brittleness of magenta or the sugariness of shocking pink – these are strident, assertive tones very far removed from the softness of baby pink.

It is natural to assume that pink is a simple colour, as it is produced by mixing red with white, but in fact the composition of pinks is very complex. Moreover, there are two distinct groups of pinks: those derived from reds on the yellow side of the colour wheel, and those derived from reds on the blue side (see pages 18–19). Warm, peachy pinks are the product of mixing scarlet, vermilion and orange-reds with white. Cool pinks are produced by mixing white with bluish reds such as crimson, carmine and cerise. The cool bluish pinks are much more numerous than the warm pinks. We find both kinds in the foxglove clan, where the species ***Digitalis purpurea*** has deep bluish-pink flowers, while those of ***Digitalis* × *mertonensis*** ♀ are a warm buff.

Warm pinks, if they contain high contents of yellow, will appear more apricot and pale orange than pink. Their inherent yellowness makes them the only pinks that will harmonize well with pale yellow. The climbing rose ***Rosa* 'Albertine'** ♀ has warm pink blooms with hints of apricot, while ***Verbascum* 'Helen Johnson'** has coppery-pink flowers that appear yellowish brown in certain light.

PINK ROSES

Many shrub and species roses have flowers in beautiful pink shades. The soft cool pinks are found in the unpretentious single flowers of *Rosa canina* (dog rose) and the many-petalled Gallica *Rosa* 'Duchesse de Montebello' ♀. For a warmer pink, the lax and spreading *Rosa* 'Raubritter' (1) has double, bright rosy flowers. *Rosa* × *centifolia* 'Cristata' ♀ has deep, silvery-pink flowers, and those of *Rosa* 'Ballerina' ♀ (2) are pale pink with white centres, while the Californian species *Rosa nutkana* 'Plena' ♀ has flowers that are deep bluish pink with a hint of lilac. For magenta flowers, among the best is *Rosa* 'Charles de Mills' ♀, which has flowers with magenta-purple petals.

Experts on using colour advise keeping the two kinds of pink apart, because they clash when seen together. Interestingly, some pink flowers seem to change from being a cool pink to a warm one, depending on their planting partners or the light shining on them. This is particularly true at sunset, when the sun has a yellow glow. When making pink harmonies, the cool pinks should be planted with blues, violets and whites, and the warm pinks with apricots and yellowish greens.

PINKS FOR ALL SEASONS

There are innumerable plants with pink flowers, some of which are suitable for shade as well as sun. For example, several hellebores have flowers in pale to deep pink and, as a breed, are shade-loving woodland plants (see page 180).

Pinks are also found in every season: the pretty winter flowers of ***Cyclamen coum*** ♀ (see also pages 168–69) appear in a range of pinks, and winter-flowering deciduous and evergreen **viburnums** sport pink flowers, too. In spring there are **tulips** in pink, from the palest cool shades to the showiest, richest magenta. Summer brings a vast array of pinks, from the flowers of the smallest alpines to the largest perennials. In autumn, some late-flowering perennials, such as the Japanese anemones ***Anemone* × *hybrida*** and ***Anemone hupehensis* var. *japonica*** (see pages 163 and 167), and **origanums** go on producing their pink flowers right up until frosts appear.

ALL-PINK PLANTINGS

With such a wealth of pink material available, it is tempting to create all-pink plantings. Since plantings of a single pink shade look too bland, it is preferable to vary shades and tones and to add interest by selecting plants exhibiting differing textures, forms and shapes. Another approach with small plantings is to select one plant whose flowers come in several pinks and grow them all together. **Diascias** or **verbenas** could be grown together in this way.

In early summer, one could create a pink planting that has great impact by combining the magenta-flowered ***Gladiolus byzantinus*** and ***Geranium psilostemon*** ♀, and interspersing them with the Oriental poppy ***Papaver orientale* 'Cedric Morris'** ♀, which has pale pink tissue-paper flowers. ***Allium cernuum***, with its pale pink to deep rose globes, and ***Geranium* (Cinereum Group) 'Ballerina'** ♀ could spill out from the front of the planting, while the knapweed ***Centaurea montana* 'Carnea'** provides pretty, pale pink star-shaped flowers over a long period.

Above, left to right: *Diascia rigescens, Digitalis* × *mertonensis, Geranium* (Cinereum Group) 'Ballerina', *Cyclamen coum, Viburnum* × *bodnantense* 'Charles Lamont', *Rhododendron* Loderi Group.

PINK-FLOWERED PLANTS

Spring

Erythronium dens-canis ♀
Magnolia × *soulangeana* 'Lennei' ♀
Rhododendron Loderi Group ♀ (see pages 132–33)
Tulipa 'China Pink' ♀

Summer

Astrantia maxima ♀
Cosmos bipinnatus
Diascia rigescens ♀
Geranium 'Ann Folkard' ♀
Lychnis coronaria ♀
Weigela 'Florida Variegata' ♀

Autumn

Anemone hupehensis 'Hadspen Abundance' ♀
Colchicum autumnale ♀ (see page 167)
Cyclamen hederifolium ♀ (see page 169)
Eupatorium purpureum
Origanum laevigatum 'Herrenhausen' ♀ (see page 74)
Phlox paniculata 'Mother of Pearl' ♀

Winter

Cyclamen coum ♀ (see pages 168–69)
Erica carnea 'King George'
Viburnum × *bodnantense* 'Charles Lamont' ♀
Viburnum farreri ♀ (see page 176)

Violet

True violet and purple are the most sumptuously rich colours a gardener will ever have to work with. The deeper shades suggest the majesty of royalty and opulence, and tend to inspire awe rather than joy. There's also something mysterious about violet – it lies at the very rim of the rainbow, next to ultra-violet rays that can't be seen by the human eye, and so it appears to melt into the void.

As a cool colour, violet has a recessive quality, which means that in a garden it may get lost in a sea of greenery or be eclipsed by stronger colours. Astute gardeners overcome this by isolating it from other colours and planting it in large masses.

Violet loses its identity as soon as it is mixed with another colour. Combined with red it becomes purple, and blue makes it into a rich blue rather than violet. When black is added, it becomes dark and sombre, the kind of colour that has overtones of melancholy – no doubt this is the reason why it is frequently associated with death and mourning. However, gardeners can capitalize on its soulful air to create plantings that bestow a meditative mood to a garden.

On the other hand, lilac and lavender (the unsaturated tones of violet) and mauve (the unsaturated tone of purple) can create an entirely different mood. When partnering pinks and blues, these understated colours make soothing, subtle harmonies that are particularly easy to create in high summer, when there are so many plants in flower. The only drawback of these paler colours is that they may be overlooked, because the tendency of violet to recede into the background is even more pronounced in the lighter shades. For this reason, it is sometimes a good idea to plant unsaturated violets and purples with other closely related colours that will not overshadow them. And remember that

DARK, MOODY COMBINATIONS

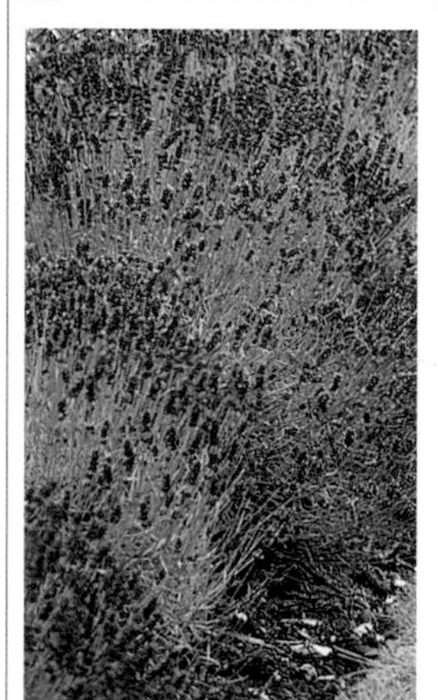

There are several tulips that have almost black flowers: *Tulipa* 'Queen of Night' (see page 38) and *Tulipa* 'Black Hero'. Planting lots of these mixed with mauve wallflowers would provide a quietly reflective setting for a seat in a small garden. On a larger scale, the seat and its planting could be the focal point for an iris walk with dark violet, tall bearded irises in parallel beds running alongside the path. A compact lavender, for example *Lavandula angustifolia* 'Hidcote' 🏆 (left), could be used to edge the path and would add its own soporific scent in high summer. *Iris* 'Blackout' has very dark violet flowers and this could be intermingled with the almost black *Iris* 'Dusky Challenger', which has ruffled falls and a delicious scent.

Above, left to right: *Syringa vulgaris* 'Katherine Havemeyer', *Clematis* 'Jackmanii Superba', *Allium* 'Globemaster', *Salvia lavandulifolia*, *Penstemon* 'Alice Hindley', *Phlox paniculata*.

SOFT HARMONIES

There are many geraniums with violet flowers that can be included in harmonies with pinks and blues. The flowers of *Geranium pratense* 'Plenum Violaceum' 🏆 (see pages 63, 141) growing with *Geranium* (Cinereum Group) 'Ballerina' 🏆 (see page 50) and *Viola cornuta* 🏆, would make a charming edging for a sunny path, and a lovely harmonious planting for summer could include *Geranium pratense* 'Mrs Kendall Clark' 🏆 growing among pink roses, together with the flowers of *Thalictrum aquilegiifolium* (right) and *Delphinium* 'Lord Butler' 🏆, which has mid-blue, semi-double flowers with hints of purple at their centres.

large masses of colour are needed to create impact. Lavender, the essential ingredient of every romantic garden, certainly looks best when it is planted in large groups, or as a hedge.

RICH, INTENSE EFFECTS

Dark violet, purple and shades of magenta planted together will produce a rich, opulent, intense effect totally removed from the soft effects of the pastel harmonies – violet and purple will calm down fiery reds and give the planting depth. Planting several **clematis** in these shades together against a wall, or to ramble over a shrub so that their flowers intermingle, will produce this kind of effect. The magenta ***Indigofera heterantha*** 🏆 makes a perfect framework for dark violet and purple late-flowering clematis to clamber through.

Violet and yellow are complementary colours, so when they are planted together a sharp contrast is set up, with the intensity of both heightened. One has only to imagine wild primroses and violets growing together in a hedgerow to see that this is the case. In these kinds of plantings, the yellows will tend to dominate and the violet will recede into the background – in order to create a balance, it is necessary to have much more of the violet than the yellow. Around a pool in early summer, such a contrast could be produced by generous plantings of ***Iris sibirica* 'Caesar's Brother'** and kingcups such as ***Trollius* × *cultorum* 'Lemon Queen'**.

VIOLET-COLOURED PLANTS

Dark and mid-violets

Allium 'Globemaster' 🏆
Allium hollandicum 'Purple Sensation' 🏆
Callicarpa bodinieri var. *giraldii* 'Profusion' 🏆 (see page 165)
Clematis 'Jackmanii Superba'
Gaultheria mucronata 'Mulberry Wine' 🏆
Iris sibirica 'Ruffled Velvet' 🏆
Lavandula angustifolia 'Hidcote' 🏆
Penstemon 'Purple Bedder'
Phlox paniculata (see page 75)
Rhododendron 'Purple Splendour' 🏆
Viola riviniana Purpurea Group

Paler, softer violets

Abutilon vitifolium
Allium cristophii 🏆
Aster amellus 'King George' 🏆
Baptisia australis 🏆 (see page 140, 141)
Iris japonica 'Variegata' 🏆
Penstemon 'Alice Hindley' 🏆 (see also pages 79, 147)
Penstemon 'Stapleford Gem' 🏆 (see page 147)
Polemonium 'Lambrook Mauve' 🏆
Salvia lavandulifolia
Syringa vulgaris 'Katherine Havemeyer' 🏆
Wisteria floribunda

White

White suggests purity, simplicity, lightness, order and romance. We marvel at pristine new snow transforming the landscape and the white tips of emerging snowdrops on a cold winter's morning. Gardens devoted to white have long fascinated gardeners for their elegance, so much so that they have become something of a cliché. However, white plants continue to cast their spell, because as well as looking beautiful in monochrome plantings, they combine well with other colours.

To satisfy this yen for white, today's gardeners have at their disposal large numbers of trees, shrubs, perennials, bulbs, grasses and alpines that exhibit the colour. Of course, numerous plants have white flowers, but there are also many that have white stems, seedpods or white-variegated leaves. Some trees, such as the **jacquemontii birches**, have striking white bark (see also pages 41, 175). There are also whites for every season, with **snowdrops** (*Galanthus*) in winter, numerous bulbs and woodland plants, such as **anemones** in spring, and white berries in autumn, for example those of ***Sorbus cashmiriana*** ♀ (see page 166) or the attractive snowberry ***Symphoricarpos albus*** (see page 166).

We tend to use the term 'white' somewhat loosely, covering colours that are, in fact, creamy or have an inherent pinkness or blueness. Nothing could be more white than the flowers of ***Lilium candidum*** ♀ (the Madonna lily), but the tulips ***Tulipa* 'Purissima'** ♀ (see page 125) and ***Tulipa* 'White Parrot'** are perhaps more ivory than pure white, and ***Geranium clarkei* 'Kashmir White'** ♀ has flowers whose petals are criss-crossed with fine purple veins so they appear pinkish grey.

The natural brilliance of white means that it stands out in any setting, and so plants with large white flowers in a mixed colour planting will dominate the picture. This may be the effect wanted in predominantly green gardens, but when using white with other colours it is preferable to use plants with smaller flowers, as their impact will be less and the rhythm and balance of the planting won't be lost. ***Gypsophila paniculata* 'Bristol Fairy'** ♀ and ***Crambe cordifolia*** ♀ (see page 138) perform the task perfectly in early

WHITE PLANTING FOR SHADY AREAS

In partial shade, one could make a white planting for spring using plants such as *Epimedium* × *youngianum* 'Niveum' ♀, *Pulmonaria* 'Sissinghurst White' ♀ and *Anemone nemorosa* ♀ for the foreground, with *Polygonatum* × *hybridum* ♀ behind. In early summer, *Dicentra spectabilis* 'Alba' ♀, *Astrantia major alba* (left) and *Campanula alliariifolia* interspersed with white foxgloves, such as *Digitalis purpurea* f. *albiflora*, will carry on the theme. Later in summer, *Monarda* 'Schneewittchen', *Aster divaricatus* and *Schizostylis coccinea* f. *alba* all provide white flowers and are happy in partial shade.

summer and, while not as light and airy, **gauras** such as ***Gaura lindheimeri*** ♀, with their thin spikes of bell-shaped flowers, can perform a similar function in late summer if scattered throughout a planting. ***Astrantia major*** also provides 'broken' white flowers, with a lightness that makes them ideal for combining with other plants. As an added bonus, if they are cut back regularly after the flowers die they will continue to bloom until early autumn.

The ethereal quality of white, and the fact that it reflects light, may be exploited in those areas of the garden that are somewhat dark and shady: plants with white flowers will always lift the mood of a dark space. Their luminosity also means that they look marvellous in moonlight. Again, you can make the most of this propensity by planting white annuals such as **cosmos**, **tobacco plants** (*Nicotiana*) and **snapdragons** (*Antirrhinum*) beside a path, in a front garden, or around a seat – anywhere in the garden where visitors or passers-by are likely to walk or sit. On balmy summer evenings there is nothing more enchanting than the feeling that you have strayed into a 'ghostly' garden.

Above, left to right: *Betula utilis* var. *jacquemontii, Tulipa* 'White Triumphator', *Crambe cordifolia, Chamerion angustifolium* 'Album', *Salvia sclarea* var. *turkestanica* white-bracted, *Zantedeschia aethiopica.*

WHITE DOGWOODS

White is well represented in the genus *Cornus* (dogwood), which includes a wide range of plants from low-growing, ground-creeping shrubs to small trees. There is the popular variegated *Cornus alba* 'Elegantissima' ♀, with its flat white flowerheads, greyish-green leaves rimmed with white, and eye-catching red stems in winter. On a smaller scale, *Cornus canadensis* ♀, the creeping dogwood, seldom grows taller than 15cm (6in) and has tiny green flowers surrounded by showy white bracts up to 2cm (¾in) long. Among the most beautiful of the small tree dogwoods, *Cornus controversa* 'Variegata' ♀ (see page 42) has tiers of shiny dark green leaves with white margins and flat heads of white flowers in early summer; it grows up to 8 x 8m (25 x 25ft). *Cornus* 'Eddie's White Wonder' ♀ (above) has showy greenish-purple flowerheads surrounded by four to six white bracts, which appear in late spring. When mature, this cornus reaches 6 x 5m (20 x 15ft).

PLANTS FEATURING WHITE

Trees and shrubs

Carpenteria californica ♀
Davidia involucrata ♀ (see page 137)
Escallonia 'Iveyi' ♀ (see pages 61, 157)
Exochorda × *macrantha* 'The Bride' ♀ (see page 123)
Magnolia stellata ♀ (see page 114)
Philadelphus 'Virginal' (see page 138)
Rosa MARGARET MERRIL ('Harkuly') ♀
Sorbus cashmiriana ♀ (see page 166)
Viburnum opulus 'Compactum' ♀

Perennials

Anthemis punctata subsp. *cupaniana* ♀
Artemisia lactiflora ♀
Hesperis matronalis var. *albiflora* 'Alba Plena'
Salvia sclarea var. *turkestanica* white-bracted (see also page 158)
Zantedeschia aethiopica ♀

Bulbs

Galanthus elwesii ♀
Leucojum aestivum 'Gravetye Giant' ♀
Trillium grandiflorum ♀ (see page 96)
Tulipa 'White Triumphator' ♀

Grey and silver

We all know that nothing sets off the colours of a shirt and tie as well as an understated, elegant dark grey suit, and the same is true in a garden setting. Grey has the capacity to make pastel shades seem more intense and to neutralize brash, strident ones. Although grey is inconspicuous and recessive in nature, it plays a major 'diplomatic' role, helping other more assertive colours to work together.

In most situations, grey seldom catches our eye, while silver (which is grey with a sheen) tends to sparkle. However, in the garden the two colours are interchangeable and will add lustre to any planting. Numerous plants have grey or silver leaves, including some trees – for example ***Olea europaea*** (olive) and ***Pyrus salicifolia* 'Pendula'**♥ (weeping pear) – as well as many shrubs, succulents and perennials. Most come from hot, dry places, so in gardens in dampish northern latitudes it is important to try and replicate as closely as possible the conditions these plants would have enjoyed in the wild, namely positions in sun in well-drained soil.

SILVER-LEAVED ARTEMISIAS

The 300 species of artemisias vary enormously, but most have grey or silver leaves with intricately cut and indented margins. The foliage of *Artemisia ludoviciana* 'Valerie Finnis'♥ (1) is silvery grey with deeply cut margins, while *Artemisia ludoviciana* 'Silver Queen'♥ (2) (see also page 79) has lance-shaped, silvery white leaves. They are ideal for weaving in and out of mixed perennial plantings, as is *Artemisia* 'Powis Castle'♥ (3), with its feathery silver leaves that billow out in soft clouds. The compact *Artemisia stelleriana* 'Boughton Silver' (4) has silky leaves and looks best at the front of a planting or as an edging for a path.

The grey or silver appearance of foliage arises because the leaves are covered with masses of tiny white hairs that grow on their surfaces – this is nature's way of preventing them from being scorched in hot sun. The texture of the leaves is variable. Some grey or silver foliage plants have leaves that are thick and felted, for instance ***Salvia argentea***♥, ***Verbascum olympicum*** and ***Stachys byzantina***, while others have feathery, intricately cut leaves, for example the **santolinas** or **artemisias** (see box, left). There are also those that have thick succulent leaves, namely the **echeverias** and **sempervivums**.

SILVER OR GREY WITH OTHER COLOURS

Silver- or grey-leaved shrubs, perennials and annuals are ideal candidates for including in plantings where the emphasis is on harmonious pastel shades, such as pinks, blues and creams. ***Artemisia*** **'Powis Castle'**♕ (see box, opposite) is the perfect companion for pale pink roses, for instance ***Rosa*** **'Mary Rose'**♕, and blue veronicas, such as ***Veronica gentianoides***♕ (see box, page 41). The silver-leaved ***Veronica spicata*** **subsp.** ***incana*** (see page 135) and the low-growing ***Anthemis punctata*** **subsp.** ***cupaniana***♕ make a pleasing and harmonious underplanting for pale yellow roses. The white daisy flowers of the anthemis have yellow centres that mirror the colour of the roses, and its silvery foliage never looks shabby.

Greys and silvers can also make a valuable contribution in all-white planting schemes, acting as softeners for the whites, which can appear almost too bright when set against a backdrop of dark green foliage. Using a single grey-leaved plant, such as ***Artemisia ludoviciana*** **'Valerie Finnis'**♕ (see box, opposite), repeated at intervals throughout a planting, will not only soften the planting but will also enrich and lighten it.

Above, left to right: *Agave americana, Stachys byzantina, Elaeagnus* 'Quicksilver', *Cynara cardunculus, Eryngium giganteum, Hebe pinguifolia* 'Pagei'.

Greys and silvers may also be used to calm down highly charged colours, such as magenta, and to provide some lightness to plantings that include dark red and plum shades. The popular oriental poppy ***Papaver orientale*** **'Patty's Plum'**, with its faded plum-coloured blooms, looks beautiful against a backdrop of grey- or silver-leaved plants such as ***Helichrysum italicum***♕ (with its yellow flowers removed) or ***Stachys byzantina*** **'Silver Carpet'**.

ARCHITECTURAL SILVER OR GREY PLANTS

One of the boons of the greys and silvers is that, among their number, there are some statuesque or architectural plants that add a great sense of theatre to plantings. The Scotch thistle *Onopordum nervosum* ♕ (right) has spiny-toothed, silver-grey leaves, to 50cm (20in) long, and thistle-like, purplish flowerheads and spiny bracts in summer. *Cynara cardunculus*♕ (cardoon) has spiny, silvery-grey, deeply cut leaves, up to 50cm (20in) long. Among the sea hollies there are also some striking silvers, for example *Eryngium giganteum*♕ (Miss Willmott's Ghost), which has 'thimble-like' flowers surrounded by prickly silver bracts, 6cm (2½in) long.

GREY/SILVER-LEAVED PLANTS

- *Agave americana*♕
- *Artemisia schmidtiana* 'Nana' ♕
- *Astelia chathamica*♕
- *Athyrium niponicum* var. *pictum*♕
- *Echeveria secunda* var. *glauca*♕
- *Elaeagnus* 'Quicksilver'♕
- *Hebe pinguifolia* 'Pagei'♕
- *Helictotrichon sempervirens*♕
- *Hippophae rhamnoides*♕
- *Pyrus salicifolia* 'Pendula'♕
- *Rosa glauca*♕
- *Salvia argentea*♕
- *Teucrium fruticans*
- *Thymus* × *citriodorus* 'Silver Queen'♕

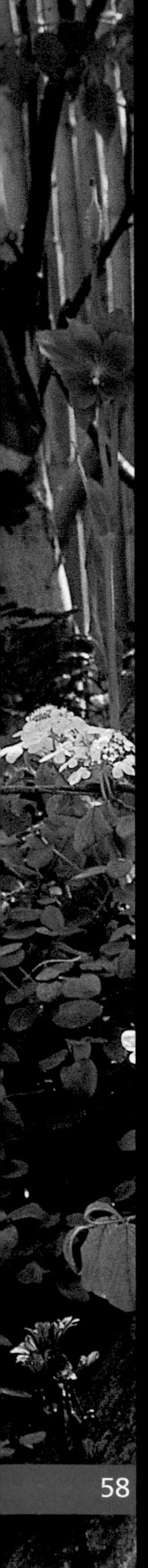

MOODS

People have long used paint to decorate their dwellings to produce specific moods. Similarly, the plants a gardener chooses, and the way they are arranged together, affect the mood of a garden. By making definite but limited colour choices, it is possible to create a range of moods, and mastering the art of exploiting colour to provide an aura of calm, subtlety, excitement, drama or sophistication enriches every gardener's experience.

RIGHT: *Viburnum plicatum* f. *tomentosum* 'Mariesii' and *Meconopsis* × *sheldonii*.

Calming

Monks of old realized that an enclosed garden with a cloister around it was the perfect place for calm reflection. Not many of us can afford to make a garden with its own cloister, but it is very easy to create a sense of enclosure, perhaps in a corner of the garden, and to construct plantings that generate a mood of calm. Not surprisingly, these plantings should be filled with harmonious rather than contrasting colours.

The word harmony suggests quietness and calm but, as we have seen, there are hot, vibrant harmonies as well as soothing, tranquil ones. Naturally, a calm planting requires the most restful harmonies – those composed largely of blues and other cool colours with blue in their make-up.

Blue harmonies show up best in shade, where the light with its bluish tinge enriches the blues. Any planting will, of course, contain a lot of green, but green is almost as soothing as blue and makes the perfect backdrop. When building blue harmonies, the most soothing plantings are made by adding other harmonious colours, such as violet, lavender, lilac, bluish-pink, broken white, pale primrose and silver – all guaranteed to enrich plantings without destroying their mood.

While orange, sulphur yellow and scarlet must be avoided, the darker, bluish reds, such as crimson and deep purples, added to blue plantings give a sumptuous feel without necessarily destroying their calming effect. In fact, dark, sultry plantings may be just what is needed if a calming garden is not to be too bland.

A FEELING OF ENCLOSURE

When creating a garden or a corner of a garden with a calming effect, it is a good idea to surround the area in some way with a hedge or fence, as enclosed spaces convey a feeling of sanctuary from the outside world and barriers may help muffle unwelcome noise. A trellis creates a similar effect, particularly if painted a colour that complements the garden scheme, as here. *Taxus baccata* ♈ (common yew) makes the most enduring and handsome of hedges and provides a rich dark green background to plantings, while *Ligustrum ovalifolium* (privet) and *Prunus lusitanica* ♈ (Portugal laurel) have lighter green leaves that are shiny and therefore reflect light.

CREATING AN ATMOSPHERE

When trying to create a calm mood it is worth remembering that a fountain or the sound of running water will add to the contemplative air. You may find wind chimes or the clattering of bamboo boxes calming too. On the other hand, you may prefer to be calmed by silence or the gentle rustling of leaves or grasses in the breeze. A garden's atmosphere can also be affected by the colour of its furniture, containers, doors, gates and walls, so take them into consideration when planning the scheme.

PLANTS TO CREATE SHADE

To provide some shade in a calm, blue planting scheme in a small area, a tree such as *Prunus padus* 'Watereri' ♈ (bird cherry) would be ideal. This small to medium-sized deciduous tree is especially attractive in spring, when it bears dangling, white, almond-scented flower clusters, up to 20cm (8in) long.

If a large enclosed area is required, use evergreen shrubs to provide weight and year-round interest when the blue plantings are not in flower. There are a number of evergreen shrubs that have attractive leaves and flowers in winter, for example *Escallonia* 'Iveyi' ♈ (1) (see also page 157), *Viburnum* × *burkwoodii* 'Anne Russell' ♈ (2) (see also page 117) and *Sarcococca hookeriana* var. *digyna* ♈ (3). All bear fragrant white flowers when little else is in bloom. *Phillyrea latifolia* (4) is an under-used evergreen with glossy, dark green leaves; it makes a very handsome addition to a shrub planting, and may also be grown as a hedge. In colder areas it should be grown against a wall.

A HARMONIOUS PLANTING FOR SHADE

There are various evergreen and deciduous shrubs that would work well in a harmonious planting in a shady area, providing some structure, a good backdrop for herbaceous plants, and various shades of green at times of year when there are no flowers present. **Philadelphus** tolerate partial shade, and their scented white, early-summer flowers add a touch of the exotic to any scheme. ***Philadelphus* 'Belle Etoile'**♕, growing to 1.2m (4ft) high, has highly fragrant white flowers with pale purple markings in the centre, while the compact, bushy ***Philadelphus* 'Manteau d'Hermine'**♕, at no more than 75cm (30in) high, suits the front of a border. **Hydrangeas** could also be used to bulk out such a planting and provide flowers over a long period from summer to autumn, when the philadelphus have ceased to flower. On acidic soil ***Hydrangea serrata* 'Bluebird'**♕ has deep, rich blue fertile flowers (they are more mauve on alkaline soil) with paler blue sterile flowers around them.

There are several low-growing shade-lovers that provide colour before the main flowering period. For the front of a border, ***Corydalis flexuosa* 'Purple Leaf'** has delicate, ferny purple leaves and pretty mid-blue, hooded flowers, and ***Brunnera macrophylla***♕ has forget-me-not flowers in powder blue. ***Pulmonaria* 'Blue Ensign'** (see also page 115 and Good Companions, page 116) has clear, deep blue flowers with dark green leaves without markings or spots. Other plants that would add to the scene in early spring, and grow in partial shade, include ***Polygonatum × hybridum***♕ (Solomon's seal) (see page 125), with its graceful sprays of bell-like flowers on stems up to 1.5m (5ft) tall, and **camassias**. These are splendid blue-, purple- and white-flowered bulbous perennials, whose star- or cup-shaped flowers emerge in erect spires from spring to summer. They provide striking vertical accents above the mounds of foliage towards the front of a border. ***Camassia cusickii* 'Zwanenburg'** has deep blue flowers.

As spring gives way to summer, the shade-loving **meadow rues** (thalictrums) come into their own. ***Thalictrum rochebruneanum*** has tiny clusters of

Top row, left to right: *Philadelphus* 'Belle Etoile', *Philadelphus* 'Manteau d'Hermine', *Hydrangea serrata* 'Bluebird', *Nepeta* 'Six Hills Giant', *Aconitum* 'Spark's Variety', *Geranium pratense* 'Plenum Violaceum'.

Bottom row, left to right: *Pulmonaria* 'Blue Ensign', *Brunnera macrophylla, Corydalis flexuosa* 'Purple Leaf', *Thalictrum rochebruneanum, Iris sibirica* 'Annemarie Troeger'.

blue and rich-mauve flowers on branching stems, which add a feeling of airiness to any planting.

Siberian irises are happy growing in partial shade; the flowers – carried on long, thin stems up to 1.2m (4ft) tall – are the height of elegance in early summer. The species, ***Iris sibirica***♀, has royal blue flowers. There are also some interesting cultivars that could be added to the planting, such as ***Iris sibirica* 'Annemarie Troeger'**♀, which has soft mauve-blue flowers with a cream throat, and ***Iris sibirica* 'Sparkling Rosé'**, with lilac-rose flowers.

The **catmints** (nepetas) are just as content growing in partial shade as in sun; ***Nepeta* × *faassenii***♀, which grows up to 45cm (18in) high, could be planted along the front of the border to provide a bluish 'haze' that would soften the border's edge from early summer to early autumn. ***Nepeta* 'Six Hills Giant'** is taller, to 90cm (3ft), with lavender-blue flower spikes.

Later in the summer, a number of **monkshoods** (aconitums) produce panicles of flowers in blue and purple. ***Aconitum* 'Spark's Variety'** has deep violet flowers on stems up to 1.5m (5ft) tall from midsummer to late summer. Some **salvias** are also happy growing in shade and, if planted in pots, could be popped into the planting to give it 'lift' in late summer or early autumn. Perhaps the best for this would be ***Salvia patens***♀, with its intense blue flowers.

Geraniums weave among other plants, and many have flowers in cool colours that would fit well into a blue harmonious planting. ***Geranium pratense* 'Plenum Violaceum'**♀ (see Good Companions, page 141) is a beautiful double cranesbill with violet-blue flowers from early to midsummer.

BLUES FOR SUN

When planting blues in sunny spots, remember that the sun will make them appear less blue and more violet. However, there are lots of plants with blue flowers that you could use to make a calming planting. Delphiniums, such as *Delphinium* 'Bluebird', could be the centrepiece for summer; later, provided the soil is well drained and not too rich, *Perovskia* 'Blue Spire'♀ provides clouds of violet-blue flowers for weeks.

Exciting, vibrant

Playing safe doesn't always pay. Treading carefully may give one a secure life but the chances are, it will be a dull one. The same is true in a garden. Playing safe with colour and always opting for restful hues will more than likely produce an uninteresting garden. How much more stimulating to throw caution to the wind now and then and experiment with bold, loud colour to produce a mood that stimulates rather than soothes.

When trying to create a mood of excitement, there is nothing to beat the brightest reds, oranges and yellows that together make hot, vibrant harmonies, unmatched for generating a spirit of *joie de vivre*. Moreover, when placed together, the individual colours seem more intense. These harmonies could not be further removed from the calm, harmonious plantings of the blues. Because they are brimming with energy, these hot colours will overpower more muted and cooler plantings so, where space permits, it is often best to create a separate area surrounded by trellis, a fence or a wall. The owners of smaller gardens will have to decide whether they want to go for broke and 'electrify' the whole garden or confine vibrant colour combinations to containers.

SPRING BORDERS

Mid- to late summer is the time when vibrant and exotic colours are most numerous, but it is also possible to make exciting schemes from mid-spring on.

(*Continued on page 66.*)

DAHLIAS

After years of being thought infra dig, dahlias have become fashionable again and rightly so, for they have wonderfully jazzy flowers in an amazing range of colours. They are native to Central America, which explains why they are usually lifted and brought into a frost-free environment for winter. The shapes of the flowers are almost as diverse as their colours, varying from daisy-like single-flowered dahlias to 'ball', 'pom-pom', 'waterlily', 'orchid', 'peony', 'decorative' and 'cactus' dahlias. Among the best for an exciting, hot planting are *Dahlia* 'Glow Orange' (1), with its small, bright orange, ball-shaped blooms, *Dahlia* 'Moonfire'♀ (2), a single-flowered variety with cream blooms that are flushed with red at the centre and dark-coloured leaves, and the spiky-looking, 'semi-cactus' *Dahlia* 'Nargold' (3), with pinkish-orange, double flowers with slightly pointed petals (see also page 153).

ADDING FOLIAGE

When creating hot plantings it is vital to achieve a balance between colour and foliage, bearing in mind that a mixture of highly charged colours needs an almost equal mass of foliage. Some of the leaves should be big and dramatic, and there should be a range of shapes and textures. The foliage in hot, exciting schemes is every bit as important as the flowers – these plantings call for bold statements.

Phormiums, with their large, spiked leaves, work well in these situations; also rheums, such as *Rheum palmatum* 'Atrosanguineum'♀ (1), with its giant rhubarb leaves. These are red when fresh, gradually becoming dark green on top; *Melianthus major*♀ makes an elegant addition, with its beautiful grey-green, toothed, pinnate leaves, as well as tall, wafting grasses such as *Stipa gigantea*♀, which has golden spikelets on 2.5m (8ft) stems (see page 67 and Good Companions, page 151). Ligularias and rodgersias, such as *Rodgersia podophylla*♀ (2) (see also page 101), have magnificent leaves, as do bananas (*Musa*), guaranteed to give a lush tropical feeling to a planting. For their calming properties, some dark red or crimson leaves are an asset, such as the leaves of *Canna* TROPICANNA ('Phasion') (3) (see also page 67), but they must be used sparingly as too many make a planting seem sombre. The inclusion of lime-green or yellow foliage will counteract this. Golden grasses such as *Milium effusum* 'Aureum'♀, bamboos including *Pleioblastus viridistriatus*♀, and golden-leaved shrubs such as *Choisya ternata* SUNDANCE ('Lich')♀ and *Cornus alba* 'Aurea' ♀ are all useful 'lighteners'.

In a planting of strong contrasting colours like this mixture of yarrows, *Centaurea montana* and poppies, it is important to have large amounts of green foliage to act as a buffer.

From mid-spring on, bulbs such as **hyacinths**, **narcissi** (see pages 120–21), **tulips** (see pages 130–31) and large **fritillaries** (see page 129), notably the orange crown imperial ***Fritillaria imperialis* 'Rubra Maxima'**♀, start flowering in earnest. Many **tulips** are also brightly coloured, and a high-octane planting could include the scarlet flowers of ***Tulipa* 'Red Impression'**, the orangey-gold of ***Tulipa* 'Generaal de Wet'**, the soft pink of ***Tulipa* 'Apricot Beauty'**, the golden yellow of ***Tulipa* 'Golden Apeldoorn'** and the scarlet-flowered ***Tulipa praestans* 'Fusilier'**♀. These would grow through a bed of emerging foliage, such as that of **aquilegias** or **euphorbias**, perhaps ***Euphorbia palustris***♀ or ***Euphorbia polychroma***♀ (see page 126), or the emerging bright yellow foliage of ***Valeriana phu* 'Aurea'**. Planting the tulips so that they emerge through the young leaves of bronze fennel or the rich crimson leaves of ***Euphorbia dulcis* 'Chameleon'** will make the scheme deeper and richer.

SUMMER COMBINATIONS

While spring offers the excitements of bulbs and emerging lush foliage, and early summer yields masses of perennials and statuesque plants such as **oriental poppies** *(Papaver orientale)*, **tall bearded irises**, **delphiniums** and **lupins**, as well as **roses** (see page 145), it is late summer that takes the prize for providing gardeners with the most dazzling palette of colours to play with. This is the time when half-hardy and tropical flowers come into their own, flowering for all they are worth. **Kniphofias** (see page 152), **cannas**, **heleniums**, **rudbeckias**, **dahlias** (see page 65) and **crocosmias**, as well as **sunflowers** (*Helianthus*), **zinnias**, **gazanias** and numerous other annuals, are at their peak now, and when combined they make the sparks fly.

At the back of a summer border you could plant pollarded ***Paulownia tomentosa***♀ for the impact of its vast leaves. ***Berberis thunbergii* f. *atropurpurea*** and ***Cotinus coggygria* Rubrifolius Group** would contribute calming red foliage. Architectural shapes for the middle of the border could consist of ***Phormium cookianum* subsp.**

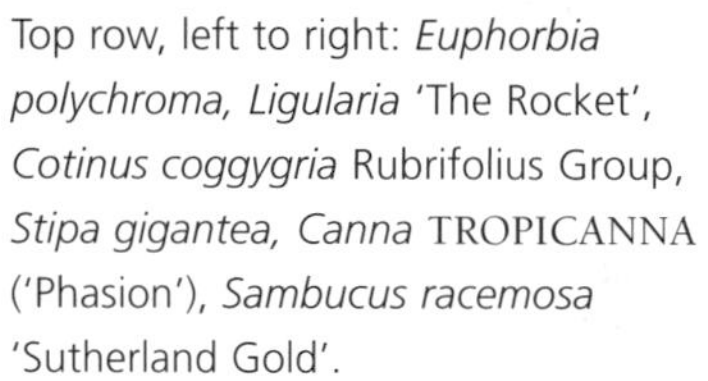

Top row, left to right: *Euphorbia polychroma, Ligularia* 'The Rocket', *Cotinus coggygria* Rubrifolius Group, *Stipa gigantea, Canna* TROPICANNA ('Phasion'), *Sambucus racemosa* 'Sutherland Gold'.

Bottom row, left to right: *Fritillaria imperialis* 'Rubra Maxima', *Tulipa* 'Red Impression', *Ligularia dentata* 'Britt-Marie Crawford', *Helenium* 'The Bishop', *Heuchera* 'Plum Pudding'.

hookeri* 'Cream Delight'**♡, with cream-striped leaves, and ***Ligularia dentata* 'Britt-Marie Crawford'**, with its red-brown, kidney-shaped leaves and deep orange flowers. For a different but equally attractive leaf form, ***Ligularia* 'The Rocket'**♡ could provide dramatic, toothed dark green leaves and spires of yellow flowers. The 'lifting' of the planting would rely on the yellow, finely cut foliage of ***Sambucus racemosa* 'Sutherland Gold'**♡ and the bamboo ***Pleioblastus viridistriatus♡. At the front of the border, the purple-leaved ***Heuchera* 'Plum Pudding'** and ***Milium effusum* 'Aureum'**♡ (Bowles' golden grass) could be interspersed with flowering perennials.

Every planting needs its stars, and here they are ***Canna* 'Wyoming'**♡, which has frilly trumpets of flowers in bright orange or vermilion red and purple foliage with darker veins, and ***Canna* 'Rosemond Coles'**, with its shimmering red flowers on stems 1.5m (5ft) high. The cannas will provide strong vertical accents throughout the planting. There are also many highly coloured daisies that would bring great charm and help to fill out the middle and front of the border. ***Helenium* 'The Bishop'** has rich yellow flowerheads, while those of ***Helenium* 'Chipperfield Orange'** are rich orange. ***Rudbeckia fulgida* var. *sullivantii* 'Goldsturm'**♡ has golden flowerheads 7–12cm (3–5in) in diameter, while those of ***Rudbeckia laciniata* 'Goldquelle'**♡ are mop-like with numerous petals in lemon yellow. **Crocosmias**, with their funnel-shaped flowers on arching spikes, would provide contrasts to the daisies and, as they are available in yellow, orange and red, would fit the scheme perfectly. ***Crocosmia masoniorum***♡ has orange-red flowers, while those of ***Crocosmia* 'Lucifer'**♡ (see page 148) are tomato red. ***Crocosmia* × *crocosmiiflora* 'Citronella'** has lemon-yellow flowers. A selection of **dahlias** would bring a touch of glamour and any gaps could be filled by annuals such as ***Bidens aurea* 'Hannay's Lemon Drop'**, with its sunny yellow flowers, and ***Tithonia rotundifolia* 'Torch'**, which is a tall Mexican sunflower with orange-red flowers. If more exotic touches are needed, pots containing yellow and orange **lilies** could be popped into the planting as and when required.

Dramatic

Plantings of rich, sultry colours capture our attention and draw us into their depths in the same way as an oil painting of an interior by a Dutch master. Dark blues, dark reds, indigo, violet, red-browns, copper, bronze, and burnt gold – all are intense colours individually, yet together they seem to coalesce into a mélange in which no one colour stands out and which holds us enthralled.

For dramatic plantings, avoid pastels and lighter colours, such as white and yellow, which draw the eye too much. Consider including some flowering shrubs – by selecting carefully, it is possible to have attractive leaves, flowers and brilliant autumn colour, thus prolonging the interest of the scheme beyond the flowering period of the herbaceous plants. All plantings need a mixture of shapes and textures, but in dramatic schemes, where the aim is to create an overall impression of rich interwoven colour, they are particularly important.

Alliums are dramatic plants in their own right and always provide strong vertical accents.

SHRUBS AND ROSES FOR DRAMATIC SCHEMES

The darker-flowered weigelas are good shrubs for dramatic schemes. They are happy in sun or partial shade, and some produce leaves in unusual dark shades to complement their funnel-shaped flowers: *Weigela* 'Eva Rathke' (see page 71) has rich green leaves and crimson flowers, *Weigela florida* 'Foliis Purpureis' ♀ has bronze-tinged leaves and dark pink flowers, and *Weigela* BRIANT RUBIDOR ('Olympiade') has yellow leaves and dark red flowers (see page 70). The smoke bushes (*Cotinus*) are perfect in these situations, too. *Cotinus* 'Flame' ♀ has light green leaves and purple-pink fluffy flowerheads, and *Cotinus* 'Grace' (1) (see also page 162) is large with purple leaves that turn brilliant shades of red in autumn.

Dark blue brings another dimension to rich plantings, as it does to Renaissance paintings, so it pays to include blue-flowered shrubs. *Ceanothus*, the Californian lilacs, are easy to grow and some bloom in late spring and early summer, others later in summer and into early autumn. *Ceanothus* 'Concha' (2) (see also page 136) has dark foliage and sapphire-blue flowers in spring. *Ceanothus thyrsiflorus* 'Skylark' ♀ is a late spring to early summer flowering shrub, growing up to about 2m (6ft), with glossy, mid-green leaves and dark, rich blue flowers. *Ceanothus* 'Autumnal Blue' ♀ bears deep sky-blue flowers from late summer to autumn.

Among the shrub roses there are ideal candidates for dark, moody plantings. The short flowering time of some cultivars is more than compensated for by the intensity and richness of colour and scent. The scented Gallica rose *Rosa* 'Tuscany Superb' ♀ blooms only once, but its velvet-textured, flattish, double flowers in deep crimson-maroon with a central boss of gold stamens make it a must. The Moss rose *Rosa* 'William Lobb' ♀ is another worthy candidate. Its moss-like, prickly, arching stems bear abundant highly fragrant, double, rich purple or deep lavender flowers; the stems may be trained over bent canes to encourage lateral branches to bear more flowers and make the flowers more visible. Another Moss rose, *Rosa* 'Nuits de Young' ♀, has upright stems covered with brownish 'moss' and scented, saucer-like flowers in a dark maroon. So dark are the blooms that this rose's common name is old black rose; it has a reputation for being prone to disease. On the other hand *Rosa* 'Roseraie de l'Haÿ' ♀ (3) is a robust Rugosa rose that grows up to 2.2m (7ft) and has healthy, light green, leathery leaves and strongly scented rich dark crimson flowers over a long period from summer to autumn (see also Good Companions, page 135, and page 145). Another long-flowering rose is *Rosa* 'Reine des Violettes', with double violet-purple, scented flowers from summer to autumn.

1 2 3

DAYLILIES

Today there are daylilies (*Hemerocallis*) in a kaleidoscope of colours and, while their individual flowers last only a day or two, the plants continue to bloom for at least a month. There are many different kinds to try for rich plantings. *Hemerocallis* 'American Revolution' has dark crimson flowers, which appear almost black, in midsummer, and *Hemerocallis* 'Bela Lugosi' has black-purple flowers with green throats from mid- to late summer. The flowers of *Hemerocallis* 'Dominic' are a sumptuous dark rich red and appear in late summer, as do those of *Hemerocallis* 'Starling', which are dark chocolate. *Hemerocallis fulva* 'Flore Pleno' (right) has double, tangerine flowers with dark orange veining, but those of *Hemerocallis* 'Missenden' ♀ are burnt marmalade with tangerine veins and centres.

ORIENTAL POPPIES

Oriental poppies, some of the *grandes dames* of the traditional herbaceous border in early summer, are blowsy and 'over the top', and they leave gaps when they finish flowering. However, they give such breathtaking performances that it is worth finding a place for them. Choice cultivars include the crimson *Papaver orientale* Goliath Group 'Beauty of Livermere' (see page 49), the dusky mauve *Papaver orientale* 'Patty's Plum' (1) and the salmon-pink semi-double *Papaver orientale* 'Garden Glory' (2). The best way to fill the gaps left in the border after the flowers are over is to plant out some annuals, perhaps zinnias or cosmea, or tender perennials such as salvias. *Salvia patens* has beautiful, saturated blue, hooded flowers.

HERBACEOUS PLANTS FOR A DRAMATIC PLANTING

You can heighten the drama by including some plants with impressive foliage, for example ***Angelica gigas*** or ***Angelica archangelica*** (see page 100), ***Acanthus spinosus***, ***Acanthus mollis*** and ***Veratrum nigrum***. However, such dominating shapes need to be offset by more unassuming, clump-forming subjects such as **astrantias** and **geraniums**. Astrantias are good-value plants, whose pincushion flowers are always decorative. And their lobed leaves are attractive. The dark red ***Astrantia major* 'Claret'** or ***Astrantia* 'Hadspen Blood'** (see page 156) would fit perfectly in this context, as would ***Geranium***

Top row, left to right: *Angelica gigas*, *Delphinium elatum* hybrid, *Weigela* BRIANT RUBIDOR ('Olympiade'), *Digitalis ferruginea*, *Weigela* 'Eva Rathke', *Eremurus stenophyllus.*

Bottom row, left to right: *Papaver somniferum* Paeony Flowered Mixed, *Hemerocallis* 'Anzac', *Astrantia major* 'Claret', *Anthriscus sylvestris* 'Ravenswing', *Crocosmia masoniorum* 'Rowallane Yellow'.

himalayense **'Gravetye'**♀, whose violet-blue flowers have reddish centres. For more ferny leaves, turn to ***Thalictrum aquilegiifolium*** **'Thundercloud'**♀ and the dark-leaved cow parsley ***Anthriscus sylvestris*** **'Ravenswing'**.

Tall, towering spires are always impressive and can bring real drama to a planting. **Delphiniums** have the showiest blooms and ***Delphinium*** **'Faust'**♀, with semi-double, rich cornflower-blue flowers with hints of purple and indigo, and ***Delphinium*** **'Blue Nile'**♀, with midnight-blue blooms with white eyes, are reliable performers. The **foxtail lilies** *(Eremurus)* have star quality also but, like some prima donnas, have a reputation for being 'tricky'. ***Eremurus* × *isabellinus*** **'Cleopatra'** is worthy of her name, with exotic reddish-orange flowers carried in 50cm (20in) spears on stems that can grow as tall as 1.5m (5ft). ***Eremurus stenophyllus***♀ is somewhat less showy but has dark, rich yellow flowers in 30cm (12in) long spikes that would blend into dark plantings. ***Digitalis ferruginea***♀, with its coppery flowers in thin spires (see also page 96), and ***Digitalis davisiana***, with pale yellow flowers criss-crossed with orange veins, are classy members of the foxglove family that could be included.

When including 'towering' plants it is wise to balance them with some glitzy perennials, for example **tall bearded irises**, **peonies** (*Paeonia*), **daylilies** (*Hemerocallis*, see page 69), **oriental poppies** (*Papaver orientale*, see opposite) and **crocosmias**, perhaps ***Crocosmia masoniorum*** **'Rowallane Yellow'**♀ or the dark orange and yellow ***Crocosmia* × *crocosmiiflora*** **'Jackanapes'** (see page 151). There are also some stalwart perennials, including **aquilegias** and **penstemons**, that are worth including as minor players. Bulbs such as **alliums** would provide interest for late spring, while grasses would provide a spectacle well into autumn; some **pennisetums**, for example, have pinkish or purple plumes.

Plantings of deep sultry colours are at their best in summer and early autumn, but one can prolong the drama by not cutting the plants down as winter approaches. Skeletons of grasses and perennials gilded with frost on a cold winter's day can be just as spellbinding as a planting in high summer.

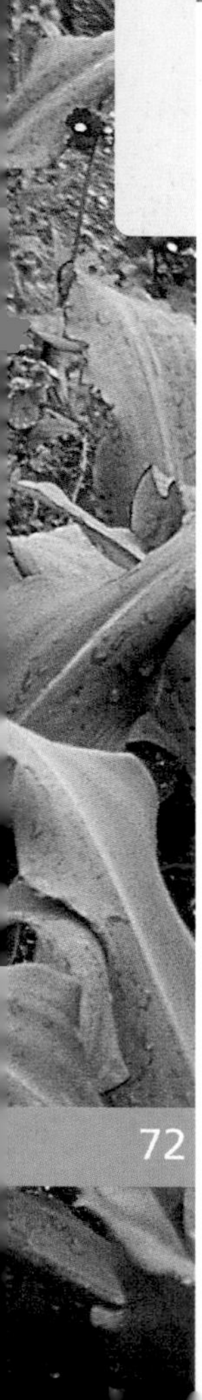

Subtle

The word 'subtle' comes from the Latin *subtilis*, meaning fine and delicate. We talk of a subtle meaning, subtle approach and subtle lighting, and in each case we mean refined and understated. Interestingly, this is the mood of many contemporary gardens, which are often designed to be as naturalistic and restrained as possible. If a naturalistic planting is not for you, there are a number of other ways to produce a subtle mood within a garden.

Restricting plants to a few choice specimens and then arranging them with great precision will produce a subtle, low-key effect. The Japanese have perfected this technique (see box, opposite), although in Japanese gardens the subtleties extend beyond the plants to embrace all the gardens' elements and symbolism. Any small, enclosed space could receive this kind of treatment, with perhaps a single, beautifully shaped tree being the centrepiece. ***Cornus controversa*** **'Variegata'**♀ (see page 42) is an elegant tree with tiered

The pendulous flowers of *Acer negundo* var. *violaceum* are a subtle shade of mauve.

branches like a wedding cake and leaves with creamy-white margins. Drifts of ***Cyclamen coum* subsp. *caucasicum* 'Album'** beneath it will provide small white flowers in winter and early spring (see pages 168–69), and intermingling the evergreen ***Asarum europaeum*** (see Good Companions, page 178), with its shiny, round or kidney-shaped, dark green leaves, ensures attractive year-round ground cover.

Green gardens or plantings can create a subtle mood, but to be sufficiently interesting they must contain plants whose leaves show marked differences of form, texture and colour. In shade, a collection of ferns including ***Dicksonia antarctica*** ♀, which produces fronds up to 3m (10ft) long, would be both spectacular and subtle at the same time. (See box, below.)

Another way of creating a subtle mood is to dedicate certain areas of the garden to flowers that are understated and muted in colour. This strategy is

JAPANESE GARDENS

Japanese gardens are perfect miniature landscapes, featuring mostly trees, shrubs, climbers, grasses, ferns and mosses. Evergreens provide a framework and bring interesting texture and strong forms, while deciduous trees and shrubs are selected for their flowers as well as their leaf forms. Interestingly, if snow settles on branches of evergreens in winter it is regarded in Japan as being another of the garden's flowers. Many gardens use the surrounding landscape as part of their composition; it may provide a view, or an element such as a large tree can provide shade. There has always been a tradition of using collected native species within Japanese gardens – a practice that has latterly been taken up by many gardeners in North America and Australia.

FERNS FOR FORM AND TEXTURE

Some hardy ferns are wonderfully architectural, for example: *Matteuccia struthiopteris* ♀ (ostrich or shuttlecock fern) (1) (see also page 43), whose upright 'shuttlecocks' of deciduous, pale green, sterile fronds, borne in spring, are at least 1.2m (4ft) long. Its fertile fronds are dark brown and less visible, only 30cm (12in) long, and appear in late summer. *Asplenium scolopendrium* Crispum Group (Hart's tongue fern) (2) has 30–60cm (12–24in) leathery, light green fronds with wavy margins. *Osmunda regalis* ♀ (royal fern) (3) is another statuesque fern that produces sterile, bright green deciduous fronds, up to 1m (3ft) long, in spring. In summer, these are joined by semi-fertile brown fronds, up to 2m (6ft) long, with wavy tassels. *Dryopteris affinis* ♀ (golden male fern) is almost evergreen and produces 'shuttlecocks' of lance-shaped, pale green fronds, finely divided into numerous small segments, or pinnae. The fronds darken as summer wears on, but often stay green throughout winter. Shorter but nonetheless elegant, *Blechnum penna-marina* is an evergreen with dark green leathery fronds up to 20cm (8in) long, that are linear or intricately divided into tiny lobes.

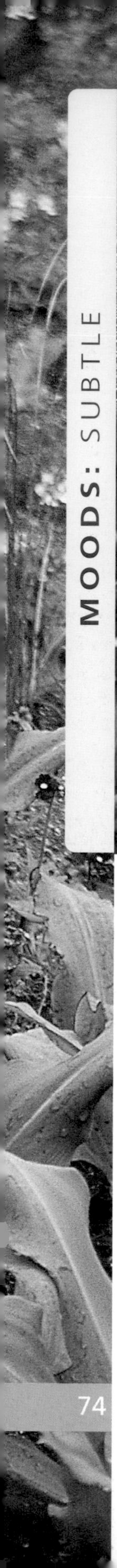

particularly suited to shady areas. On a larger scale, these kinds of plants will produce a perennially satisfying picture in a woodland garden. Woods look best if they are left to look as natural and uncluttered as possible.

Plantings of single colours in pastel shades, in which there are fine gradations of tone and shade, will create a subtle mood, too. The most delicate effects are produced using pale blue, bluish pinks, violets, greys and silvers, and beiges and browns, or harmonies of these colours. However, it is a mistake to believe that bright colours should always be banished from subtle-mood plantings. Nothing is more understated than a wildflower meadow, despite the fact that some of its flowers are highly coloured.

A subtle mood can be created using pastel-coloured flowers in various tones and shades, as seen in this drift of candelabra primulas.

Top row, left to right: *Miscanthus sinensis* 'Morning Light', *Liatris spicata, Calamagrostis* × *acutiflora* 'Karl Foerster', *Dierama pulcherrimum, Phlox paniculata.*

Bottom row, left to right: *Monarda* 'Croftway Pink', *Veronicastrum sibiricum, Origanum laevigatum* 'Herrenhausen', *Sanguisorba officinalis, Echinacea purpurea.*

A PLANTING OF PINK-FLOWERED PERENNIALS AND GRASSES

Grasses always bring elegance and lightness to a planting. ***Calamagrostis* × *acutiflora* 'Karl Foerster'** is an excellent grass, with pinky-bronze inflorescences, 0.6–1.8m (2–6ft) tall, which gradually fade to beige and light brown in autumn. ***Miscanthus sinensis* 'Morning Light'**🏆 (see also page 170) is another delicately beautiful grass, reaching 1.2m (4ft). It bears fine curved leaves with white margins and midribs that make the foliage appear silvery. Its flowerheads are produced in autumn and are grey tinted with maroon.

Like grasses, umbellifers – plants that resemble cow parsley, with umbrella-shaped inflorescences – can be relied on to help create subtle effects. An elegant umbellifer to add to a midsummer pink planting is ***Anthriscus sylvestris* 'Ravenswing'** (see page 71), which has white flowers and bronze ferny foliage.

Perennials to provide large areas of colour in this late-summer planting could include ***Echinacea purpurea,*** with its pink daisies (see also page 156), and the phloxes ***Phlox paniculata* 'Eva Cullum'**, a free-flowering form with rich, bright pink flowers and deeper pink centres, and ***Phlox paniculata* 'Norah Leigh'**, which has variegated leaves and pale pinkish-lilac flowers. All reach about 1m (3ft). Monardas, too, are worthwhile, though susceptible to mildew: ***Monarda* 'Croftway Pink'**🏆 has mid-pink flowerheads on stems up to 1m (3ft). ***Sanguisorba officinalis*** has fluffy 'bottle-brushes' carried 1.2m (4ft) high; they are maroon so appear as darker 'dots' through the planting. Held on stems up to 1.5m (5ft) tall, the bells of ***Dierama pulcherrimum*** also provide subtle specks of colours, ranging from pink to dark purple, over the lower plants.

For strong vertical accents, add ***Liatris spicata***, which has long, tapering flower spikes in purplish pink or white, and ***Veronicastrum sibiricum***, with spikes of lavender-blue flowers above whorls of horizontally held leaves. ***Origanum laevigatum* 'Herrenhausen'**🏆, with its clusters of bluish-pink flowers, is a good candidate for weaving in and out of plants at the front of the planting.

To create a subtle, naturalistic look, repeat the plants throughout the border.

Sophisticated

Sophistication is the antithesis of naturalness, so perhaps the most sophisticated gardens ever created in Britain were 18th-century landscapes made by aristocrats, inspired by the classical landscape paintings that they had seen on their Grand Tours in Italy. They filled their gardens with temples and statuary, whose relevance would have been apparent only to those who had a classical education or had been on the Grand Tour. But sophistication comes in many guises.

A great modern garden to which the epithet might apply was created by the late David Hicks, in Buckinghamshire. There are classical influences here – the design consists of strong, formal lines, and both the colour palette and the range of plant material are restricted. Green predominates and, while there are the browns, greys and black of bark and hard landscaping, other bright colours make only guest appearances. So perhaps the lesson for creating sophisticated moods is that less is more, and green handled carefully can be the epitome of chic.

Sophisticated plantings can be unpretentious, like this hollyhock with *Vitis vinifera* 'Purpurea'.

PLANTS FOR A SOPHISTICATED LOOK

The 'little black dress' has long been the simplest way for a woman to ensure that she looks sophisticated, and the equivalent in a garden is perhaps the clipped evergreen hedge. ***Taxus baccata*** ♕ (English yew) has been the traditional formal hedge of English gardens for centuries, no doubt because, being an indigenous species, it has always been close at hand. Making hedges of shrubs with variegated foliage brings lightness to a garden. **Hollies** (*Ilex*), with their shiny leaves, also make good hedges (see box, right).

Pleaching – the ancient art of creating hedges on stilts by training branches of standard trees (usually hornbeam or lime) along horizontal wires or bamboo canes – brings a definite air of sophistication.

Topiary is another way of introducing some distinction to a garden. **Yew** (*Taxus*) and **box** (*Buxus*) topiaries are ubiquitous because they make such perfect subjects, but there are other plants that respond well to clipping. In milder areas, ***Phillyrea angustifolia***, a Mediterranean and South-West Asian species with handsome lance-shaped, glossy, rich dark green leaves and insignificant greenish-white flowers, is a good choice. ***Prunus lusitanica*** ♕ (Portugal laurel; see also page 82) also adapts well to being clipped and is less susceptible to cold weather than ***Laurus nobilis*** ♕ (bay laurel or sweet bay), which it closely resembles. Evergreen shrubs with eye-catching glossy leaves and flamboyant flowers, for example **camellias** (see page 78), are also sophisticates and, whether grown in pots or in the soil, won't fail to bring an air of distinction to a garden. Adding a knot of low hedges, perhaps of **box**, a **lavender** such as ***Lavandula × intermedia*** **'Grosso'** or

HOLLIES FOR HEDGES

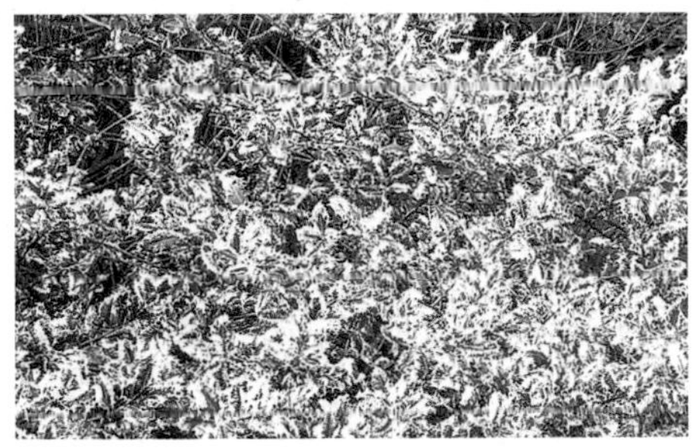

Some evergreen hollies, especially cultivars of *Ilex aquifolium* ♕ and *Ilex × altaclerensis*, make handsome hedges. Variegated forms are choice subjects, such as *Ilex aquifolium* 'Handsworth New Silver' ♕ (see page 1/4), a female holly with distinctive dark purple stems and narrow, mid-green leaves finely edged with cream; the similarly variegated but broader-leaved (and male) *Ilex aquifolium* 'Silver Queen' ♕; and *Ilex aquifolium* 'Ferox Argentea ♕ (above, see also page 173), a male holly with wide creamy-white margins. Planting male and female hollies together ensures berries.

The neatly clipped box hedges at Bourton House and the pleached hornbeam at Hidcote bring an air of sophistication to these Gloucestershire gardens.

BAMBOOS

The more compact bamboos are useful for including in smaller-scale plantings as well as in containers. They should be trimmed and the older canes thinned from time to time. *Shibataea kumasasa* is a well-behaved evergreen bamboo that is suitable for growing in a pot; it grows up to 60cm (24in) and has rich dark green, lance-shaped leaves. *Pleioblastus auricomus* has hollow purple and green canes and its leaves are bright yellow striped with green; it grows up to about 1.2m (4ft) and has a tendency to spread. *Pleioblastus variegatus* (see page 79) is another small bamboo, about 1m (40in) tall, with attractive cream-striped leaves. *Pleioblastus pygmaeus* 'Distichus' has hollow mid-green canes with purple tips and produces many linear, mid-green leaves; it grows up to about 75cm (30in) and is excellent as ground cover under other shrubs. *Sasaella masamuneana* 'Albostriata' reaches about 1.5m (5ft) and is sometimes invasive but may be confined to a pot. It has slender green or brown canes and narrowly elliptic, apple-green leaves with conspicuous white stripes; the stripes become more yellow as the leaves age.

CAMELLIAS

The camellias that have the widest range of flower colour, size and form are the cultivars of *Camellia japonica*. Most need some protection from midday sun and perform best if grown in free-draining acid soil with lots of leaf mould or well-rotted horse or cow manure added. They prefer to be fairly dry when dormant but well watered in the growing season.

Camellia japonica 'Inspiration'♕ (top left) bears miniature, soft pink flowers in what is known as a formal double configuration (flowers that have lots of rows of regular, overlapping petals with no stamens present). For those who like striped flowers, *Camellia japonica* 'Lavinia Maggi'♕ (bottom left) has medium-sized, formal double white flowers striped with pink and red. *Camellia japonica* 'Adolphe Audusson'♕ makes a compact bush, with large, semi-double red blooms in early spring.

a grey-leaved plant such as ***Santolina chamaecyparissus*** **'Lambrook Silver'** or ***Teucrium fruticans*** adds another layer of sophistication.

Minimalist gardens, with their strong emphasis on the cohesiveness and quality of all their elements, can be the height of sophistication. Plants that are interesting throughout the year and possess strong shapes are important in these settings. **Cordylines** and **yuccas**, and in warmer spots **aloes**, all have spear-like leaves so have instant impact. ***Fatsia japonica***♕ (see also page 83) is another classy but very good-tempered evergreen shrub with stunningly large shiny leaves. Its great advantage is that it is quite happy growing in deep shade, and so it makes an ideal specimen for a dark courtyard garden. In recent years

Top row, left to right: *Fatsia japonica, Camellia japonica* 'Adolphe Audusson', *Pleioblastus variegatus, Penstemon* 'Alice Hindley', *Clematis montana* var. *rubens* 'Tetrarose'.

Bottom row, left to right: *Lavandula* × *intermedia* 'Grosso', *Scabiosa caucasica* Perfecta Series 'Perfecta Alba', *Ophiopogon planiscapus* 'Nigrescens', *Tulipa* 'Black Hero', *Artemisia ludoviciana* 'Silver Queen'.

bamboos have become more popular, and the smaller ones make good pot plants that look very stylish in modern minimalist compositions. (See page 77.)

A FORMAL PLANTING FOR SUN IN BLACK, WHITE AND SILVER

Simple, clean-cut water features, such as rectangular pools, canals or rills with a paved surround, immediately say 'sophisticated' and would be the perfect setting for this type of planting scheme. The garden, or area of the garden, could be enclosed by trellis painted in a neutral colour, such as a soft grey.

Beds around a pool, or a paved area, could be edged with low hedges of ***Buxus sempervirens*** **'Suffruticosa'**♕, which might also perhaps zigzag through the beds to form a simple 'knot garden'. The spaces could be filled with white **grape hyacinths** (*Muscari*), the black-leaved grass ***Ophiopogon planiscapus*** **'Nigrescens'**♕ (see also pages 36–37 and 39), and, in spring, ***Tulipa*** **'Black Hero'** and ***Tulipa*** **'Snow Parrot'**. The bulbs could then be replaced with white annuals such as **snapdragons** (*Antirrhinum*). Standard roses planted at regular intervals always add a touch of formality, and a good choice here would be the white-flowered and scented English rose ***Rosa*** **WINCHESTER CATHEDRAL ('Auscat')**. These could be underplanted with the green- and silver-leaved ***Heuchera*** **'Mint Frost'**, the grey-leaved ***Artemisia ludoviciana*** **'Silver Queen'**♕ (see page 56), ***Viola*** **'Bowles' Black'** and the prolific white-flowered ***Penstemon*** **'White Bedder'**♕. The white-flowered scabious, ***Scabiosa caucasica*** **Perfecta Series 'Perfecta Alba'** and the black-flowered ***Scabiosa atropurpurea*** **'Ace of Spades'** would be good alternatives.

An arbour makes an attractive feature, and here it could host the dark-leaved ***Clematis montana*** **var.** ***rubens*** **'Tetrarose'**♕, with its sugar-pink flowers in late spring, and ***Solanum laxum*** **'Album'**♕, whose sweetly scented flowers appear in summer and autumn. Large pots of ***Yucca filamentosa*** **'Variegata'**♕ and the black-flowered ***Aquilegia vulgaris*** **var.** ***stellata*** **Barlow Series 'Black Barlow'** or, for a subtle touch of lilac blue, ***Penstemon*** **'Alice Hindley'**, would complete the picture.

SITUATIONS

In our minds we associate certain colours with specific situations. For example washed-out, sun-bleached pale blues and yellows seem to be appropriate in gardens beside the sea, as does an array of greens in woodland. When planning a garden's colours, the wise gardener bears in mind the situation and takes into consideration the colours of the hard landscaping and any containers. These are all factors that play a part in creating a satisfying overall picture.

RIGHT: Candelabra primulas.

Town gardens

Many town gardens are pocket-handkerchief size, but it's amazing what can be achieved using a bit of imagination, a few pots and plants, and perhaps some paint. Part of the fun of walking around a city is seeing the way people personalize their outdoor spaces, including making the most of the areas around front doors and windows.

By training climbers (here, *Rosa* 'Albertine') on the front wall of a townhouse, it is possible to create a verdant look even when there is no front garden.

It is always good to highlight the entrance to a house or flat. One way to do this is to pick out the colour of the door in the planting: a purple front door could be complemented by plants sporting pink, mauve, magenta and purple flowers or foliage. Another idea would be to train climbers around the door – a dark green **ivy**, such as ***Hedera helix* 'Parsley Crested'**♕, trained into diamond trellis looks wonderful on a brick wall, as does ***Jasminum nudiflorum***♕, the winter-flowering jasmine, trained into an arch on a stone façade. Pots containing matching plants placed either side of the door will transform an entrance. Try something dramatic, like **cordylines**, or topiary (see page 84). Trimmed **hollies** (*Ilex*), such as the variegated ***Ilex aquifolium* 'Silver Queen'**♕, always look smart as liveried doormen; contorted **hazels** in large pots or, on a north-facing aspect, trimmed ***Garrya elliptica*** work just as well.

Cordyline australis 'Torbay Dazzler'

URBAN JUNGLE OR MINIMALIST STYLE?

Many back gardens in towns don't have a view. There may be tall buildings nearby or overhanging trees that create permanent shade. One way to treat this kind of garden is to create a green 'jungle', using large-scale plants and climbers. With a few big specimen plants and some tall evergreen shrubs, it is possible to create a totally private domain, rich in atmosphere, where an adventurous and imaginative gardener can experiment with exotic plants and vivid but ephemeral 'tropical' colour.

Background foliage could be provided by evergreen shrubs such as ***Viburnum tinus***, ***Prunus lusitanica***♕, ***Elaeagnus* × *ebbingei* 'Gilt Edge'**♕ and the much-maligned Japanese laurels – the

Viburnum tinus

Prunus lusitanica 'Variegata'

Musa lasiocarpa

A jungle effect has been created in this garden by planting evergreen shrubs, including *Fatsia japonica*, in close proximity to the seating area.

Lapageria rosea

most elegant are ***Aucuba japonica* 'Nana Rotundifolia'**, with handsome, rounded, lance-shaped leaves, and ***Aucuba japonica* 'Crotonifolia'**🏆, with gold-streaked foliage. Principal players should be more exotic plants, such as large-leaved **hostas, ferns, tree ferns, phormiums, bamboos** and **bananas**. The most suitable banana for general cultivation, if space allows, is ***Musa* 'Dwarf Cavendish'**🏆; it has mid-green, paddle-like leaves up to 1.5m (5ft) long; it grows to 3m (10ft) high, with a similar spread. ***Musa lasiocarpa***, regarded as the hardiest banana, has shorter leaves, up to 1m (40in) long, reaches only 1.5m (5ft) and is suitable for growing in a pot.

A pergola draped with the Chilean climber ***Lapageria rosea***🏆, with its waxy, bell-shaped, pinkish-red flowers, will add to the subtropical feel, and large pots of ginger lilies would provide vivid spots of colour in late summer. ***Hedychium densiflorum* 'Assam Orange'** has rich dark orange, erect, bottlebrush-like flower spikes and long, shiny leaves. It is hardier than many people think.

The antithesis of the urban 'jungle' is the minimalist garden. Simple, streamlined gardens make the perfect accompaniment to building schemes where steel, concrete and glass are used in the construction and interiors are characterized by bleached wood, stainless steel and neutral colours. Plantings of white, cream, sand and grey (bamboos and grasses have stems and flowers in the appropriate neutral shades) work well in these settings alongside bold architectural plants such as **agaves, yuccas, phormiums** and **cordylines** (see box, page 84).

This sophisticated garden uses a restricted colour palette of green and white. The stark geometric lines of the hard landscaping have been softened with pale-flowered plants.

TINY TOWN GARDENS

In those town gardens where space is severely limited, it is often worth keeping permanent plantings of foliage plants to a minimum while making maximum use of the garden's perimeter walls or fences to support wall shrubs and climbers.

Another option is to train espalier trees around the perimeter, using plants like **beech**, **hornbeam** or **pyracantha**. This will give a formal, almost French feel to a garden, and that could be

In small urban gardens it is important to make maximum use of the vertical elements, namely the walls or fences and any dividers. Here, a painted trellis adds a splash of colour to a dark urban garden; its colour is repeated in the planting.

ARCHITECTURAL PLANTS FOR POTS

When selecting succulents and other architectural plants for pots, it is important to choose slow-growers. These include the succulent *Agave americana* 🏆 (see page 56), with its spiky, greyish-green leaves (in the ground these reach 2m/6ft eventually), and the dwarf fan palm *Chamaerops humilis* 🏆 (above), with its broad, bluish-green leaves divided into many long, pointed leaflets (it grows up to about 3m/10ft in the ground). Yuccas also grow slowly and make good potted specimens. The variegated *Yucca filamentosa* 'Bright Edge' 🏆 is eye-catching, with long, pointed, dark green leaves edged with bright yellow.

Architectural potted plants should be fed with blood, fish and bone and watered regularly. Check periodically to ensure they are not frozen in winter or dried out and overheated in summer.

POTTED TOPIARY

The most obvious choice for potted topiary is *Buxus sempervirens* 🏆 (common box). It can be trained into a wide variety of shapes including balls, pyramids and spirals. However, there are also flowering plants that respond well to being trimmed and will grow happily in containers.

Syringa meyeri 'Palibin' 🏆 is a slow-growing lilac with pale mauvish-pink flowers in late spring; it makes an elegant specimen when trained into a standard with a 'lollipop' head. Winter-flowering *Viburnum tinus* (see page 82) has dark green, shiny leaves and flattened clusters of white flowers in late winter and spring, and also makes a good lollipop shape. Another option is *Ligustrum delavayanum* (left), which is semi-evergreen in milder areas.

The expert advice on trimming plants in pots and containers is 'little and often'.

reinforced by placing painted Versailles containers or other decorative pots of topiary around the garden.

SHADY TOWN GARDENS

Many urban gardens are permanently shady. Damp shade results when overhanging trees allow little or no sun to warm the soil, and drips from the trees dampen the ground. Luckily, there are many plants that are happy to grow in these conditions.

For a planting scheme in damp shade, a lovely centrepiece would be a ***Cercidiphyllum magnificum***, a medium-sized, Japanese tree with large rounded leaves that turn brilliant shades in autumn. Alternatively, for smaller spaces, use a witch hazel such as ***Hamamelis* × *intermedia* 'Jelena'**♀ (see page 179), which has large, burnt orange, 'spider-like' flowers in winter and leaves that turn bright red in autumn, or a dogwood such as ***Cornus kousa* var. *chinensis* 'China Girl'**. This has tiny, spherical green flowerheads surrounded by elegant white bracts in early summer, and the leaves become dark reddish-purple in autumn.

A small enclosed town garden with few plants can be dull in winter but planting some evergreens can overcome this. Here, clipped box hedges surround a sundial and variegated ivy covers the wall, providing colour and structure all through the year. Growing shrubs in containers allows the owner to ring the changes, bringing them to the fore when they are in flower.

Good-looking evergreen shrubs that would give background foliage in a scheme for damp shade include **camellias**, **hollies**, **laurels** and **privets**, such as ***Ligustrum quihoui***♀, with its fragrant white flowers in late summer. **Hellebores** have flowers in winter and early spring and could be interspersed with low, carpeting plants such as ***Soleirolia soleirolii*** (mind your own business), the shiny-leaved ***Asarum europaeum*** (see page 178), ***Anemone nemorosa***♀ (see page 96), with its white flowers, and the creeping dogwood, ***Cornus canadensis***♀. The attractive perennial ***Astelia chathamica***♀, with its arching, sword-shaped foliage, could provide silvery vertical accents in the foreground planting.

PLANTS FOR DRY SHADE

Dry shade is caused by overhanging plants that prevent rain from reaching the ground. Fewer plants are happy growing in these conditions than in damp shade, but certain trees, including robinias, gleditsias and *Amelanchier lamarckii*♀, will grow, as will shrubs such as the flowering currant *Ribes sanguineum* (1), *Hippophae rhamnoides*♀, berberis, euonymus and *Lonicera pileata*. Perennials that spread happily include lamiums, brunneras, vincas, bergenias and *Liriope muscari* 'Variegata' (2).

Country gardens

When considering the English country garden, people often conjure up the vision of a traditional cottage garden with winding paths and old-fashioned flowers, or perhaps a country-house garden with spectacular herbaceous borders and sweeping lawns reminiscent of grand Edwardian estates. However, while there are still a lot of gardens that fit these descriptions, country gardens today tend to be as diverse and idiosyncratic as the people who make them.

Many gardens today, especially rural ones, are looking more 'natural' than they did a generation ago. The reason for this is that there is great interest in naturalistic planting, that is planting schemes that use grasses, biennials and perennials, including umbellifers (whose thousands of tiny flowers are carried in flat-topped clusters or umbels, like those of cow parsley). In addition to this, many gardeners have responded to calls from gardening and environmental experts to make their gardens more eco-friendly and attractive to wildlife by growing native plants alongside garden cultivars. These trends have inevitably had repercussions on the colours found in these gardens.

NATURALISTIC PLANTING

Plantings containing grasses and wildflowers (see pages 88–89), or those close in appearance to their native ancestors, generally have more restrained colours than schemes made up of garden cultivars. This is because the flowers of grasses are muted in colour, and wildflowers tend, on the whole, to have smaller flowerheads and less brilliant colours than cultivars. Also, in naturalistic plantings, plants are generally intermingled rather than planted in large masses, so the colours are more diffuse.

For many people the classic English country garden has roses and a mixture of cottage-style perennials billowing over a path like the one shown here. The effect is informal, intimate and enticing and, although the colours are mixed, the garden has a distinctly harmonious feel.

Close planting of a mixture of perennials with grasses has become popular in recent years: an informal effect like the one shown here works well in country gardens.

NATURALISTIC DESIGN

Wildflowers are the inspiration for the planting schemes designed by many contemporary designers. In Britain, Dan Pearson uses wildflowers in his designs, which are renowned for blending seamlessly into the landscape. His philosophy is that gardeners should work *with* nature rather than trying to dominate it. Similarly, nature is what inspires Piet Oudolf, one of Europe's most famous contemporary garden designers, acclaimed for his naturalistic plantings of grasses and tall perennials. For Oudolf, successful plant combinations rely primarily on shapes, particularly those of flowers and seedheads. Leaf shape and texture are of secondary importance, and colour is only the third consideration.

Some advocates of the naturalistic gardening style argue that gardeners should restrict themselves to growing only native species. There are situations in a country garden where planting nothing but native species can be a good idea, for example at a garden's boundaries, when the garden merges into the surrounding countryside, or in an area devoted to wild plants. Elsewhere, however, intermingling native plants with introduced species and cultivars generally makes for a more interesting and perhaps more personal garden. **Primroses** (*Primula*), **violets** (*Viola*) and **forget-me-nots** (*Myosotis*) are ubiquitous in country gardens, and are often found among spring bulbs or **snowdrops** (*Galanthus,* see page 177). And many gardeners happily allow the native **foxglove** (*Digitalis purpurea*) to seed itself around their borders.

On the other hand, planting introduced species and cultivars in wilder parts of the garden can work well too. In outer areas of his garden, garden designer Tom Stuart-Smith has native plants such as **cranesbills** (*Geranium*), **teasels** (*Dipsacus*), **scabious** (*Scabiosa*) and **wild carrot** (*Daucus*). But he mixes them with introduced plants that have a delicate, wild look, such as ***Persicaria amplexicaulis***, with its spiky purple, red or white flowers, ***Veronicastrum virginicum* 'Album'**, with its spikes of veronica-like, white flowers, and the grass ***Hakonechloa macra***, which has smooth, arching, mid-green leaves and pale green flower spikes from late summer to early autumn. He likes the idea of having a gradient of naturalness in a garden, from the highly cultivated areas close to the house to the semi-wild in its outer reaches. This is a gardening practice particularly well suited to country gardens.

Umbellifers are a key ingredient in any naturalistic planting scheme.

Planting bulbs such as narcissi in grass gives a country garden the feeling that it is rooted in the surrounding landscape.

Enormous herbaceous borders were often features of large country-house gardens in the past. Today, many borders are mixed, that is they that include shrubs, trees, grasses and bulbs as well as herbaceous perennials. In this border at White Windows, in Longparish, Hampshire, shrubs are planted among perennials, in a colour scheme featuring flowers in blue, cream and yellow.

COUNTRY-GARDEN BORDERS

In the past, many country gardens had very large herbaceous borders, the grandest of which contained thousands of plants and required an army of gardeners to tend them. We can still see these kinds of border in some National Trust gardens, for example Barrington Court in Somerset, and large private gardens such as Rodmarton Manor in Gloucestershire and Arley Hall in Cheshire, but the herbaceous borders created in country gardens today tend to be far less grand and orchestrated than those of old. The trend towards naturalistic gardening is as obvious here as elsewhere, and newer borders often sport selections of umbellifers and grasses as well as the more traditional perennials. At Kingston Maurward, in Dorset, the grass ***Calamagrostis* × *acutiflora* 'Karl Foerster'** (see page 75) is repeated along the length of impressive double herbaceous borders, and the pampas grass, ***Cortaderia***, is used as dramatic vertical accents.

Dark blue sweet peas and the flat heads of a yarrow provide contrasts of shape and colour.

Planting randomly using plants with a wide selection of flower colour can look wonderful in a country garden, but it is wise to include large amounts of green in the form of foliage plants as this will soften the impact of lots of bright colours and meld them together. **Aquilegias**, **thalictrums**, **heucheras**, **hostas**, **geraniums**, **epimediums** and spotted-leaved **pulmonarias** all have attractive leaves. For the front of a bed, ***Stachys byzantina* 'Big Ears'** (see page 138) is a handsome silver-leaved, low-growing plant with distinctly furry leaves. More spectacularly, ***Cynara cardunculus***♕ (see page 57) has 50cm

MAINTAINING HERBACEOUS BORDERS

It used to be the practice for herbaceous borders to be heavily fed with well-rotted manure, cut back in autumn and dug over annually. With an eye to practicality (most people have to tend their own gardens today or manage with minimal help) and another to ecology, current practice is for borders not to be cut back until spring, for them to be fed sparingly, if at all, and for them to be mulched once a year in spring to improve the condition of the soil and suppress weeds. Fewer nutrients mean the plants don't get too leggy and don't need staking and there is less disease. Also, the skeletons of plants in winter can be attractive.

In a corner of the garden at Little Court, in Crawley, Hampshire, there is a selection of cottage-garden perennials, including sweet rocket (*Hesperis matronalis*), geranium (*Geranium psilostemon*) and forget-me-nots. There are also alliums (*Allium nigrum* and *Allium hollandicum*), plants that are great favourites with many of today's country gardeners. The modern shrub rose *Rosa* 'Constance Spry' covers the wall behind.

(20in) long, greyish-green leaves, while those of ***Acanthus spinosus***♀ are spiny, dark green and up to 1m (40in) long. In larger borders, these dramatic 'greens' could be planted at regular intervals to provide strong vertical accents. Adding more foliage plants and grasses will make a planting look even more untamed and natural.

Large silver-leaved plants (in this case an onopordum) can soften a mixed-colour planting as well as providing drama in their own right.

COTTAGE GARDENS

Mixed plantings, in which woody plants are interspersed with perennials and bulbs, is very much the look of the traditional cottage garden, where plants are all jumbled together in higgledy-piggledy fashion without much thought being given to their form or colour.

It was in the latter half of the 19th century that Helen Allingham's and Myles Birket Foster's watercolours of cottage gardens opened the British public's eyes to their charms. Old cottage gardens were probably never quite as pretty as those in the paintings, but they were as crammed with plants of all kinds as we imagine.

For centuries cottagers relied on home-grown vegetables for their staple diet and any flowers in their gardens would have been wildflowers collected from hedgerows, including primroses and violets, or hand-me-downs from the local monastery garden or manor house. Every plant was welcome but, before the days of modern medicine, those that could cure ailments or make life more comfortable were most prized. Many cottage-garden flowers only became so because they were useful in one way or another. For example **mullein** (*Verbascum*), **columbine** (*Aquilegia*), **mallow** (*Malva*) and **St John's wort** (*Hypericum*) were grown for their medicinal properties. **Wormwood** (*Artemisia absinthium*), **meadowsweet** (*Filipendula*), and also

Roses and geraniums were often found in traditional cottage gardens, the geranium's foliage helping to disguise 'leggy' rose bushes.

Planting wild and cultivated plants together, in large informal plantings or in borders, is becoming increasingly popular. Here, the wild white valerian is mixed with cultivated grasses, white aquilegias, delphiniums and dark-leaved fennel.

southernwood (*Artemisia abrotanum*) were valued for strewing, keeping flies and fleas at bay, while **Hyssop** (*Hyssopus*), **lavender** (*Lavandula*), **sage** (*Salvia*) and **rue** (*Ruta*) were grown for their scent as well as for their medicinal properties. **Primroses** (*Primula vulgaris*) and **cowslips** (*Primula veris*) were used for flavouring drinks, and the flowers of **violets** (*Viola*) were put in salads.

Many plants arrived in cottage gardens because they had gone out of fashion in grander circles, explaining perhaps how more 'exotic' plants such as **lilies**, **peonies**, **roses**, **delphiniums**, **oriental poppies**, **dahlias** and **pelargoniums** first arrived on the scene. Unlike their grander neighbours, cottage-garden owners seldom threw out plants and so, unwittingly, became the conservers of strains of our best-loved, old-fashioned flowers: plants such as **sweet Williams**, **pinks**, **double primroses**, **gold-laced polyanthus**, **old ranunculus** and **shrub roses**.

During the 17th century Huguenot émigrés to Britain started the cultivation of 'florist's' flowers – **anemones**, **auriculas**, **carnations**, **hyacinths**, **pinks**, **polyanthus**, **ranunculus** and **tulips** – and, in time, these too found their way into cottage gardens, adding to the colourful mixture.

PLANTING PARTNERS FOR SHADE

The native lady's smock, *Cardamine pratensis* (1), is happy in dampish shade and could be included in plantings of shade-lovers such as hellebores or epimediums, including *Epimedium × versicolor* 'Sulphureum'♡ (2). It would also go well with *Corydalis flexuosa* 'Père David' (3) and *Dicentra spectabilis* 'Alba'♡ (see page 139).

WILDFLOWER MEADOWS

Increasing development on the fringes of towns and villages over the past 50 years, combined with modern farming methods, means that Britain has lost many of its beautiful wildflower meadows. This may be the reason why they have become such a cherished countryside image, and why so many contemporary country gardeners want to try to create meadows within their own boundaries. The plants for wild meadows vary in different parts of the country, depending on the soil type, but when making a meadow in a garden, there is no reason not to 'cheat' and add plants from different areas, as well as introduced species and cultivars. Purists may baulk at including plants that are not native, especially larger-flowered cultivars, but 'meadow' is a loose term.

CUTTING WILDFLOWER MEADOWS

While meadow-style plantings look natural, they cannot be left entirely to their own devices. It was the custom for traditional meadows to be cut down from early summer to midsummer and animals grazed on them afterwards. However, this is too early for the seed of plants such as cowslips and fritillaries to set, and many summer-flowering plants are at their peak.

Today, the advice is to cut in mid- to late summer and to leave the hay *in situ* to allow the early-flowering plants to seed. Cutting then also allows summer-flowering perennials to make new leaf and flower again later.

A second cut in early autumn is a good idea if there are spring-flowering bulbs in the meadow. This enables the flowers to burst through the grass more easily in spring, while a thick thatch left in place through the winter may act as a barrier.

Poppies in Claude Monet's garden at Giverny. Wildflower meadows are the inspiration for some contemporary garden designers who interweave perennials into their plantings. Making even a simple wildflower meadow is more difficult than it appears.

For those country gardeners who don't have the inclination or space for a meadow, an alternative is to plant drifts of small bulbs for spring colour. Masses of **snowdrops** (*Galanthus*) mingled with **winter aconites** (*Eranthis*) and **crocuses** will give an early 'meadow effect'. ***Narcissus pseudonarcissus***♀ (Lent lily, see pages 121, 178) or one of the smaller daffodil cultivars such as ***Narcissus* 'Topolino'**, which has creamy-yellow petals and lemon-coloured trumpets, could be added. Later in the spring, the dainty, nodding heads of the **snakeshead fritillary** (*Fritillaria meleagris*) naturalized in grass are pure delight, and drifts of tulips under trees can look 'meadow-like', especially the smaller species, perhaps the scarlet-flowered ***Tulipa sprengeri***♀ or ***Tulipa orphanidea* Whittallii Group**♀, which produces tangerine flowers tinged with a colour similar to tarnished brass. Gardeners with space and patience might like to try to create drifts of ***Lilium martagon***♀, the martagon lily, in the dappled shade of large trees. At Iford Manor, in Wiltshire, and at Spetchley Park, in Worcestershire, these charming lilies, with their pink turkscap flowers, come out in their thousands in the early summer months and never fail to steal the show.

Fritillaria meleagris, the snakeshead fritillary, is a wildflower of the British Isles but can be naturalized in a garden easily, bringing touches of the countryside into a country garden. In Oxford, Magdalen College gardens and Christchurch Meadows are famous for their fritillaries in late spring.

Fritillaria meleagris

Seaside gardens

A flower-filled garden that looks out over a dramatic seascape is the dream of many would-be seaside gardeners. The great advantage of a seaside situation, in addition to the view, is that temperatures are higher and there is little or no risk of frost. Also, in hot sunshine bright colours don't seem out of place, which means the gardener can be more adventurous with colour, inventing plantings that would not look right in a town or country setting.

Despite these attractions, anyone gardening on the coast has to battle against the ravages of wind, salt and, sometimes, very poor soil. The wind strips plants of moisture and 'wind prunes' them, so they appear lop-sided. Salt draws water out of plants when it lands on their leaves and shoots. Salt damage may even be a problem for gardens a few miles inland, too – in a storm, salt may be carried as far as 24 kilometres (15 miles).

Most plants resent being exposed to strong winds, so the first thing to consider when making a seaside garden is the provision of some protection from wind: contouring the land, building screens, or planting tough, wind-resistant plants as the garden's 'outer defences' (see box, right) will all help to minimize its effects. However, implementing any of these may obscure a wonderful view, so it may be necessary to protect only part of the

SPRING BULBS IN SAND

Many bulbs thrive best in gritty, free-draining soil with scarce nutrients, so they grow happily in sand. This is especially useful for those who garden by the sea. Here, grape hyacinths and chionodoxa flower profusely in a seaside setting.

WIND-RESISTANT PLANTS

Trees that withstand strong winds and are suitable for outer defences in a coastal garden include the evergreen oak *Quercus ilex* 🏆, *Cupressus macrocarpa* (Monterey cypress) and pines. Wind-resistant shrubs include the mountain pine, *Pinus mugo* (1), an architectural conifer with a spreading, irregular habit, and *Griselinia littoralis* (2), a glossy-leaved shrub with unusual ochre-coloured stems and round mid-green leaves.

1

2

In this seaside garden a low wall gives the plants in its lee some shelter against wind and salt without obscuring the view of the sea.

garden and leave the rest exposed so the view can be enjoyed. If hedges are to be included, keep them trimmed below eye-level; alternatively, cut 'windows' through them to allow glimpses of the panorama beyond the garden. A pergola draped with climbing plants will help to filter the wind around a sitting area – **roses**, **clematis**, **passion flowers** (*Passiflora*) and ***Solanum crispum*** all thrive in the milder temperatures around the coast.

Once the outer defence plants have become established, the other plants that are not so wind-resistant can be planted within their lee, for example trees such as **hawthorn** (*Crataegus*), **whitebeams** (*Sorbus aria*) and **poplars**, in particular ***Populus alba*** and ***Populus tremula***♕. Other plants that grow well in these situations are evergreens with leathery leaves, such as **hollies** (*Ilex*), ***Phillyrea latifolia*** (see page 61), ***Arbutus unedo***♕, and cultivars of ***Escallonia***, ***Choisya ternata***♕ and ***Euonymus fortunei***.

Silver-leaved plants seem especially well suited to coastal gardens; one only has to think of the native vegetation on the Mediterranean coast to see how beautiful greys and silvers look in that sunny setting. All **santolinas** thrive in coastal regions, and ***Atriplex halimus*** (tree purslane), with its leathery, silvery-grey leaves, is happy being exposed to any sea winds; it grows up to 2m (6ft) and makes a good hedge.

Crambe maritima♕ (sea kale) is a denizen of coastal regions, with bluish-green leaves and clusters of tiny, star-shaped white flowers in early summer. It makes mounds up to 75cm (30in) tall and is a good companion to other plants with white and yellow blooms, such as **evening primroses** (*Oenothera*), **mulleins** (*Verbascum*) and many of the **daylilies** (*Hemerocallis*), particularly the lemon-flowered species ***Hemerocallis lilioasphodelus***♕. ***Centranthus ruber*** has white, pink or red flowers.

Centranthus ruber

Crambe maritima

GOOD COMPANIONS

In coastal gardens, light, jazzy colours never look out of place. A simple but effective way of making a colourful planting is to scatter seeds of poppies (*Papaver*) and eschscholzias (1) among clumps of lavender (*Lavandula*), *Mesembryanthemum* (2) and sea hollies (*Eryngium*), such as the violet-blue-flowered *Eryngium maritimum* (3).

PROSPECT COTTAGE, DUNGENESS

The late Derek Jarman's garden at Prospect Cottage, near Dungeness in Kent, is a fine example of how to garden successfully beside the sea. Displaying an artist's skill, Jarman arranged plants such as poppies, santolinas and *Crambe maritima*♕ (sea kale), which are happy in the almost pure shingle of the site, among an eclectic mix of driftwood, fishing floats and other weathered objects, to produce a garden that complements the unpretentious cottage and fits seamlessly into its stark surroundings.

Woodland gardens

Woods are atmospheric and beautiful, especially in late spring, when shafts of sunlight, filtering through unfurling leaves, gild tree trunks and small plants growing on the woodland floor. Woodland gardening can be the most pleasurable kind of gardening, and the good news is that it is not necessary to possess a wood in order to indulge in it. A single small, spreading tree planted in a garden can, when mature, provide shade for about a hundred woodland plants.

Erythroniums (here, *Erythronium californicum*) are some of the most beautiful of spring-flowering woodland plants. They like fertile, rich soil that does not dry out and dappled light or partial shade.

In northern temperate regions, native trees mostly have flowers in muted, recessive colours, as do many shade-loving plants found on the woodland floor. However, woodland in other parts of the world is far more colourful. When creating a woodland garden, the choice is between making one similar in character to your own native woodland (using indigenous or introduced species, or a mixture of both), or a much more colourful garden containing exotic plants with vibrant-coloured flowers, for example **Asiatic rhododendrons**, **azaleas** and **camellias**.

PLANTS FOR WOODLAND GARDENS

Many herbaceous and bulbous plants that thrive in woodland have a refined charm. The great boon of a woodland garden is that lots of these flowering plants bloom at a time when the rest of the garden has not yet sprung back into life. Even in a small area, it is possible to have a wide selection of simple but beguiling flowers from the middle of winter through to late spring. ***Cyclamen coum***♕ (see pages 51 and 168–69),

(Continued on page 97.)

Some woodland plants (here, *Helleborus foetidus*) flower long before many other plants.

TREES FOR WOODLAND GARDENS

The perfect trees for a woodland garden are those with deep roots, such as oaks (*Quercus*), or those with canopies that allow shafts of sunlight to reach the ground, for example larches (*Larix*) and the Scots pine, *Pinus sylvestris* 🏆 (1). However, it isn't necessary to plant large trees when making a woodland garden. There is a range of trees and shrubs better suited to smaller gardens that will provide dappled shade within a relatively short time. Among the best are magnolias, maples (*Acer*), whitebeams (*Sorbus aria*) and crab apples (*Malus*), all of which are eye-catching in more than one season. For example, *Magnolia wilsonii* 🏆 (2) has red-purple shoots, dark green leaves that have felted, reddish-brown undersides, and white, cup-shaped flowers with a prominent boss of bright red stamens in early summer. The snake-bark maples *Acer capillipes* 🏆 (3) and *Acer davidii* colour intensely in autumn and have attractive green- and white-striped bark that shows up beautifully in winter. *Sorbus hupehensis* var. *obtusa* 🏆 (4) has attractive pinnate, bluish-green leaves, white flowers in late spring, and creamy-white berries flushed with pink in autumn. *Malus toringo* subsp. *sargentii* produces masses of white flowers in spring and dark red fruits that stay on the tree for weeks in autumn.

COLOURFUL AND SUBTLE WOODLAND GARDENS

With the introduction of many Asiatic trees and shrubs in the latter part of the 19th century and early 20th century, many beautiful and highly colourful gardens were created in Britain and the USA, for example the Sir Harold Hillier Gardens, Hampshire (above), Savill Garden, Windsor, and, in the USA, the Arnold Arboretum in Massachusetts. More recently, there has been a move towards more naturalistic woodland gardens, such as the one created by Beth Chatto in Essex. Here, she has planted shade-loving species from all around the world to produce a garden of mixed but subtle colours in which foliage plays the principal part.

One of the most attractive features of a woodland garden is the way the leaves and branches of the trees create dappled light that changes throughout the day. Here, the young leaves of the fern *Matteuccia struthiopteris* are gilded by early morning sunlight and appear a luminous yellow.

Anemone nemorosa

Trillium grandiflorum

Lilium martagon var. *album*

Digitalis ferruginea

Hyacinthoides non-scripta

Dicentra 'Stuart Boothman'

PLANTS FOR DRY SHADE

In very dry shady areas, ivies (*Hedera*), *Helleborus foetidus* ♡ (see page 94), *Iris foetidissima* ♡, honesty (*Lunaria annua*) (above), comfreys such as *Symphytum caucasicum* ♡ (see page 127) and dead nettles (*Lamium*) can be relied upon to perform consistently.

IMPROVING CONDITIONS FOR WOODLAND PLANTS

When creating a woodland garden under mature trees, it may be necessary to 'lighten' the shade. Cutting out some lower branches to raise the trees' canopies and removing branches to thin out their crowns will allow more light to reach the ground, making it easier for plants beneath to flourish. It is also a good idea to try to create some patches where there is little or no shade, as this will permit a wider range of plants to be grown.

The soil under mature trees is often dry and poor in nutrients, especially on the sides facing north and east, and so it is good practice to mulch the ground with organic matter, preferably leaf mould, each spring – this will provide a reservoir of moisture for the plants' developing roots. A balanced slow-release fertilizer applied regularly in spring will make the soil less impoverished.

winter aconites (*Eranthis*) and snowdrops (*Galanthus*) will start the show by flowering in midwinter and late winter, and are followed soon after by **Lenten roses** (*Helleborus* × *hybridus*) and **lungwort** (*Pulmonaria*). **Primroses** (*Primula*), **navelworts** (*Omphalodes*), **wood anemones** (*Anemone nemorosa*), **erythroniums**, **tiarellas**, **trilliums**, **epimediums**, small **narcissi** and **bluebells** (*Hyacinthoides*) will ensure there is a continuous display from early spring to mid-spring, while **Solomon's seal** (*Polygonatum*), **dicentras** and **lily-of-the-valley** (*Convallaria*) will carry the flowering period through into late spring. If you intersperse these flowering woodlanders with foliage plants such as **hostas**, **asarums** and ***Arum italicum*** **subsp.** ***italicum*** **'Marmoratum'**♕ (see page 124), you will enrich the plantings and highlight the jewel-like colours.

By midsummer, when the trees are fully decked out in new leaves, there may not be sufficient light for many plants to flower. So, just when the rest of the garden is resplendent with colour, a woodland garden is at its most green. However, there are plants that will go on producing flowers in deep shade, ***Geranium macrorrhizum*** and ***Geranium phaeum*** for example. In the less shady areas, ***Alchemilla mollis***♕ (lady's mantle, see page 154), **sweet woodruff** (*Galium odoratum*, see page 124) and cultivars of **periwinkle** (*Vinca*) will colonize the ground and produce flowers. In areas where the shade is not too dense, and the soil is moist, the green summer scene will be enlivened by planting **foxgloves** (*Digitalis*) and **bugbanes**, such as ***Actaea simplex***, with its bottlebrush white flowers. **Lilies** add real class to woodland plantings, especially the giant lily ***Cardiocrinum giganteum***; patience is needed to grow this dramatic lily as it takes several years to reach maturity.

SHRUBS FOR WOODLAND PLANTINGS

While it is possible to create beautiful woodland plantings of small bulbs and perennials under trees, in larger spaces it is a good idea to create an understorey by including shrubs as well. Shrubs bring more contrast of leaf form and texture and, if evergreens are included, year-round interest. Hollies (*Ilex*) are perfect candidates for woodland planting, especially those with all-green leaves. *Ilex aquifolium* 'J.C. van Tol'♕ is a self-fertilizing holly with dark purple stems, dark green, non-prickly leaves and scarlet berries. (The variegated cultivars produce the best leaf colour if planted in sun.) *Lonicera pileata* is a handsome evergreen with small, shiny green leaves; it grows little more than 60cm (2ft) tall but spreads over an area of 2.5m (8ft) and is happy in poor soils. *Daphne laureola*, the spurge laurel, is another small shrub that flourishes in deep shade; it has shiny dark green leaves and small, scented green flowers in winter. Also small but wide-spreading, the glossy-leaved *Daphne pontica*♕ (1) has fragrant yellow flowers in spring. Sarcococcas are excellent shrubs for woodland as they have attractive evergreen leaves and fragrant flowers that appear in winter; plant them beside a path so their scents may be enjoyed at close hand. *Sarcococca confusa*♕ has tapering dark green, shiny leaves and highly scented white flowers. It grows up to 1.2m (4ft) tall with a spread of 1m (40in). *Sarcococca hookeriana* var. *digyna* 'Purple Stem' (see page 173) has narrower leaves and young shoots flushed with purple-pink; it grows up to 1.5m (5ft) and its sweetly scented flowers are white tinged with pink.

1 2 3

Among the deciduous shrubs, *Forsythia* × *intermedia* (2) and most deutzias are happy growing in light dappled shade, as is the enchanting *Exochorda* × *macrantha* 'The Bride'♕ (see page 123), which grows into a mound 2 x 3m (6 x 10ft) and produces abundant white, cup-shaped flowers on its arching stems in late spring and early summer. Golden-leaved and variegated shrubs can help to 'lift' dark areas in a wood. The golden-leaved privet *Ligustrum* 'Vicaryi' is a semi-evergreen that has golden yellow leaves, and panicles of white flowers in summer. *Philadelphus coronarius* 'Aureus'♕, the golden mock orange, has yellow leaves that become light green as they age and the bonus of sweetly scented flowers. *Sambucus racemosa* 'Plumosa Aurea' (3) is an elder with finely cut golden leaves.

Water gardens

Ancient Egyptian and Persian gardens always contained pools because gardens were considered to be sanctuaries from the harsh conditions of the desert. Today, gardeners value water not only for its soothing qualities, but also because even a small pond or pool can bring huge ecological benefits, providing havens for wildlife such as frogs, toads and dragonflies. In addition, water offers opportunities to experiment with some beautiful aquatic and moisture-loving plants.

When creating a naturalistic water garden, it is important to grow aquatic and moisture-loving plants with leaves in varying shapes and textures as these will long outlast the flowers. Here, the giant leaves of *Gunnera manicata* provide a dramatic contrast to those of water lilies and irises.

When thinking about the colours for watery situations, it is important to consider whether the water feature is natural or artificial. If the body of water is a natural asset, perhaps a boggy area, stream or pond, it is preferable to construct plantings that appear to be part of the immediate surroundings – green should be the predominant colour, flowers should be mostly on the small side and their tones should be muted. If, on the other hand, a water feature is artificial, there is no reason for not embellishing it with plantings that are both dramatic and highly colourful, especially if it is the centrepiece of its own area within a garden. Here, one could experiment with hot harmonies, mixing plants with flowers in reds, oranges and yellows, for example **cannas**, and interspersing them with large, highly textured and coloured leaves. Try the giant rhubarb cultivar ***Rheum* 'Ace of Hearts'**, bronze-leaved ligularias such as ***Ligularia dentata* 'Desdemona'**♀ or ***Ligularia* 'Zepter'**, and large-leaved hostas like ***Hosta* 'Sum and Substance'**♀.

Whatever the situation, it is always important not to obscure the water totally and to have a range of foliage forms, textures and sizes, as leaves will be present for far longer than flowers.

NATURAL SCHEMES

Naturalistic plantings may, of course, be constructed by selecting only indigenous species, but this may be too restrictive for some gardeners. For those who want to try growing non-native plants, it is possible to create natural-looking plantings by mixing indigenous species with carefully selected introduced ones. Grasses always bring an air of informality, and moisture-loving

Ligularia 'Zepter'

The damp ground around a naturalistic pool is the perfect place to grow moisture-loving perennials. In the boggy ground around this pool, candelabra primulas, irises, hostas, rodgersias and billowing foliage plants provide a lush and tranquil setting for the water. Even though the flowers' colours are mixed, the effect is harmonious and calm.

ones, such as **molinia**, can be used successfully in association with plants with pastel-coloured flowers. The cultivar of the purple moor grass ***Molinia caerulea* subsp. *arundinacea* 'Karl Foerster'** has purple flowerheads on 1.2m (4ft) tall stems, and a graceful habit. It blends perfectly with the indigenous meadowsweet ***Filipendula ulmaria***, which has fluffy cream flowerheads in summer, and the native water plantain ***Alisma plantago-aquatica***, with its gypsophila-like, pinkish-white flowers in mid- to late summer (it flowers best when planted in 15cm/6in of water). A lovely addition would be the beautiful Eurasian flowering rush ***Butomus umbellatus***♀; this has bluish-pink flowerheads, somewhat like those of an allium, which appear in late summer.

PONDS AND POOLS

In artificial ponds or pools, plants should be grown in containers – either troughs built into the sides of the pond, or removable baskets filled with heavy clay soil and covered with gravel to prevent the soil from floating away. In the past, formal pools were usually accompanied by formal plantings, which featured a few species in recurring patterns. A much more relaxed approach is in vogue today, and many formal pools now include random, bold plantings of plants such as bamboos, ferns, hostas, rushes and grasses.

WATER LILIES

The aristocrats of aquatic plants, water lilies are both beautiful and useful, as their large flat leaves help to provide essential shade for the water, thus preventing algae from developing.

Water lilies come in sizes to suit any expanse of water, from a lake to a large tub. Pygmy cultivars grow in less than 30cm (12in) of water, while the largest need a depth of about 1m (40in).

There are subtle contrasts of form and colour between the yellow flowers of *Primula florindae* and *Iris ensata* in this waterside planting.

Common cotton grass, ***Eriophorum angustifolium,*** could be added to naturalistic plantings in peaty soil, as it thrives in or beside shallow water in acid conditions. It has silky white flowerheads, reminiscent of cotton wool balls, which are carried on stems 30–45cm (12–18in) long.

For a natural-looking planting that features creams and yellows, the statuesque umbellifer ***Angelica archangelica*** (often grown as a biennial), with its domed flowerheads of greenish-yellow flowers, is hard to beat. It would make a handsome companion for ***Caltha palustris*** (marsh marigold), with its egg-yolk yellow flowers, or perhaps a creamy-coloured cultivar such as ***Trollius × cultorum* 'Cheddar'** or ***Euphorbia palustris*** ♀, which has deep yellow bracts carried on 1m (40in) tall stems in spring. For elegant foliage one could include the little South American perennial ***Gunnera magellanica***, which has kidney-shaped, glossy dark green leaves borne on 7–15cm (3–6in) stalks. ***Nymphoides peltata*** would also make an attractive and useful addition to this kind of planting, as its rounded leaves form a floating carpet on water; by shading the water surface, the leaves help to keep the water clean and free from algae. As well as attractive leaves, it has funnel-shaped, bright yellow flowers that are carried on long stalks in summer.

TENDER MARGINAL AQUATIC PERENNIALS

There are some highly decorative, subtropical aquatic plants that will add much to water's edge plantings but, as they are too tender to withstand frost, they must be brought indoors for winter in colder areas.

Cyperus papyrus ♀, the Egyptian paper rush, is a graceful plant that grows to over 2m (6ft) in warmer summers. Its three-angled stems, which were flattened out by ancient Egyptians to make paper, carry globes of thin threads, on the end of which are tiny brown flowers. It grows best in 10–15cm (4–6in) of water.

Thalia dealbata is an elegant North American perennial found in the southern states of the USA and Mexico; it has evergreen, often lance-shaped, greyish-green leaves, 50cm (20in) long, and violet flowers that are carried in slender panicles on stalks up to 3m (10ft) tall, in summer. It should be grown either in an aquatic basket or in fertile, loamy mud in water up to 15cm (6in) deep.

The buttercup family contains perennials that thrive at the margins of pools. *Trollius chinensis* is one, here growing beside a pink astilbe.

Some umbellifers, such as *Angelica archangelica*, thrive in damp soil and can be used to add height and structure to a waterside planting.

DRAMATIC FOLIAGE PLANTINGS

The obvious choice for dramatic foliage plantings beside water would be ***Gunnera manicata*** ♀; however, many gardeners may well decide this South American giant, with its massive leaves, 2m (6ft) in diameter, on stems up to 2.5m (8ft) tall, is far too large. **Rodgersias** have much smaller leaves than this gunnera, but they are nonetheless striking foliage plants with

The South American perennial *Gunnera manicata* makes an impressive architectural plant beside a pool or stream but its huge leaves need plenty of room to look their best. Here, they provide a sumptuous backdrop for *Primula florindae*.

Rodgersia podophylla

large, dramatic leaves. As they are happy growing in damp positions, they make good stream- or poolside plants. ***Rodgersia pinnata*** **'Superba'**🏆 has glossy, dark green, deeply veined leaves, 1m (40in) long, which are purple or bronze when they first unfurl. Its flowers, which appear in mid- to late summer, are tiny bright pink stars carried in tapering clusters up to 70cm (28in) long on stems 1.2m (4ft) tall. ***Rodgersia podophylla***🏆 has leaves 40cm (16in) long, which are purplish and wrinkly when young but become smoother as they age. Its greenish-cream flowers appear in late summer, carried in 30cm (12in) plumes on stems up to 1.5m (5ft) tall; in autumn its leaves turn rich brownish-red. ***Rheum palmatum*** is a wonderfully colourful foliage plant. Its leaves have reddish stems and veins, and it bears tall plumes of cream or pinkish flowers. The leaves of ***Rheum palmatum*** **'Atrosanguineum'**🏆 (see page 65) have plum-red undersides and deep pink flowers.

Rheum palmatum

Plants with spiky leaves always add a touch of drama, and **phormiums**, with their sword-shaped leaves, are especially well suited to moist waterside plantings because they thrive in damp soil. There is now a wide choice of cultivars with attractively coloured and variegated foliage. ***Phormium*** **'Sundowner'**🏆 has leaves that are up to 1.5m (5ft) long, in brownish green with deep rose-red margins. Its spikes of yellowish-green flowers are carried on stems up to 2m (6ft) tall. ***Phormium cookianum*** **subsp.** ***hookeri*** **'Tricolor'**🏆 bears arching, light green leaves with clearly defined cream and red margins that grow as long as 1.5m (5ft). Another dramatic foliage plant is ***Lysichiton americanus***🏆 (skunk cabbage), an inhabitant of streams in the USA. Despite its musky smell, this perennial is worth growing for its vivid yellow spathes that appear in early spring, as well as for its thick, shiny leaves, which are sometimes 1.2m (4ft) long.

Lysichiton americanus

Hard landscaping

The debate about the most important constituents of a garden has raged among the gardening fraternity for a long time. Some think that plants should always take precedence, while others believe that design incorporating hard landscaping is all-important and that plants are incidental. In fact, it takes both to make a good garden and, just as the plants we choose affect the character and mood of our gardens, so too does the hard landscaping.

The term 'hard landscaping' refers to a garden's walls, fences, dividers, paths and paving, as well as structures such as pergolas, arbours, arches, raised beds, garden buildings and any decorative elements such as pots, fountains and statuary. Today, hard landscaping elements are made from a bewildering selection of different-coloured stones, woods, metals, plastics and composite materials, and there are numerous outdoor paints and timber stains available in a kaleidoscope of colours. It can be difficult to decide which will look best in your garden.

The secret of good garden design is simplicity and appropriateness, and this applies particularly to hard landscaping. Remember to limit the number of materials and to select those with a colour, texture and finish that suits your garden's setting and character. Owners of Cotswold stone cottages should therefore be choosing gravel or paving stones whose colour mirrors that of the local stone, whereas owners of redbrick houses will be aiming to match the texture, colour and finish of the house bricks. Materials indigenous to an area should be used whenever possible, and when restoring old gardens any new materials should match what is already there. This applies as much to paving and gravel as it does to walls, screens and arches. A garden near the sea might include decking, local pebbles, shingle, sand and driftwood, as these are the kinds of materials normally found at the seaside, but they would look somewhat out of place in a Scottish moorland garden. In the same way, shiny engineering bricks would make stylish paving for a high-tech modern house but would not sit well in a traditional rural garden.

The hard landscaping in this 2004 Chelsea Flower Show garden shows how inventive one can be: the wall in the background is made from sawn logs, held in a wire frame. Green- and grey-leaved plants, some with flowers picking out the colours in the hard landscaping, soften the whole effect.

Choosing the hard landscaping to suit a particular situation is important. Weathered wood decking makes the perfect foil for the moisture-loving perennials in this water garden.

Garden designer Christopher Bradley-Hole chose a rich crimson red for the walls in this contemporary garden and, very cleverly, mirrored it in the planting by including the perennial *Cirsium rivulare* 'Atropurpureum'.

WALLS AND FLOORS

Traditionally, a garden's boundaries are made from natural or reconstituted stone, brick, concrete, metal or wood. However, some garden designers are now making walls of stone or timber encased in steel mesh. Perspex and glass are also being used.

Walls are a garden's most important piece of hard landscaping and give a feeling of security and permanence. Both boundary walls and retaining walls should be made from the same materials as the house. This not only makes the house and garden seem like a single entity, but can also set the property in its wider landscape. Walls made from natural materials, such as brick and stone, get more beautiful as they age because they acquire a patina that adds to their character. For this reason, it is important not to obscure them totally with climbers or shrubs.

Placing painted trellis on walls will produce different effects, depending on the colour of the wood and of the wall itself.

WALLS IN URBAN GARDENS

Marylyn Abbott, in her book *Thoughts on Garden Design,* recommends painting walls in urban gardens in bright colours. She suggests deep Pompeii red as a backdrop for a series of pale-coloured urns or a row of yuccas, and recommends paint the colour of thunder clouds, marketed as 'Thunderclap', for a backdrop to terracotta and sandstone items. In her garden at West Green House, in Hampshire, she has replicated the intense Islamic blue of the Majorelle Gardens in Marrakesh, Morocco, in her fragrant herb garden.

This old stone wall with its terracotta coping provides the perfect backdrop for a pink-flowered hollyhock.

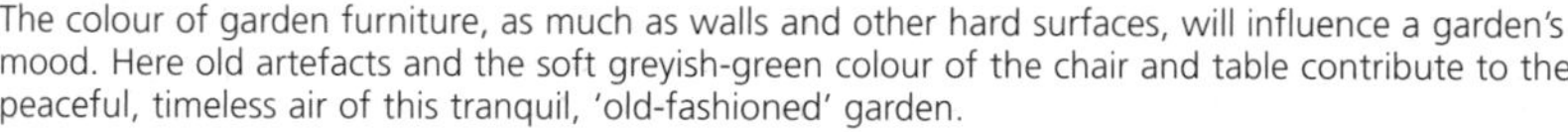
The colour of garden furniture, as much as walls and other hard surfaces, will influence a garden's mood. Here old artefacts and the soft greyish-green colour of the chair and table contribute to the peaceful, timeless air of this tranquil, 'old-fashioned' garden.

The colour of a garden's paving should never overshadow any planting. Rocks and shingle (top) are a good foil for sempervivums; brick pavers (middle) complement the pink sedum; and pale apricot-coloured slabs blend in well in a contemporary water garden (bottom).

Walls made of concrete or concrete blocks may be greatly improved by painting them or rendering them with coloured cement. A perimeter wall painted a pale colour will reflect light, giving a dark garden a more cheerful atmosphere. Similarly, laying a light-coloured paving in a dark corner instantly makes it seem less sombre. As the majority of plants do not thrive in dark shady conditions, using hard landscaping to lighten spaces often enables the gardener to grow a wider, more interesting and colourful range of plants.

Walls painted white or pale cream will make the garden seem smaller. But this need not necessarily be seen as a disadvantage. In fact, light colours are a perfect foil for dark evergreen foliage, making the leaves seem even greener. Trees or shrubs with finely dissected foliage look beautiful in front of pale walls, especially when the sun throws their shadows on to the walls. ***Acer japonicum*** (the Japanese maples), ***Acer palmatum*** cultivars and ***Rhus typhina* 'Dissecta'**🏆 have beautifully shaped leaves. These all sit happily in smaller gardens as they never get too large.

White walls can seem cold and stark in cool northern climates, where in winter the light is often grey. Cream, pale yellow or sand will cast a warmer feel than white.

Painting a garden's perimeter walls in a vivid colour, from the warm side of the spectrum, will instantly bring a feeling of heat. For example, a garden surrounded by burnt orange or terracotta walls will seem to be bathed in perennial sunshine and the feeling will be reinforced if Mediterranean-style terracotta pots and paving tiles are used as well. Introducing plants with bluish-green or glaucous foliage and plants with blue flowers (blue and orange are complementary colours) in such a garden will provide a sharp contrast to the walls, pots and paving. In areas where there is little risk of frost, Mediterranean-style plants will tend to emphasize the garden's mood, especially as many of them have bluish-green or grey foliage. An **olive tree** (*Olea*) could be the centrepiece of a planting featuring **cistus**, **lavender**, **teucrium**, blue grasses such as ***Helictotrichon sempervirens***🏆, and succulents like **echeveria**.

FENCES AND FEATURES

Fences used as garden boundaries are of two sorts – solid, which make complete

Painting garden structures such as fences, railings, arches or obelisks a dark colour, perhaps black or dark green, will lessen their impact and may even make them 'disappear' into the surrounding greenery. The arches in the rose tunnel shown here are almost invisible when they are covered with the foliage of rambler roses.

Painting garden structures in subtle colours (top) will allow pale-coloured flowers growing against them to show up well. A strong colour, like the purplish-blue of the door shown above, will draw the eye but will harmonize well with green plantings placed in front.

barriers, and open, which allow you to have a view of the landscape beyond. Open fences are especially useful for rural settings, where a garden sits in a beautiful landscape, whereas solid fences come into their own in urban settings, providing privacy and hiding unsightly surroundings. The painting of fences and trellis, as well as garden buildings and other wooden features such as arbours and arches, can also greatly affect the mood and feel of a garden. Painting them in light colours, say cream or white, has the effect of drawing the eye to them, thereby lessening the effect of what lies beyond or around them. This can be useful if the view beyond a fence is dull or if a structure is helping to mask an eyesore. On the other hand, painting wooden structures in muted, cool colours lessens their impact, and paler-coloured flowers growing against them seem even brighter.

Metal railings vary from the very simple to the highly ornate and, again, the choice should be based on what is right for the setting. Ornate wrought-iron railings do not look out of place as boundaries for the front garden of a Victorian terraced house but would be totally inappropriate on the balconies of ultra-modern flats. In a country setting, a metal fence painted a dark colour, for example black or dark green, will tend to disappear into the landscape. This is useful for disguising an unsightly fence or for drawing the eye to a landscape beyond it. It is also useful for disguising the metal netting around a tennis court, particularly against a green backdrop.

DUMBARTON OAKS

The garden at Dumbarton Oaks in Georgetown, Washington DC, USA, designed by the famous landscape architect Beatrix Farrand, has exquisite elements of hard landscaping, demonstrating Mrs Farrand's meticulous attention to detail. Its steps, paths, pergola, fences, gates, pots, handrails, and even its water spouts are beautifully crafted and reinforce the overall formality and Italianate feel of the garden.

Containers

Whatever the style and size of garden, it will be made more beautiful and more interesting by including pots and other containers. Container gardening is simply gardening in a different, and very practical, way. It allows the gardener to play at being flamboyant, sophisticated, quirky, experimental or just plain outrageous with plants. The beauty of a container is that if a planting doesn't match up to expectations, it can easily be dismantled and replanted. And it is mobile.

Perhaps the greatest advantage of containers is that they can bring colour into the garden in every season. This is especially valuable for those with a very small garden, where there isn't sufficient room in beds and borders to grow plants for year-round interest. Another huge bonus of container gardening is that it allows gardeners to grow plants that are not suited to their particular soil type. For example, anyone with an alkaline soil can enjoy growing acid-loving plants such as **rhododendrons**, **camellias** and **azaleas**, and exquisite woodlanders such as **trilliums** and **bloodroot** (*Sanguinaria*). In the same way, those gardening on heavy clay soil can raise plants, including **tulips**, that will only succeed in free-draining soil. For those gardening in colder areas, containers provide the chance to indulge in a little subtropical gardening, raising plants such as **citrus fruits**, **oleanders**, **aloes**, **agaves**, **echeverias** and numerous others. Naturally, these tender creatures have to be brought into a frost-free environment in winter.

In this all-green composition, painted terracotta containers planted with box add another dimension to the planting and provide colour and structure when the flowering plants have ceased to bloom.

Containers can be used for all sorts of purposes: to disguise eyesores, lighten dark and dull corners, provide focal points, and embellish garden features such as doors, gates, seats, arches or niches. They may also be popped into flowerbeds and borders that are looking past their best to give them a 'lift' (Gertrude Jekyll used to put pots of lilies into her borders when she thought they needed it) or to provide 'movable' colour. Sometimes simply shifting a container with flowers in full bloom to a position to catch the falling light, or to emphasize a part of the garden that is often overlooked, can transform it.

At its best, container gardening is an art form and, like artists, container gardeners have to consider the style, form, texture, proportion and, of course, the colour of the elements of their creations and how they relate to each other. It goes without saying that the most successful are those who can arrange a 'happy marriage' between the container and its planting.

CHOOSING CONTAINERS

When choosing pots and containers, it is important to remember that, as with other elements of hard landscaping, simplicity and appropriateness pay off; a few large pots look more effective than lots of small ones, and containers whose style matches that of the garden will never look out of place. So, large and ornate terracotta or stone pots that would look at home on the terrace of a Georgian country house would not meld well into a minimalist roof garden, and wooden containers might not look right in a classical parterre – unless, like the famous pots at the Palace of Versailles, they were especially designed and painted to match other features within the garden.

Of course, one does not have to choose conventional containers. A collection of old utensils, tools, pottery and disused artefacts can make eye-catching planters and are a fun way of personalizing the garden, often in a unique way. A medley of old baskets hung from the branches of a tree near a sitting area can look attractive in a cottage garden and, if filled with fragrant annuals, would add to the garden's atmosphere. In the same way, large tree stumps lying in a woodland garden can make interesting and appropriate containers for shade-loving woodland plants such as **wood anemones** (*Anemone nemorosa*, see page 96), **primroses** (*Primula*) and **violets** (*Viola*). Metal pots and pans no longer used in a kitchen would make quirky but practical containers for herbs in a vegetable garden, while old terracotta chimney pots filled with **grasses** always make an eye-catching feature on a roof garden or terrace.

Placing containers near a seating area ensures that the plants will be admired at close hand, and you can ring the changes throughout the seasons. Individual pots, like the one shown below, can be given centre stage as their flowers appear and can be moved or replanted when they are over.

NATURAL OR SYNTHETIC?

When it comes to deciding between synthetic or natural materials, there is no right or wrong. The late David Hicks, whose garden in Buckinghamshire is the epitome of good taste, removed all the terracotta pots from his garden and replaced them with plastic ones, which he had painted green. He was firmly of the opinion that no one ever noticed the difference. Synthetic materials have the advantage of being cheap, lighter to lift and move, and do not get damaged by frost but, unlike natural materials, they do not acquire a patina as they age.

For a stylish and eye-catching effect, match the colour of the containers with that of the flowers or foliage of their plants. No one could ignore these bright orange pots and their early-flowering miniature tulips and daisies.

Many people use containers for bedding plants, bringing instant colour in the summer months. Nurseries and garden centres are constantly expanding the range and you can now buy plants with flowers in an array of both brilliant and subtle colours.

Growing hardy perennials in pots has the advantage that the containers can be treated as nurseries, where the plants are left to grow to a size where they can be split and planted out in the garden. A planting for a shady area might include **ferns**, **pulmonarias** and **Solomon's seal** (*Polygonatum*), while one for a sunny spot could include **daylilies** (*Hemerocallis*), **grasses** and perhaps late-flowering daisies such as **heleniums**. All-foliage plantings are stylish too; mixing spiky- or glossy-leaved plants with felted or ferny ones will emphasize their differences and highlight their various attributes. A planting in this vein could, for example, feature the dramatic ***Agave americana*** ♕ (see page 56), which has thick, fleshy, spiky, greyish-green foliage, the lovely, delicate, hairy-leaved ***Lotus hirsutus*** ♕, ***Mentha suaveolens*** (apple

PLANTS FOR CONTAINERS

Virtually any plant may be grown in a container, provided it is fed and watered regularly and grown in its ideal medium. However, most plants that are kept permanently in containers need to be repotted from time to time to keep them in good shape. As a rule of thumb, shrubs need repotting every year or two in spring until mature, then they just need to be top-dressed in spring; trees need repotting every three to five years either into the same container or a larger one, and top-dressing each spring; bulbs need to be repotted only when they have become overcrowded.

Silver-leaved plants, such as eryngiums, do not need frequent watering, so they thrive in pots.

HOSTAS FOR POTS

Hostas are exquisite foliage plants. Sadly, however, they are favourite fare for slugs and snails. Growing hostas in containers is one way of counteracting the activity of these pests and is especially effective if the pots are placed on a hard surface, some way away from flowerbeds and bare earth. An array of containers in all shapes and sizes filled with different varieties of hosta can look very effective and, as most fare best in partial shade (yellow-leaved ones perform better in sun with some midday shade), a collection of them will always give a lift to a darkish corner of a garden. Copper strips and/or Vaseline placed around the perimeter of the containers provides extra defence.

Naturally, a container's position will determine the kind of plant that can be grown in it. A pot placed in shade, for instance, must be filled with shade-lovers, such as **hostas**. Containers in hot spots should be filled with sun-worshippers that are happy to be baked dry, as soil in containers dries out rapidly in warm weather. **Agaves**, **aloes**, **agapanthus**, **echeverias** and silver-leaved plants thrive in hot, dry places.

A tall pot with a spiky-leaved plant such as this *Cordyline* 'Torbay Red' will make a dramatic focal point at the centre of a small garden.

Containers do not have to be filled with flowering plants. A pot, or a group of pots, planted with a mixture of differently coloured foliage plants can be very satisfying visually. And they do not need much maintenance to keep them looking good.

mint), which has wrinkled, greyish-green leaves, and the grey-leaved ***Artemisia* 'Powis Castle'**♕ (see page 56).

Grasses look elegant in containers, either in mixed plantings or solo, perhaps in individual pots arranged as a group. A collection of grasses can be surprisingly colourful in a subtle way:

Choosing containers and plants for a situation can be an art form. These simple unadorned steps have been much enhanced by the series of flat containers filled with grape hyacinths.

those with bluish foliage include ***Helictotrichon sempervirens***♕ and cultivars of ***Festuca glauca***; yellows include ***Milium effusum* 'Aureum'**♕, ***Hakonechloa macra* 'Alboaurea'**♕, and ***Carex elata* 'Aurea'** ♕ (see page 45). ***Holcus mollis* 'Albovariegatus'** and ***Carex oshimensis* 'Evergold'**♕ (see page 172) have, respectively, white-variegated and yellow-variegated leaves. For showy pinkish flowers choose ***Pennisetum orientale***.

A large container filled with a mixture of flowering plants looks good with a big foliage plant as its focal point. This might be a young shrub with dark leaves, perhaps a purple-leaved **cotinus**, a spiky-leaved specimen such as a **cordyline**, an especially handsome foliage plant such as ***Melianthus major***♕, or a plant with strikingly large leaves, for example a **canna**, a **datura** or ***Petasites japonicus* var. *giganteus***, whose kidney-shaped leaves may grow as long as 60cm (2ft).

When it comes to choosing colour combinations, you have to consider the container's position and the effect you want to create – restful or vibrant harmonies, or high-octane contrasts? It may be that you are looking for a planting to stand out against a dark background, such as an evergreen hedge; here, use plants with red leaves or flowers, as red is the complementary colour of green. Similarly, a mixture of yellow-flowering plants in a container will stand out against the backdrop of a blue fence or garden building.

Placing containers planted with flowers that come into their own in late summer or autumn, like these agapanthus, is an easy way to rejuvenate somewhat jaded borders.

SEASONS

Clever gardeners make their gardens colourful all through the year, using plants whose hues are appropriate to the season. When selecting plants it is wise to follow nature's example, remembering that spring has a preponderance of yellows and blues, while summer offers an abundance of pastels in pinks and violets early in the season and a profusion of reds later on. Autumn abounds with fiery oranges, browns and reds, and winter is rich with greys, browns, silvers, whites and numerous shades of green.

RIGHT: *Hyacinthoides non-scripta* in a spring woodland garden.

Narcissi come in all shapes and sizes but few have such elegant flowers as *Narcissus cyclamineus*.

Early spring

There is often a day in early spring when, as you stroll around your garden, you become aware that the restrained palette of winter, with its predominance of whites, silvers, greys, beiges and browns, has been eclipsed by a brighter, jazzier one. Lemon-yellow and greens seem to dominate, but there are also numerous blues and the odd splash of red, orange, pink and purple.

The freshness and cool clarity of many of early spring's colours are intoxicating. Every day, the garden reveals something new – perhaps a group of crocuses opening their flowers wide in the sun, or a favourite shrub suddenly showered in blossom, or a crown of fresh young leaves peeping above ground; this is a time of incomparable excitement for a gardener. For me, it is the time to revel in whatever nature has to offer and so, for the most part, I am happy to let the colours that emerge intermingle to produce kaleidoscopes of pure colour.

YELLOW FLOWERS

The predominance of yellow in the early part of the year comes for the most part from early-flowering bulbs and shrubs such as **witch hazels** (*Hamamelis*, see pages 177–79), **forsythias**, and some kinds of **berberis**.

Daffodils are kings and queens in the spring garden and many begin flowering now (a few flower in autumn and winter). There are some real gems among them – tiny narcissi, such as the dwarf species ***Narcissus cyclamineus***🏆, whose flowers have swept-back petals and long, narrow trumpets, and ***Narcissus minor***🏆, whose pure yellow flowers grow on stems only 10cm (4in) tall. Also, elegant cultivars such as ***Narcissus* 'February Gold'**🏆 (see pages 115, 120), with its welcome early, bright yellow flowers on long stems, and ***Narcissus* 'Jenny'**🏆, whose flowers have creamy-white petals and lemon-yellow trumpets that fade to match the petals. There are narcissi to suit every taste but, for me, it is the smaller species and cultivars that steal the show (see pages 120–21).

Some of the earliest **tulips** also have yellow in their flowers. The short-stemmed species ***Tulipa kaufmanniana*** has creamy-yellow and pink flowers that open wide in the sunshine, and some of its cultivars also feature yellow, for example ***Tulipa* 'Berlioz'**, which has citron-yellow petals flushed with red. (For other early spring tulips, see page 117.)

We find yellow in the flowers of several early spring flowering shrubs, the most popular being **forsythias**, which are easy to grow and not too choosy about soil. However, to my mind there are other yellow-flowered, early spring flowering shrubs that may be more of a challenge but are much more rewarding, because they have more subtly beautiful flowers. **Corylopsis**, for instance, are deciduous shrubs related to witch hazels and, like them, produce their flowers before the young leaves emerge. They require an acid soil that is fertile and moist and, being woodland shrubs, they prefer a semi-shaded site. ***Corylopsis pauciflora*** ♀ has sweetly scented, bell-shaped, primrose yellow flowers arranged in hanging clusters, up to 8cm (3in) long, on a spreading shrub, 1.5 x 2.5m (5 x 8ft) when mature. ***Corylopsis glabrescens*** grows up to 5 x 5m (1.5 x 1.5ft) and its flower clusters are only 2.5cm (1in) long. The flowers of ***Corylopsis sinensis*** ♀ (see page 44) are lemon-yellow and 8cm (3in) long, and this vigorous species becomes a bushy shrub, 4 x 4m (12 x 12ft) when it reaches maturity.

Stachyurus is another genus of unusual but delightful early-flowering woodland shrubs. They produce pendent clusters of flowers on bare branches. Like corylopsis, they need to be grown in acid soil that is fertile, humus-rich and well-drained, but they will grow happily in either sun or light shade and look especially effective when trained against a wall. ***Stachyurus praecox*** ♀ (see page 178) is a deciduous species with arching stems with pale greenish-lemon flowers in hanging clusters, like dangly earrings, up to 18cm (7in) long. It grows into a widely spreading open shrub. Those gardeners who like variegated foliage may prefer to plant ***Stachyurus* 'Magpie'**, which has mid-green leaves with a wide edging of cream; it is less vigorous than *Stachyurus praecox*, and a mature specimen grows to only 1.5m (5ft) with a spread of 2m (6ft).

Magnolia 'Elizabeth'

Corylopsis pauciflora

Magnolia* 'Elizabeth'** ♀ is a mid-spring flowering magnolia with pale yellow flowers opening before or just as the leaves emerge. It is conical in habit, reaching 10 x 6m (30 x 20ft) and making a fine specimen tree where there is space to admire it. (For more magnolias, see pages 118–19.) If space is limited, use a smaller shrub, such as ***Forsythia × intermedia* 'Weekend'** or ***Forsythia suspensa.

Forsythia × intermedia 'Weekend'

As the ground is only just beginning to warm up in early spring there aren't yet many perennials in flower, especially those with yellow flowers. An exception is ***Lysichiton americanus*** ♀ (American skunk cabbage, see page 101), a marginal aquatic perennial that produces bright yellow spathes up to 1m (40in) tall before the leaves appear. The somewhat curious ***Valeriana phu* 'Aurea'** is another perennial that appears yellow in early spring, but here it is the intricately divided, ferny leaves that are a pale yellow as they emerge above ground. Their yellow colour is short-lived, however, as they become a greener shade with age until, by midsummer, they are lime green.

WHITE FLOWERS

While yellow explodes into our gardens in early spring it is not, by any means, the only colour that transforms them. White features prominently in the flowers of many early spring flowering plants. We find it in the smallest bulbs, such as **crocuses**, the handsomest of shrubs, such as ***Magnolia stellata***🏆 (for other magnolias, see pages 118–19), and choice trees, for example ***Prunus incisa*** (Fuji cherry). However, none of these plants produces more beautiful flowers than the late-flowering **snowdrops** that can still be in bloom now, for example ***Galanthus* 'S. Arnott'**🏆 and ***Galanthus* 'Magnet'**🏆 (see page 177). The **flowering quinces** also produce a white-flowered cultivar, ***Chaenomeles speciosa* 'Nivalis'**. This is

Chaenomeles speciosa 'Nivalis'

less attention-grabbing than the red and pink cultivars (see page 117) but is a better colour to use against brickwork.

Some **crocuses** have white and cream flowers, too, and make excellent accompaniments to smaller narcissi. ***Crocus sieberi* 'Albus'**🏆 (formerly *Crocus sieberi* 'Bowles' White', see Good Companions, opposite) has flowers with pure white petals and orange stigmas, while the petals of ***Crocus biflorus* 'Miss Vain'** are white with pale lemon-yellow throats. ***Crocus chrysanthus* 'Snow Bunting'**🏆 has ivory flowers with a hint of greyish blue on the insides of the petals, but those of ***Crocus vernus* subsp. *albiflorus* 'Jeanne d'Arc'** are white with purple bases. White is also found in some **pulmonarias**, most noticeably in those with spotted leaves and in the flowers of certain cultivars such as ***Pulmonaria* 'Sissinghurst White'**🏆.

Hellebores hybridize freely and sometimes white-flowered types are produced. White ***Helleborus* × *hybridus*** flowers may be pure white or embellished with pink spots at the base of their petals.

Crocus chrysanthus 'Snow Bunting'

Pulmonaria 'Sissinghurst White'

Magnolia stellata

Helleborus × *hybridus*

FRAGRANT PLANTS FOR EARLY SPRING *Acacia dealbata* • *Chimonanthus praecox* var. *luteus* •

Ajuga reptans 'Atropurpurea'

Pulmonaria 'Blue Ensign'

Scilla mischtschenkoana

BLUE- AND PURPLE-FLOWERED PLANTS

The blues of early spring are especially welcome as a contrast to all the yellows now appearing, and they are found in the flowers of perennials and bulbs. Among the easiest to grow are the **bugles**, perennials that are related to the blue-flowered ***Ajuga reptans***, beloved by generations of cottage gardeners. There are numerous cultivars, some having bronze, green, or even variegated leaves, and some producing white or pink flowers. ***Ajuga reptans* 'Atropurpurea'** is a particularly fine cultivar, with dark bluish-purple flowers and bronze-purple leaves.

Crocus chrysanthus 'Blue Pearl'

GOOD COMPANIONS

The cheery, bright yellow flowers of *Eranthis hyemalis* ♀ (1) (winter aconite) harmonize beautifully with the white and orange flowers of *Crocus sieberi* 'Albus' (2).

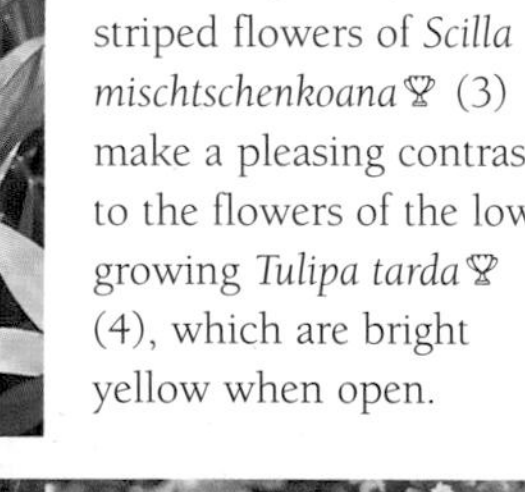

The silvery-blue, darker-striped flowers of *Scilla mischtschenkoana* ♀ (3) make a pleasing contrast to the flowers of the low-growing *Tulipa tarda* ♀ (4), which are bright yellow when open.

Narcissus 'February Gold' ♀ (5), with its golden flowers, makes a striking contrast to the blues of *Anemone blanda* blue-flowered (6).

Like ajugas, **pulmonarias** are easy to grow and hybridists have produced some excellent cultivars with all-blue flowers; among them are the dark blue ***Pulmonaria* 'Mawson's Blue'** and ***Pulmonaria* 'Blue Ensign'**, with violet-blue flowers. (See also page 62 and Good Companions, page 116.)

Among the most intense blues of early spring are the flowers of the bulbous perennial ***Scilla siberica*** ♀, which are a deep, rich azure colour. ***Scilla mischtschenkoana*** ♀ (see Good Companions, left) is pale silvery-blue, and ***Chionodoxa forbesii*** ♀ produces flowers in a pale blue with white eyes. The flowers of ***Anemone blanda* blue-flowered** (see Good Companions, left) are a rich bright blue, and their corms produce flowers whether planted in sun or in the shade of large trees. ***Crocus chrysanthus* 'Blue Pearl'** ♀ is a pale lavender-blue.

Iris unguicularis

Crocus tommasinianus 'Ruby Giant'

Crocus tommasinianus

Violet or purple may not be colours we instantly think of as having major associations with early spring, but violet is the colour of the wild ***Viola riviniana*** (wood violet or dog violet) and of some early-flowering irises, such as ***Iris unguicularis***🏆, which produces mauve flowers with paler lilac standards, and ***Iris unguicularis*** **'Mary Barnard'**🏆, with its dark purple falls and gold streaks. Purple also features in the flowers of some cultivars of ***Anemone blanda***🏆 and in some crocuses, for instance ***Crocus tommasinianus*** and its darker-flowered cultivars: ***Crocus tommasinianus*** **'Ruby Giant'**, in violet-blue, and the reddish-purple ***Crocus tommasinianus*** **'Whitewell Purple'**.

Ipheion uniflorum 'Wisley Blue'

Ipheions may not be as familiar as crocuses, but these South American bulbs are just as easy and rewarding to grow and deserve to be much better known. Their principal flowering time is mid-spring, but milder weather will bring them into flower earlier. The cultivar ***Ipheion uniflorum*** **'Wisley Blue'**🏆 has lilac-blue flowers that sometimes appear as early as late winter.

Later in the season, these blue- and purple-flowered plants will be supplemented by many more, when perennials such as brunneras, forget-me-nots, gentians and omphalodes, and bulbs including bluebells and mertensias all come into their own.

GOOD COMPANIONS

The blue flowers of grape hyacinths (*Muscari armeniacum*) appear in early spring, at the same time as the canary-yellow trumpets of *Narcissus* 'Hawera'🏆 (see also page 120).

The blue-violet flowers and dark green leaves of *Pulmonaria* 'Blue Ensign' (1) provide a perfect foil for the creamy and yellow flowers of the early-blooming *Tulipa turkestanica*🏆 (2).

OTHER EARLY SPRING FLOWERING SHRUBS *Azara microphylla* • *Berberis* 'Goldilocks' • *Daphne laureola* •

Viburnum × *burkwoodii* 'Anne Russell'

PINKS AND REDS

When it comes to pinks for early spring, we need look no further than the purplish-pink ***Daphne mezereum*** and some cultivars of ***Helleborus* × *hybridus*** (Lenten rose) and ***Cyclamen coum***♀ (see pages 51, 168–69). Pinks, cream and white are also the colours of the winter-flowering viburnums, such as the evergreen ***Viburnum tinus*** (see page 82) and the deciduous ***Viburnum bodnantense* 'Dawn'**♀ (see page 180), which continue to flower into early spring. Later, their flowers will be joined by others, for example the evergreen ***Viburnum* × *burkwoodii* 'Anne Russell'**♀ (see also page 61), whose flowers are fragrant, pink in bud, but white when open fully.

EARLY-FLOWERING TULIPS

Tulips bring a range of rich, dazzling colours to our gardens. By choosing judiciously, it is possible to grow blooms in colours that range from darkest purple to the purest white, and to experiment with violets, reds, oranges, pinks, apricots and yellows. The earliest tulips begin blooming at the end of winter so, by selecting some from each of the early-, mid- and late-flowering groups, it is possible to have these gorgeous flowers in the garden for about four months, from late winter to the end of spring.

Among the early-flowering kinds is *Tulipa turkestanica* (see Good Companions, opposite), a species that has as many as 12 star-shaped ivory flowers, striped with green, on each of its stems. The flowers have a somewhat unpleasant scent, but that should not put you off this understated tulip. Other early tulips include the free-flowering *Tulipa saxatilis* Bakeri Group 'Lilac Wonder'♀ (above), with lilac-mauve tepals, yellow at the base, and the elegant *Tulipa clusiana*, known as the lady tulip. Its flowers are mostly white, but the tepals have dark purplish-pink stripes on their outsides and their bases are crimson or purple. The flowers are bowl-shaped when they first appear, but as their tepals open wide they become flat stars. One or two flowers grow on each stem, which are up to 30cm (12in) tall. *Tulipa biflora* (formerly *Tulipa polychroma*) produces star-shaped fragrant flowers that appear relatively early, often in late winter; they are white tinged with greenish pink, and when open reveal golden yellow centres. *Tulipa humilis* 'Eastern Star' also has yellow centres, but its tepals are magenta with bronzy-green flames on their outer surfaces.

FLOWERING QUINCES

Early spring is the time when flowering quinces begin to reveal their captivating cup-shaped flowers, and among them there is an eye-catching array of colours – vermilion, scarlet, bright pink and white. Among the most reliable performers are *Chaenomeles* × *superba* 'Nicoline'♀ and *Chaenomeles* × *superba* 'Knap Hill Scarlet'♀, both producing scarlet flowers (those of 'Nicoline' are sometimes semi-double). *Chaenomeles* × *superba* 'Crimson and Gold'♀ (1) produces darker red flowers and grows into a compact but spreading shrub (see also page 48), while *Chaenomeles* × *superba* 'Pink Lady'♀ has dark pink flowers that appear earlier than most. *Chaenomeles speciosa* 'Moerloosei'♀ (2) is a paler-coloured cultivar, whose attractive, soft pink and cream flowers could be mistaken for apple blossom.

Jasminum nudiflorum • *Prunus mume* 'Beni-chidori' • *Ribes sanguineum* 'Pulborough Scarlet' •

Magnolias

Magnolias are some of the most breathtaking trees and shrubs a gardener can grow, and they bring an air of distinction to any garden. With their magnificent goblet-shaped, cup-shaped or star-shaped flowers, in pink, purple, white, cream, yellow or green, they are perfect candidates for specimen planting, uncluttered by other plants. Many magnolias flower before the leaves appear, in winter or early spring, while others bloom later in spring, or in summer or autumn.

There are both evergreen and deciduous magnolias among the 125 species (all those shown on these pages are deciduous), but perhaps the most popular – seen in urban settings as often as rural ones – is *Magnolia* × *soulangeana*, which grows into a widely spreading tree or large shrub. As a mature specimen, it may have a diameter as wide as 6m (20ft), so is best suited to a larger garden. For those with smaller gardens, the good news is that there are lots of delightful magnolias that make ideal specimens for more restricted spaces. *Magnolia stellata* ♈ is a beautiful white specimen shrub for a small garden (see page 114).

While they appear to be the epitome of sophistication, magnolias are in fact easy to grow, preferring soils that are moist, well-drained and humus-rich, with a neutral pH or a slightly acidic one. However, most will tolerate a degree of alkalinity, especially *Magnolia* × *loebneri* and *Magnolia stellata* and their cultivars. Magnolias should be planted in positions where they may grow to their full extent without pruning, which is unnecessary and destroys their elegant shape. The flowers of those magnolias that bloom in early spring are susceptible to damage from frost and wind, so it is important to select a spot for them that is as sheltered from the elements as possible.

***Magnolia* × *loebneri* 'Leonard Messel'** ♈ has pale lilac-pink, star-shaped flowers with 12 wavy petals that appear before the leaves. It grows into a rounded shrub, 8 x 6m (25 x 20ft).

Magnolia* × *soulangeana, 6 x 6m (20 x 20ft), bears goblet-shaped flowers with petals that have deep purplish-pink bases and paler pink tips. Its flowers appear just before the leaves.

Magnolia **'Susan'** ♕ has scented, slender, goblet-shaped flowers with narrow petals. The petals twist and are deep purplish pink on the outside and paler pink inside. It is relatively compact, at 4 x 3m (12 x 10ft) when mature.

Magnolia campbellii grows into a large spreading tree, eventually producing beautiful, big cup-and-saucer-shaped flowers in white and pink. A magnolia for favoured locations away from strong winds and hard frosts.

OTHER GOOD MAGNOLIAS

Magnolia **'Galaxy'** ♕**,** a cone-shaped deciduous tree, 12 x 8m (40 x 25ft), with rich purplish-pink, tulip-shaped flowers, 12cm (5in) in diameter, which appear on bare branches.

Magnolia **'Heaven Scent'** ♕, a large shrub or tree, 10 x 10m (30 x 30ft), with fragrant flowers, flushed pink with a deeper stripe outside and white within; blooms well into early summer.

Magnolia wilsonii ♕, a spreading shrub or small tree, 6 x 6m (20 x 20ft). Exquisite white flowers hang from the branches, revealing a central boss of dazzling crimson stamens.

Magnolia stellata **'Centennial'** is a compact magnolia with decorative silky buds opening to reveal pure white, double, star-shaped flowers, up to 14cm (5½in) in diameter, with many petals in each bloom. They flower profusely before the leaves appear.

Dwarf and miniature narcissi

Narcissus **'February Gold'** ♥ is a popular yellow daffodil, with slightly swept-back petals. (See Good Companions, page 115.)

Narcissus **'Thalia'** is a mid-spring flowering daffodil with up to three exquisite pure white flowers per stem.

Narcissus **'Hawera'** ♥ has pale lemon-yellow, drooping flowers that sway in the wind. (See Good Companions, page 116.)

The garden daffodils, or narcissi, we all love to grow are descended from the 50 wild species found in areas of southern Europe and the Mediterranean region, North Africa and western Asia. Narcissi grow from bulbs and are characterized by flowers that have six spreading perianth segments (petals) that surround the cup or corona, sometimes known as the 'trumpet'. The corona may be flat or prominent, widely flared, or long and thin. Wild daffodils have widely differing flower shapes, but few grow more than 30cm (12in) tall. They are found in meadows in situations as diverse as mountain crags and coastal plains, and their colours are white, cream and yellow.

Cultivars display a much wider selection of colours than wild narcissi, despite the fact that many of them – especially the dwarf and miniature varieties – are only one or two generations removed from their species ancestors. To distinguish between the many thousands of cultivars, horticulturists divide narcissi into 12 divisions, each of which has distinct characteristics. The species are placed in Division 10, and Division 12 includes daffodils not in any other division.

Narcissus pseudonarcissus ♀ (Lent lily) has flowers with yellow trumpets and creamy-white petals. Although it may take some time to get established, this charming daffodil is suitable for naturalizing in grass and woodland. (See Good Companions, page 178.)

Narcissus 'Canaliculatus' is sweetly scented, with swept-back white petals and rounded yellow trumpets. It needs a well-drained site and good summer baking.

Narcissus 'Minnow' ♀ has cream-coloured petals and pale yellow cups. It is up to 18cm (7in) high, with four or five flowers per stem.

USING NARCISSI IN THE GARDEN

Like their larger relatives, small narcissi may be grown in pots, borders, rock gardens, or naturalized in grass. *Narcissus triandrus* ♀ and *Narcissus jonquilla* ♀ hybrids thrive in borders and rock gardens and will add colour early in the season. The bulbocodiums and tazettas are better grown in containers, raised beds and frost-free greenhouses, where they can be given ideal growing conditions. The species *Narcissus pseudonarcissus* ♀ and *Narcissus cyclamineus* ♀ (see page 112) may be naturalized in grass (*Narcissus cyclamineus* will only flourish in damp acid soil) and so too the cultivar *Narcissus* 'Jack Snipe' ♀. The latter has the advantage of not being too choosy about soil.

Narcissi grow best in moderately fertile, well-drained soil that is moist during the growing season. They should be planted in autumn at one and a half times their own depth. Bulbs to be naturalized in grass should be planted slightly deeper.

Groups of pots, each containing a single dwarf or miniature narcissus, look effective, but those in borders or beds associate well with later-flowering snowdrops, forget-me-nots, blue- or white-flowered pulmonarias and crocuses, and foliage plants such as asarums.

Narcissus 'Jetfire' ♀ is an early-flowering hybrid that produces neat plants with masses of flowers on 20cm (8in) stems. The petals are bright golden yellow and the long trumpets are bright orange.

OTHER GOOD NARCISSI

Narcissus 'Baby Moon' ♀, deep yellow, scented flowers, with as many as six flowers on its 15cm (6in) long stems.

Narcissus 'Fairy Chimes', dark lemon-yellow flowers on stems 20cm (8in) long.

Narcissus jonquilla ♀ (wild jonquil), up to five golden yellow scented flowers per 30cm (12in) stem.

Narcissus 'Mite' ♀, golden yellow flowers with long, straight trumpets and swept-back petals.

Narcissus 'Small Talk', tiny golden yellow flowers carried on stems to 10cm (4in) tall.

Narcissus 'Sundial', one or two golden yellow flowers on stems up to 20cm (8in) tall.

Narcissus tazetta, many sweetly scented blooms with flat white petals and small yellow cups on each of its stems; these vary considerably in length.

Narcissus 'Tête-à-tête' ♀, very early golden yellow flowers, 15cm (6in) high, with slightly deeper trumpets.

Narcissus triandrus ♀ (angel's tears), nodding cream-coloured flowers with rounded cups and swept-back petals.

Prunus 'Taihaku', the great white cherry, in full bloom.

Late spring

As the days lengthen and there is some warmth in the sun's rays, the atmosphere in the garden is one of luxuriant and abundant freshness, with colour everywhere you look. Blossom has appeared on trees and shrubs, and an increasing number of perennials are producing flowers to add to those of bulbs.

As was the case earlier in the season, the principal colours of mid- to late spring tend to be yellows, whites and blues, but now there are many more pinks as the blossom of trees such as **crab apples** (*Malus*), **magnolias** and **cherries** (*Prunus*) reach their peak. Since this is the time when the majority of **tulips** flower too (see pages 130–31), there is also much more apricot, orange, red and purple, and gardeners can enjoy creating hot harmonies or striking contrasts with them. In gardens where the soil is acid, yet more exciting and dramatic combinations are possible with **azaleas** and **rhododendrons**, which produce flowers in hot, vibrant yellows, apricots, pinks and reds as well as cooler pinks, violet, mauve, cream and white. (See pages 132–33.)

WHITE-FLOWERED SHRUBS AND TREES

For those who prefer their colours to be more subtle than rhododendrons', late spring is the time when many white-flowering shrubs and small trees produce their flowers; there are kinds to suit every situation. Some **viburnums** produce white flowers in late spring, for example ***Viburnum* × *carlcephalum*** ♕ and the widely spreading ***Viburnum plicatum* f. *tomentosum* 'Mariesii'** ♕, whose flowers are carried in horizontal tiers. **Amelanchiers** may still be producing masses of white flowers, sometimes flushed with pink, and some

Viburnum plicatum f. *tomentosum* 'Mariesii'

Cornus 'Norman Hadden'

Osmanthus delavayi

Fothergilla major

Exochorda × *macrantha* 'The Bride'

crab apples also produce white blooms: ***Malus toringo*** (formerly *Malus sieboldii*) and ***Malus toringo* subsp. *sargentii*** are choice shrubs or small trees that flower copiously in mid- and late spring; ***Malus transitoria***♕ is an elegant larger tree, with pink buds that become white as the flowers open.

Many **dogwoods** are resplendent in white too, but principally in those areas where the soil is neutral or acid. ***Cornus* 'Norman Hadden'**♕ and ***Cornus florida*** are excellent choices for smaller gardens. For those who love scent, now is the time to enjoy the flowers of fragrant shrubs, such as those of ***Osmanthus delavayi***♕, ***Amomyrtus luma*** (formerly *Myrtus lechleriana*) and ***Choisya ternata***♕ (Mexican orange blossom). The North American native ***Fothergilla major***♕ may not produce such heavily scented flowers but its tiny white, powder-puff flowers are some of the prettiest of the season.

WHITE-FLOWERING CHERRIES
Prunus 'Shirotae'♕
Prunus avium 'Plena'♕
Prunus glandulosa 'Alba Plena'

***Spiraea* 'Arguta'**♕ is one of those invaluable shrubs that are easy to grow and flower reliably without too much cosseting. Its tiny, saucer-shaped white flowers, carried in clusters on short branches, are an asset to any garden in late spring.

Pieris are evergreen shrubs with handsome leaves, colourful young shoots (pink, red or bronze in some kinds) and clusters of small, urn-like flowers. ***Pieris japonica*** and its cultivars, such as ***Pieris japonica* 'Scarlett O'Hara'**, have white flowers carried in densely packed clusters.

Attractive as all these are, to my mind one of the most beautiful of all the white-flowered shrubs for late spring is ***Exochorda* × *macrantha* 'The Bride'**♕, which produces a profusion of flowers that look like white apple-blossom. It grows into a spreading bush, which reaches up to 2 x 3m (6 x 10ft) when mature. It needs fertile soil, so gardeners with poor, chalky soil could grow it in a large pot.

WHITE WOODLAND PERENNIALS

Late spring is when more and more woodland perennials are bursting into flower, and many have white flowers. **Epimediums** are beautiful perennials that spread happily in shade and are useful for ground cover under trees and shrubs. They produce small, intricately shaped flowers in many colours including white. ***Epimedium* × *youngianum* 'Niveum'**♕, ***Epimedium pubigerum*** and ***Epimedium grandiflorum* 'White Queen'**♕ all have white flowers and pretty young leaves. Sometimes old foliage completely hides the new flowers; to prevent this, cut back last year's leaves in early spring (taking care not to snip tender new shoots). Some epimediums, for example ***Epimedium grandiflorum***♕ and its cultivars, have foliage that is bronze when young.

Arum italicum* subsp. *italicum* 'Marmoratum'**♕ produces beautifully marbled leaves, white on dark green, that start emerging in late winter, so it makes the ideal foliage plant to accompany those woodlanders whose flowers appear in mid- and late spring, such as **erythroniums** (dog's-tooth violets) and **trilliums** (wood lilies). Some of the American species erythroniums have white or creamy-white flowers, with pretty, backward-sweeping petals, on slender, upright stems; ***Erythronium californicum♕ shows up well in a shady corner; ***Erythronium californicum* 'White Beauty'**♕ is a choice, large-flowered cultivar, which increases well in suitable humus-rich soil. ***Erythronium oregonum*** is a similar, rather exotic-looking woodlander. All of these dog's-tooth violets would be assets in any woodland or rock garden.

Trillium grandiflorum

Smilacina racemosa

Among the trillium clan there are some beautiful white-flowered species, such as ***Trillium grandiflorum***♕, ***Trillium grandiflorum* 'Flore Pleno'**♕, which is even more captivating than the species, and the pretty, smaller-flowered ***Trillium ovatum***. The flowers are three-petalled, and they turn pink as they age, but ***Trillium chloropetalum*** produces flowers in a range of colours from white to pink to purple. ***Trillium cernuum*** has white flowers with maroon centres, sometimes hidden beneath its luxuriant mid-green leaves.

Some trillium species also hail from North America, and this is the home of

Arum italicum subsp. *italicum* 'Marmoratum'

GOOD COMPANIONS

An attractive all-white planting for woodland in late spring would include the dainty, bell-shaped flowers of the summer snowflake *Leucojum aestivum* (1) planted among the saucer-shaped yellow and white blooms of the buttercup *Ranunculus aconitifolius* (2). Star-shaped white flowers add interest to the planting, in the form of *Asphodelus albus* (3) and the scented sweet woodruff *Galium odoratum* (4).

MORE WOODLAND PERENNIALS *Anemone nemorosa* • *Asarum splendens* • *Convallaria majalis* •

Polygonatum × hybridum

another charming woodland plant, ***Smilacina racemosa***♀, which carries elegant white 'candles' of flowers above its leaves in mid- to late spring. Somewhat similar are the **Solomon's seals** (*Polygonatum*), which produce their pendent, bell-like flowers on arching stems as spring progresses. ***Polygonatum* × *hybridum***♀ (common Solomon's seal) has creamy-white, green-tipped flowers that grow on stems up to 1m (40cm) tall (see Good Companions, below), while its cultivar ***Polygonatum* × *hybridum* 'Striatum'** also has white flowers tipped with green, and its leaves are striped with creamy white.

One of the loveliest white-flowered bulbs is the curiously named summer snowflake, ***Leucojum aestivum***, which produces its snowdrop-like blooms on stems up to 60cm (2ft) tall in mid- to late spring. It flowers best in full sun, and all-white plantings always benefit greatly from its presence. (See Good Companions, opposite.)

YELLOW IN THE GARDEN

Spring would not be spring without catkins, and late spring is when the **birches** and the **willows** produce them in large numbers. Most birches produce yellow or yellow and brown male catkins, but willows produce grey, silver and green as well as yellow ones; the males are always more striking than the females. Particularly stunning yellow male catkins are produced by ***Salix lanata***♀ (woolly willow). They are golden and 5cm (2in) long, while those of ***Salix repens*** (creeping willow) are 2cm (¾in) long in a silvery grey with prominent yellow anthers.

Yellow is also the colour of various flowering shrubs, such as **kerrias** and **mahonias**, for example the evergreen

Mahonia aquifolium

Cytisus × praecox 'Warminster'

Mahonia aquifolium (Oregon grape), and some **brooms** (*Cytisus*). Brooms are magnificent when showered in their pea-like flowers but need to be grown in full sun in well-drained, moderately fertile soil to perform well. ***Cytisus* × *praecox*** produces pale yellow flowers, while those of its cultivar ***Cytisus* × *praecox* 'Allgold'**♀ are dark rich yellow. Other yellow-flowered brooms include ***Cytisus scoparius* 'Cornish Cream'**, ***Cytisus decumbens***, ***Cytisus* 'Golden Sunlight'**, ***Cytisus* × *beanii***♀, ***Cytisus* 'Firefly'** and ***Cytisus* × *praecox* 'Warminster'**♀.

GOOD COMPANIONS

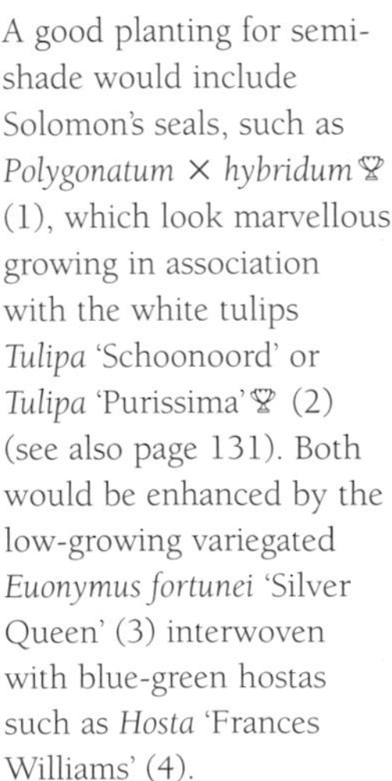
A good planting for semi-shade would include Solomon's seals, such as *Polygonatum* × *hybridum*♀ (1), which look marvellous growing in association with the white tulips *Tulipa* 'Schoonoord' or *Tulipa* 'Purissima'♀ (2) (see also page 131). Both would be enhanced by the low-growing variegated *Euonymus fortunei* 'Silver Queen' (3) interwoven with blue-green hostas such as *Hosta* 'Frances Williams' (4).

Hyacinthoides non-scripta • *Oxalis oregana* • *Tiarella wherryi* • *Trillium erectum* f. *luteum* • *Viola odorata* •

Uvularia grandiflora

Doronicum × excelsum 'Harpur Crewe'

There are numerous other garden-worthy, late spring flowering perennials that could be included either in all-yellow plantings or in contrasting schemes of yellow and blue. ***Uvularia grandiflora***♀, with its bell-shaped yellow flowers tinged with green, likes to be grown in deep or partial shade, while ***Asphodeline lutea*** (yellow asphodel), a native of the eastern Mediterranean, needs a sunny position to thrive. It has upright, narrow flower spikes, like tapering candles, which could be used as vertical accents for a planting of yellow-flowered perennials with rounded, daisy-like flowerheads such as doronicums. ***Doronicum* × *excelsum* 'Harpur Crewe'** has golden yellow flowers on 60cm (2ft) stems and attractive heart-shaped leaves. The **anemones** that produce yellow flowers in late spring are much less imposing but make ideal carpeting plants in sun and partial shade. The small, refined ***Anemone* × *lipsiensis*** has pale yellow flowers on stems 15cm (6in) long and ***Anemone ranunculoides***♀ produces deep yellow, buttercup-like blooms on 20cm (8in) stems.

So much yellow appearing around the garden could be overwhelming if it were not tempered by the green of emerging foliage of perennials and shrubs. **Hostas** and **geraniums** provide an abundance of fresh green leaves in late spring, and some **spurges** (euphorbias) produce their complex and curious-looking yellow, green or lime-green flowerheads now. ***Euphorbia amygdaloides* var. *robbiae***♀ and ***Euphorbia cyparissias*** are lime green, ***Euphorbia polychroma***♀ (see also page 66) and ***Euphorbia myrsinites***♀ are bright yellow, and ***Euphorbia seguieriana*** produces flowerheads that are yellowish green.

For those with water gardens, late spring is when marginal plants really begin to make a show, and nothing could be more appealing than **marsh marigolds**, with their cup-shaped flowers. ***Caltha palustris***♀ has bright golden yellow blooms, and those of ***Caltha palustris* var. *palustris*** (giant marsh marigold) are twice the size of the species. ***Caltha palustris* 'Flore Pleno'**♀, with its double flowers, is especially beguiling. Just as beautiful are the **globeflowers** (*Trollius*), which produce buttercup-like flowers and like to grow in dampish conditions. ***Trollius* × *cultorum* 'Alabaster'** has pale primrose-yellow flowers on 60cm (2ft)

Trollius chinensis

Euphorbia polychroma

CLIMBERS FOR LATE SPRING *Actinidia kolomikta* • *Akebia quinata* • *Ceanothus impressus* •

stems, while **Trollius × cultorum 'Earliest of All'** bears intense yellow flowers on 50cm (18in) stems and **Trollius chinensis** has light orange-yellow blooms.

BLUE-FLOWERED PLANTS

As we have seen in the 'blue' section of the book (see pages 40–41), blue-flowered plants are always treasured by gardeners as true blues are few. Late spring is when some of the best reveal their wares – plants such as the gentians ***Gentiana verna***, with bright blue, funnel-shaped flowers, and ***Gentiana acaulis*** 🏆, whose flowers are an intense blue. Less glamorous are **forget-me-nots** (*Myosotis*), which, once established in a garden, set seed indiscriminately. ***Mertensia virginica*** 🏆 will be familiar to many American readers, as it grows wild in woods in North America, but less so to the majority of British gardeners. It produces violet-blue (sometimes white)

Brunnera macrophylla

Omphalodes cappadocica 'Starry Eyes'

flowers above mid-green leaves in late spring. Somewhat similar are the **brunneras**, perennials that produce flowers resembling forget-me-nots in airy clusters above heart-shaped leaves. ***Brunnera macrophylla* 'Dawson's White'** has bright blue flowers and leaves margined in white, while ***Brunnera macrophylla* 'Jack Frost'** bears attractive, green-veined silver leaves and pale blue flowers.

GOOD COMPANIONS

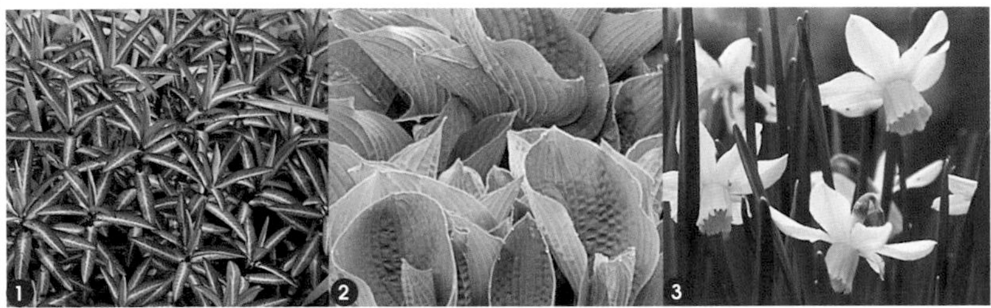

Spurges such as *Euphorbia schillingii* 🏆 (1) look wonderful in all-green plantings; mixing them with *Hosta sieboldiana* var. *elegans* 🏆 (2) and ferns works well, and they also combine beautifully with narcissi, such as the white and yellow *Narcissus* 'Surfside' 🏆 (3).

The silver foliage and pinkish flowers of *Lamium maculatum* 'Beacon Silver' (4) combine beautifully with the pinkish leaves of the elephant's ears *Bergenia* 'Rosi Klose' (5) (see also page 129) and the crushed raspberry blooms of *Pulmonaria saccharata* 'Leopard' (6).

Symphytum caucasicum

Navelworts (omphalodes) are related to mertensias and brunneras and most produce flowers in mid- to late spring. ***Omphalodes verna*** (blue-eyed Mary) produces bright blue flowers with white eyes on 20cm (8in) stems, while ***Omphalodes cappadocica*** 🏆 and its cultivars have azure-blue flowers on 25cm (10in) stems. The flowers of ***Omphalodes cappadocica* 'Starry Eyes'** are larger than those of the species, with a white margin to each petal, and ***Omphalodes cappadocica* 'Parisian Skies'** has very deep blue flowers. Also useful as ground cover for a shady border or for a woodland garden is the bright blue comfrey ***Symphytum caucasicum*** 🏆.

Hydrangea anomala subsp. *petiolaris* • *Lonicera japonica* 'Halliana' • *Rosa banksiae* 'Lutea' • *Wisteria sinensis* 'Alba' •

Early-flowering clematis

One of the joys of mid- to late spring is watching the emergence of bell-shaped, nodding flowers on clematis of the alpina and macropetala types. They flower for about six weeks. Among them are cultivars with captivating blue flowers, such as *Clematis* 'Frances Rivis'♀, whose mid-blue flowers have twisted tepals, *Clematis* 'Columbine', with powder-blue flowers, and *Clematis* 'Frankie'♀, whose light Oxford blue flowers have white stamens that look more like petals. *Clematis macropetala* is similar to *Clematis alpina*♀, but its flowers have longer stamens that resemble petals, so they appear to have double rather than single flowers.

Clematis montana also blooms in late spring and into early summer, bearing a profusion of small white flowers. It has many cultivars, some of which have pink flowers, for example *Clematis montana* var. *rubens* 'Tetrarose' (see page 79). They are all very vigorous so should be planted where they can scramble freely.

Clematis macropetala has blue or violet-blue, bell-shaped flowers from spring to early summer. The flowers are followed by silver seedheads.

***Clematis macropetala* 'Blue Bird'** has slightly drooping, mauve-blue flowers with cream-coloured stamens.

OTHER GOOD ALPINA AND MACROPETALA CULTIVARS

Clematis alpina 'Pamela Jackman'
Clematis 'Constance'♀
Clematis 'Jacqueline du Pré'♀
Clematis 'Jan Lindmark'
Clematis 'Markham's Pink'♀
Clematis 'White Swan
Clematis 'Willy'

ALPINA AND MACROPETALA CULTIVARS: CULTIVATION AND PRUNING

Clematis alpina♀ and *Clematis macropetala* and their cultivars are easy to grow but prefer free-draining, fertile soil that does not dry out in summer. They should be mulched with well-rotted manure in spring and appreciate a liquid feed throughout the summer. A position in full sun produces the best flowers. Less vigorous than *Clematis montana*, they are good for small gardens and can be grown in containers.

Alpina and macropetala cultivars grown in pots should be fed regularly and hard-pruned annually after flowering. Those grown in the ground benefit from being pruned after their first flowering, as this will encourage new shoots to grow from the base and make training easier. After this initial flowering, they do not need regular pruning, but it is a good idea to cut them to the ground every few years after flowering, as otherwise they become a jumbled mass of stems with the newer ones covering the older ones.

Daphne tangutica Retusa Group

Bergenia 'Rosi Klose'

Lamium maculatum 'Beacon Silver'

PINK-FLOWERED PLANTS

Those wanting to grow pink flowers for late spring have an assortment of **flowering cherries** (*Prunus*), **crab apples** (*Malus*), shrubs, perennials and bulbs at their disposal, and there are some aristocrats among them – for instance **daphnes**, some of which produce lovely scented pink flowers at this time, namely ***Daphne tangutica*** ♀, ***Daphne tangutica* Retusa Group** ♀, ***Daphne × burkwoodii* 'Somerset'**, ***Daphne* 'Valerie Hillier'**, ***Daphne arbuscula*** ♀ and ***Daphne petraea* 'Grandiflora'**. **Staphyleas** may not be as familiar as daphnes, but they are intriguing shrubs, whose pink and white flowers make a welcome contribution to a late-spring garden. ***Staphylea holocarpa* 'Rosea'** has bell-shaped, pale pink flowers and bronze young leaves, and ***Staphylea pinnata*** has white flowers tinged with pink. Staphyleas are known as bladdernuts because they produce curious bladder-like, two- or three-lobed fruit.

Bergenias belong to the saxifrage family. With their handsome evergreen 'elephant's ears' leaves and clusters of funnel-shaped or bell-shaped flowers, they are striking plants that should not be overlooked when perennials with pink, red or magenta flowers are required for a late-spring planting. ***Bergenia* 'Rosi Klose'** has large pink flowers in mid- to late spring and is one of the bergenias that looks good in winter, when its foliage becomes a glossy bronze-red colour. (See Good Companions, page 127.) ***Bergenia cordifolia*** has dark pink or pale rose-red flowers in late spring, and purple-flushed leaves in winter. ***Bergenia* 'Morgenröte'** ♀ produces reddish-pink flowers that are carried on rigid red stems. Bergenias make handsome companions for taller white, cream or pink tulips (see pages 130–31).

The **deadnettles** (lamiums) may not be everyone's first choice when it comes to selecting perennials, but not all are invasive and some have prettily mottled leaves. ***Lamium maculatum* 'Beacon Silver'** is one of the more choice species; it is non-invasive and has attractive silver leaves with a narrow green margin, and pale pink, two-lipped flowers from late spring to summer. (See also Good Companions, page 127.)

FRITILLARIES

The fritillaries are bulbous plants that produce bell-shaped, tubular or cup-shaped, pendulous flowers in spring and early summer. Some are suitable for raised beds or borders, while others look best in a woodland garden. They vary in size and colour, and often the blooms are chequered. Flowers range from *Fritillaria meleagris* (see page 91), denizen of meadows, with its pinkish-purple and white flowers on 30cm (12in) stems, to the dainty maroon-purple, yellow-tipped *Fritillaria michailovskyi* ♀ (1) at 20cm (8in) high, the creamy *Fritillaria pallidiflora* ♀ (2) at 40cm (16in) high, and the imposing *Fritillaria imperialis* (crown imperial, see page 66), with yellow, orange or red blooms and a cluster of dark green bracts, on stems up to 90cm (3ft) tall.

OTHER GOOD FRITILLARIES

Fritillaria acmopetala ♀
Fritillaria persica
Fritillaria persica 'Adiyaman' ♀
Fritillaria pontica
Fritillaria raddeana

PLANT PROFILE

Tulips

Tulips are among the most captivating of spring flowers, and their blooms, which are composed of six petal-like tepals, come in various shapes and sizes. They may be cup-shaped, star-shaped or goblet-shaped. Some are single and have tepals that open widely, while others are double with tightly packed tepals resembling old cottage-garden peonies. Some have fringed tepals, and others have complex shapes with twisted or elongated tepals. However, their principal appeal lies in the clarity and opulence of their colours. There are tulips in sumptuous reds, mouth-watering oranges, scintillating pinks, subtle mauves, cool whites, and some that are striped or whose colours are swirled together like different flavours of ice-cream.

To distinguish between them, tulips are divided into 15 groups, which reflect their flowers' characteristics and, to a lesser extent, their flowering times. For example, the Rembrandt Group consists of single, cup-shaped flowers in white, yellow or red, with other colours such as black, brown, bronze, purple, red or pink superimposed as stripes or feathers. These were the kind of tulips that commanded enormous sums during the height of tulipomania in Holland in the 1630s. (Now we know that these so-called 'broken' tulips owe their colour variations to a virus.) Striped tulips are found in the Viridiflora Group and the Parrot

Tulipa 'Blue Diamond' *Tulipa* 'Attila'

Left: *Tulipa* 'Orange Emperor'
Below: *Tulipa* 'Pink Impression'

Group, and tulips whose petals have fringed edges are placed in the Fringed Group. Many tulips are marked with strong, contrasting colours. The leaves of most tulips are mid-green or grey-green, but they vary in length and width, and some have wavy edges.

When choosing tulips, it is important to consider their flowering time and whether they are suitable for tubs, beds, borders or – in the case of the smaller species – a rock garden, and whether they are suitable for naturalizing – some thrive in fine grass. Tulips dislike excessive wet and almost all like to grow in fertile, well-drained soil in full sun in positions sheltered from strong winds. The species *Tulipa sprengeri*♀ and *Tulipa tarda*♀ (see Good Companions, page 115) prefer humus-rich, peaty soil. (For a further selection of early-flowering tulips, see page 117.)

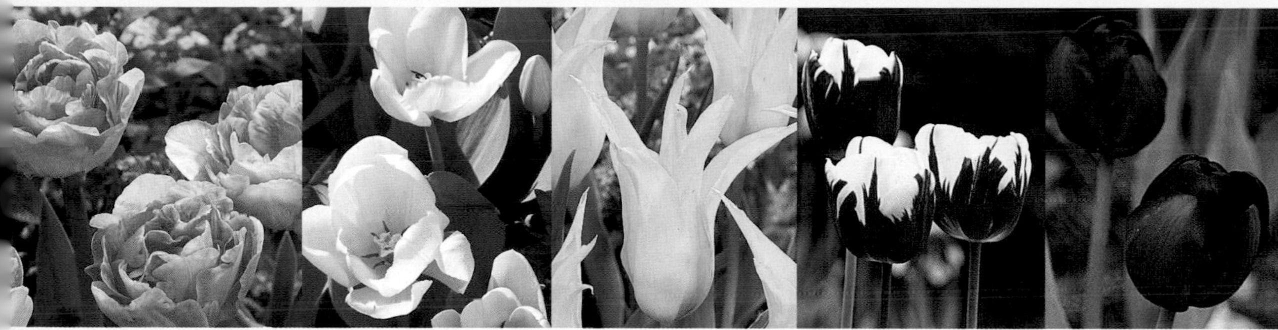

Tulipa 'Angélique' *Tulipa* 'Purissima' *Tulipa* 'West Point' *Tulipa* 'Blueberry Ripple' *Tulipa* 'Queen of Night'

APRICOT FLOWERS

***Tulipa* 'Apricot Beauty'** 🏆 has cup-shaped flowers in salmon-pink in early or mid-spring. The tepals' margins become orange as they age. Useful for bedding or mixed borders.

***Tulipa* 'Cape Cod'** has single, bowl-shaped, apricot-yellow flowers, with red central stripes, in early or mid-spring. Its leaves are bluish grey splashed with dark maroon. Good for the front of a border or in a rock garden.

PINK FLOWERS

***Tulipa* 'Angélique'** 🏆 bears peony-like flowers in pale pink in late spring. The tepals are suffused with paler and deeper pinks. The blooms may be damaged by rain, so provide shelter from wet. Suitable for bedding or a border.

***Tulipa* 'Attila'** has cup-shaped, purplish-violet flowers that appear in mid- to late spring. Suitable for bedding and for cut flowers (See also Good Companions, page 173.)

***Tulipa* 'China Pink'** 🏆 bears goblet-shaped pink blooms in late spring. The flowers' tepals have swept-back, pointed tips, which makes them look very elegant. Makes a good bedding plant in a formal setting.

WHITE FLOWERS

***Tulipa* 'Purissima'** 🏆 produces single, bowl-shaped, pure white flowers in mid-spring. Suitable for a border. (See also Good Companions, page 125.)

***Tulipa* 'Schoonoord'** produces fully double, bowl-shaped, pure white flowers in mid-spring. Good for bedding and containers.

VIOLET OR BLUE FLOWERS

***Tulipa* 'Blueberry Ripple'** has single, cup-shaped flowers in late winter or early spring. The petals are violet or lavender with contrasting white or near-white markings. Suitable for cut flowers and for bedding.

***Tulipa* 'Blue Diamond'** has bowl-shaped flowers, full of dark bluish-purple tepals, that appear in mid- to late spring. Suitable for use as bedding or for a border.

***Tulipa* 'Blue Parrot'** produces single, cup-shaped, bright violet-blue flowers with the characteristic 'cut' tepals of parrot tulips, in late spring. The insides of the tepals are shaded with bronze. It is excellent for cutting and may also be grown in a border.

RED FLOWERS

***Tulipa* 'Apeldoorn'** produces single, ovoid, cherry-red flowers in mid-spring. The inside of the flowers is orangey red with black and yellow marks and prominent black anthers. It is useful for bedding and for cut flowers.

***Tulipa praestans* 'Fusilier'** 🏆 has single, bowl-shaped, bright red flowers in early and mid-spring. Several blooms are produced on a single stem. Good for growing in a rock garden. Keep bulbs dry in summer.

YELLOW FLOWERS

Tulipa sylvestris produces single, star-shaped yellow flowers in mid- and late spring. The flowers' outer surfaces are tinged with green and the blooms are sweetly scented. Suitable for growing in a rock garden.

***Tulipa* 'West Point'** 🏆 produces clear yellow, goblet-shaped flowers in late spring. Makes a good bedding plant for formal settings.

GREEN FLOWERS

***Tulipa* 'Groenland'** produces single, bowl-shaped green blooms with rosy-pink margins in late spring. Good for using for cut flowers and for planting in mixed borders.

***Tulipa* 'Spring Green'** 🏆 produces single, white bowl-shaped flowers, marked with green on the outside, in late spring. Suitable for planting in mixed borders and also excellent for cutting.

PURPLE-BLACK FLOWERS

***Tulipa* 'Arabian Mystery'** has single, cup-shaped, deep purple flowers with white-margined tepals, in mid-spring. Ideal for bedding and also good for cut flowers.

***Tulipa* 'Queen of Night'** produces single, cup-shaped, velvety dark purple or maroon flowers in late spring. The 'blackest' of all tulips to date, it is good for cut flowers as well as bedding. (See also page 38.)

PLANT PROFILE

Rhododendrons and azaleas

Rhododendron 'Peste's Fire Light' (left) is a compact hybrid evergreen rhododendron reaching 1.5m (5ft) in height and spread. The loose trusses of hose-in-hose flowers, the colour of ripe peaches and flecked with coral and mahogany, appear in mid-spring.

The genus *Rhododendron* is one of the largest in the plant kingdom, with between 500 and 900 species. Within the genus there are plants as diverse as trees, growing up to 25m (80ft) tall, and small prostrate shrubs, only a few inches high. Azalea is the common name given to all the deciduous species and hybrids and many of the small-leaved evergreens.

All rhododendrons produce spectacular blooms, and they flower between late autumn and late summer depending on the species or cultivar, and some are sweetly scented. The flowers occur singly or in racemes, known as trusses, and vary widely in size and shape. They may be tubular or trumpet-, funnel-, saucer- or bell-shaped, or something in between. Some have hose-in-hose flowers, with one flower tube inside the other. Most rhododendrons produce lance-shaped, mid- or dark green leaves, varying greatly in size from 4mm (⅛in) to 75cm (30in).

Rhododendrons must be grown in acid soil that is fertile and humus-rich with excellent drainage. Most prefer cool woodland conditions, but some dwarf ones thrive in more open positions. Many adapt well to being grown in pots and, once established, need feeding only occasionally and mulching annually.

WHITE FLOWERS

***Rhododendron* 'Cunningham's White'** is an old hybrid evergreen rhododendron with white flowers marked with yellow and brown. Although not the showiest of rhododendrons, it is hardy and tolerant of slightly alkaline soil.

***Rhododendron* 'Polar Bear'** 🏆 is a superb hybrid evergreen rhododendron making a large shrub or small tree at least 4m (13ft) tall. In late spring it bears large trusses of lily-like fragrant, white flowers delicately marked with green. Flowers are produced only on mature plants, but it's worth the wait.

***Rhododendron* 'Silver Slipper'** 🏆 is a deciduous azalea reaching 2m (6ft) in height and spread. The young leaves are copper-coloured, the flowers white flushed pink with an orange flare in the throat. It flowers in mid-spring.

***Rhododendron* Loderi Group** produces very large, fragrant flowers. The colours are variable.

***Rhododendron* 'Irene Koster'** 🏆, a deciduous azalea, has fragrant flowers of delicate salmon pink marked with yellow and orange.

PINK FLOWERS

Rhododendron calophytum ♀ is a large-leaved evergreen, species rhododendron, reaching 5m (16ft) or more. The loose cluster of large, bell-shaped flowers are pale pink with darker throat markings.

Rhododendron 'Homebush' ♀ is a deciduous azalea reaching 1.5m (5ft) in height and spread. The round clusters of double, strawberry-pink flowers open at the tips of the upright branches in late spring.

Rhododendron 'Mrs Furnivall' ♀ is fine evergreen rhododendron at least 3m (10ft) in height and spread. The pale rose-pink flowers are delicately marked with crimson and sienna, and are carried in large clusters.

RED FLOWERS

Rhododendron 'Cynthia' ♀ is a large, hardy, hybrid evergreen rhododendron reaching 5m (16ft) in height when mature. In mid- to late spring it bears big, pyramid-shaped clusters of rosy-crimson flowers with darker markings. This is regarded as one of the easiest rhododendrons to grow.

Rhododendron 'Scarlet Wonder' ♀ is a low-growing, compact evergreen shrub reaching 1m (40in) in height and spread. The frilled trumpet flowers are ruby red and are freely produced even on young plants.

Rhododendron 'Fireball' ♀, a magnificent deciduous azalea reaching at least 2m (6ft), has copper-tinted foliage and bears glowing orange-red, dense clusters of fragrant blooms in early spring. Brilliant autumn foliage.

MAUVE-BLUE FLOWERS

Rhododendron Blue Diamond Group is a compact shrub slowly reaching 1m (40in) in height. In early spring open, lavender-blue flowers appear in clusters against the small, neat leaves.

Rhododendron 'Blue Danube' ♀ is an evergreen azalea; a spreading shrub up to 90cm (3ft) by 1.2m (4ft). The large blooms are blue-violet – striking against the dark green leaves. It flowers in mid-spring.

YELLOW FLOWERS

Rhododendron luteum ♀ is perhaps the loveliest deciduous azalea, an elegant shrub of open habit at least 2m (6ft) high. In mid- to late spring it bears delicate clusters of honeysuckle-scented, soft yellow flowers at the branch tips. Superb autumn foliage.

Rhododendron 'Hotei' ♀ is a compact evergreen reaching 1m (40in) or more, with clear yellow, bell-shaped flowers in loose clusters in mid-spring.

Rhododendron 'The Hon. Jean Marie de Montague' ♀ bears masses of bright red flowers in mid- to late spring.

Rhododendron 'Colonel Coen' ♀ is a compact evergreen producing deep purple flowers in mid-spring.

Rhododendron 'Horizon Monarch' ♀ is a superb hardy evergreen, with large soft yellow flowers opening from salmon-tinged buds early to mid-spring.

Early-summer plantings like this have a translucent, harmonious beauty, with pink, violet, silver and white much to the fore.

Early summer

There is something magical about early summer. Queen Anne's lace in the hedgerows, fresh, soft green leaves on the trees, and a feeling of lushness everywhere. The sap has risen and suddenly we are seeing the results. In gardens, flowers of every description are appearing daily and the colour palette seems to have transformed into one where pinks are vying with purples, violets and blues to be most numerous. White flowers add to the general feeling of airiness.

This is the time of year when harmonies seem to be more appropriate to the freshness of the season, and in those gardens that feature perennials these are easily created, especially when mixing pinks with mauves, violets and blues. If these schemes seem to be too predictable, it can be fun to experiment with single-coloured borders, random effects or stark contrasts, perhaps of purples and yellows. Whichever colour approach is taken, one thing is certain and that is that there is an enormous amount of plant material to play with.

BLUE FLOWERS

While in spring many of the blues are found in the flowers of bulbous plants, in early summer it is mainly perennials whose flowers are blue, for example ***Anchusa azurea* 'Loddon Royalist'**♀, a cultivar that has deep gentian-blue, tubular flowers in clusters on 90cm (3ft) stems. This anchusa has the advantage of not always needing to be staked. (See Good Companions, opposite.)

Among the **veronica** (speedwell) clan there are also some that produce blue

Anchusa azurea 'Loddon Royalist'

flowers. Veronicas vary in habit from creeping, mat-forming plants to tall kinds over 1m (40in) tall, but all produce tiny flowers in tapering spikes. ***Veronica gentianoides***♀ (see page 41) has pale blue, cup-shaped flowers in racemes up to 25cm (10in) on stems up to 45cm (18in) tall, and is an excellent plant for the front of a border. Its cousin ***Veronica spicata* subsp. *incana*** (silver speedwell) may be used in similar situations, as it has especially decorative silvered leaves and dark blue flowers with a hint of purple on 30cm (12in) tall stems. Mat-forming veronicas, such as ***Veronica prostrata***♀ and ***Veronica peduncularis***, are useful plants for

Veronica spicata subsp. *incana*

carpeting in a rock garden and both produce pretty blue flowers. ***Veronica peduncularis* 'Georgia Blue'** is a good cultivar; easy to grow, it has deep blue flowers with white eyes that appear most abundantly in spring and occasionally until late summer or autumn.

Traditional English gardens would not be complete without at least a few **delphiniums**. These magnificent plants cannot be ignored wherever they are planted, especially those whose flowers are an intense deep, rich blue. Among the best of the blue-flowering kinds are

Delphinium 'Kestrel'

Delphinium* 'Kestrel'**, which is one of the earliest to flower and is a light gentian blue colour with a black eye; ***Delphinium* 'Oliver'**♀, which bears pretty semi-double, mid-blue flowers with contrasting black eyes (see also Good Companions, below); ***Delphinium

Delphinium 'Oliver'

'Blue Nile'♀, with striking semi-double, rich blue flowers with white eyes; ***Delphinium grandiflorum* 'Blue Butterfly'**, with azure-blue flowers; and ***Delphinium* × *bellamosum***, with deep purple-blue flowers.

While not possessing the stateliness of delphiniums, **campanulas** – those traditional herbaceous border plants beloved of cottage gardeners – are well worth growing for their pretty bell- or cup-shaped flowers, some of which are blue. One of the most exquisite of all is ***Campanula persicifolia* 'Telham Beauty'**, which has pale powder-blue, cup-shaped flowers in slender spires. (*Continued on page 137.*)

GOOD COMPANIONS

Anchusa azurea 'Loddon Royalist'♀ (1) makes a good companion for pink-flowered geraniums and purple-red roses, for example *Rosa* 'Roseraie de l'Haÿ'♀ (2) (see also pages 69, 145).

Delphinium 'Oliver' (3) provides a strong vertical accent so it is ideal with rounded or clump-forming plants, such as *Paeonia lactiflora* 'Sarah Bernhardt'♀ (4) (see also page 142).

Ceanothus

Some clematis produce blue flowers in early spring and late summer, but it is to the California lilacs, or *Ceanothus*, that we must turn if we are looking for shrubs with blue flowers in early summer. Ceanothus may be grown in shrub borders, against walls or, if they are prostrate or low-growing, as carpet-forming ground cover for borders or in rock gardens. A wall-trained shrub could provide the backdrop for an all-blue or mixed-colour planting scheme featuring white, cream, pink or violet. Ceanothus should be grown in fertile, well-drained soil in a site in full sun and where they are sheltered from cold winds. They do not fare well in shallow chalk soils. The best time to prune evergreen kinds is after flowering; deciduous ones should be pruned in spring.

***Ceanothus* 'Blue Mound'** ♀, as you might expect, grows into a dome shape or mound reaching 1.5 x 2m (5 x 6ft) when mature, so it may be grown as ground cover at the front of a shrub border. It is an evergreen shrub with glossy, dark green leaves, and its flowers, which are produced from late spring to early summer, are bright blue.

***Ceanothus* 'Concha'** ♀ is a dense, evergreen shrub, 3 x 3m (10 x 10ft) when mature, with dark green leaves and reddish buds opening into deep blue flowers in tightly packed, rounded clusters. (See also page 69.)

***Ceanothus arboreus* 'Trewithen Blue'** ♀ is an evergreen that grows vigorously up to 6 x 8m (20 x 25ft) if left unpruned, and so is a suitable candidate for a large shrub border; it has dark green, rounded leaves, and large deep blue, scented flowers.

***Ceanothus thyrsiflorus* 'Skylark'** ♀ has large glossy, evergreen leaves and masses of mid-blue flowers carried in loose clusters; upright in form, it makes a good wall shrub, growing to 2 x 1.5m (6 x 5ft).

Ceanothus impressus, a fast-growing California lilac, has soft blue flowers and dark green, rounded evergreen leaves; it makes an excellent wall shrub as it reaches only 1.5 x 2.5m (5 x 8ft).

***Ceanothus* 'Cascade'** ♀ is well named, as its bright blue flowers tumble down from arching stems that carry evergreen, dark green leaves; it is 4 x 4m (12 x 12ft) when mature, and looks effective cascading over a bank or down a slope.

The flowers grow on tall stems, about 1m (40in) high, above rosettes of bright green, lance-shaped leaves. Another excellent kind is ***Campanula lactiflora* 'Prichard's Variety'**♡, which has rich violet-blue flowers carried in conical clusters on 75cm (30in) stems. On a considerably smaller scale, ***Campanula cochlearifolia***♡ (Fairies' thimbles) is a charming, creeping, rock-garden

Campanula lactiflora 'Prichard's Variety'

Campanula 'Samantha'

campanula, whose slate-blue flowers appear all through summer on short stems, only 8cm (3in) long. ***Campanula* 'Samantha'** is another low spreader, forming mats of blue-violet, upward-facing flowers.

There are also plenty of less well-known early-summer perennials with blue flowers that are well worth seeking out. ***Cichorium intybus*** (chicory) is a captivating perennial, with toothed leaves and light blue or, occasionally, white or pink flowers reminiscent of dandelions, on branching stems up to 1.2m (4ft) tall. **Amsonias** are perennials found in grassland and woods in Japan, south-eastern Europe and central and north-eastern USA and they too deserve to be more widely grown in gardens. ***Amsonia orientalis*** produces narrow, willow-like leaves and panicles of tiny, funnel-shaped, violet-blue flowers on 30cm (12in) stems, while ***Amsonia tabernaemontana*** has dense clusters of pale blue flowers from late spring to summer on taller stems, 60cm (24in) high. Amsonias will grow in any moist but well-drained soil in full sun.

Linum narbonense (flax) produces beautiful saucer-shaped, rich blue flowers with white eyes; it needs well-drained, moderately fertile, humus-rich soil, and tends to be short-lived, but is well worth growing. ***Myosotidium hortensia*** is an evergreen perennial from Chatham Island, New Zealand, with large, heart-shaped, glossy leaves; it bears forget-me-not, pale to dark blue flowers in dome-shaped clusters on 60cm (24in) stems in early summer. The main disadvantage of this charming plant is that it is half hardy and so has to be lifted in winter if grown outdoors in frost-prone areas. A position in dappled shade suits it best, in moist but well-drained soil with added grit and humus.

WHITE FLOWERS

Plants as large as trees and as small as mat-forming alpines provide the wealth of white available to gardeners in early summer. White-flowering trees include ***Davidia involucrata***♡ (handkerchief tree), whose insignificant flowers are surrounded by prominent white bracts that resemble fluttering white handkerchiefs, and the elegant ***Stewartia pseudocamellia***♡, with its rose-like white flowers with prominent creamy-yellow stamens. ***Cornus controversa* 'Variegata'**♡ (see page 42) is an elegant tree with tiered branches and attractive leaves with wide, creamy-white margins; it looks its best in early summer. This is also the time when the leaves of the whitebeam ***Sorbus aria* 'Lutescens'**♡ appear at their most white; as summer wears on, they become greener.

Early summer is when shrubs such as **philadelphus**, the mock oranges, are flowering to perfection too. Among them are shrubs that produce single or

Davidia involucrata

Stewartia pseudocamellia

Sorbus aria 'Lutescens'

Philadelphus 'Virginal'

Cistus × *obtusifolius* 'Thrive'

double, cup- or bowl-shaped flowers, most of which are sweetly scented. Some good performers are the double-flowered ***Philadelphus*** **'Virginal'** and ***Philadelphus*** **'Buckley's Quill'**, the single ***Philadelphus*** **'Beauclerk'**♀ and ***Philadelphus*** **'Burfordensis'**, and the low-growing ***Philadelphus*** **'Manteau d'Hermine'**♀ (see page 62).

Cistus, such as ***Cistus*** **×** ***obtusifolius*** **'Thrive'**, and **deutzias** also provide white flowers in early and midsummer, and there are white-flowered varieties of both tree and herbaceous **peonies**. The single-flowered herbaceous peony ***Paeonia lactiflora*** **'White Wings'**, with fine, tissue-like white petals and

Gillenia trifoliata

prominent yellow stamens, is particularly appealing and is also fragrant.

When it comes to white-flowering perennials for early summer the choice is wide. ***Gillenia trifoliata***♀ is a graceful perennial for semi-shade on soil with adequate moisture. Its pretty, divided leaves and reddish stems are the perfect background for the dainty white flowers, which open from red buds all through the summer, Some **cranesbills** have white flowers, such as ***Geranium clarkei*** **'Kashmir White'**♀, ***Geranium renardii***♀ and ***Geranium sylvaticum***

Geranium clarkei 'Kashmir White'

'Album'♀. Any of these would be suitable companions for the silver-leaved, daisy-like ***Anthemis punctata*** **subsp.** ***cupaniana***♀. For airy effects, there is ***Gypsophila paniculata*** **'Bristol Fairy'**♀ or the much taller ***Crambe cordifolia***♀, which grows as tall as 2m

Crambe cordifolia

GOOD COMPANIONS

The yellow-centred flowers of *Tanacetum parthenium* (feverfew) (1) harmonize beautifully with the lime-green flowers and foliage of *Nicotiana* 'Lime Green'♀ (2) (see also page 43).

The soft grey leaves of *Stachys byzantina* 'Big Ears' (3) provide the perfect foreground for the stiff white spikes and feathery foliage of the monkshood *Aconitum* 'Ivorine' (4).

MORE COTTAGE-GARDEN PLANTS *Aquilegia vulgaris* • *Centaurea montana* • *Digitalis purpurea* •

Dictamnus albus

Digitalis purpurea f. *albiflora*

(6ft) and has large, dark green leaves. Both these perennials produce delicate branched stems with tiny white flowers in loose, spreading clusters resembling light white clouds.

Thalictrums have the advantage of delicate, ferny leaves and fluffy flowers that look like powder puffs; ***Thalictrum aquilegiifolium* var. *album*** has white flowers arranged in flat-topped clusters on 1m (40in) tall stems. The pyramidal flower panicles found on **rodgersias**, statuesque moisture-loving perennials from Asia, are much more solid and look like thick, tapering candles. Their flowers are star-shaped, and ***Rodgersia podophylla***♡ (see pages 65, 101) produces white ones tinged with green in 30cm (12in) panicles. ***Rodgersia aesculifolia***♡, on the other hand, produces white or pink flowers in longer panicles (see page 143)

Plants that produce spires of flowers are always welcome in a planting, and ***Dictamnus albus,*** with its open racemes of five-petalled flowers in white or pink, and the white form of the common foxglove, ***Digitalis purpurea* f. *albiflora,*** add an elegant dimension to any planting scheme. (See Good Companions, below.)

***Dicentra spectabilis* 'Alba'**♡ is a white-flowered form of bleeding heart, whose charming heart-shaped flowers

Dicentra spectabilis 'Alba'

dangle from arching stems in late spring and early summer. This perennial will grow happily in sun or light shade. ***Hesperis matronalis*** (sweet rocket, see page 89) is just as obliging. This old cottage-garden favourite is a vigorous self-seeder, but its sweetly scented, four-petalled, white or pale lilac flowers are so charming that they are an asset wherever they appear. Its white double-flowered form, ***Hesperis matronalis* var. *albiflora* 'Alba Plena'** is even lovelier. ***Galium odoratum*** (sweet woodruff) is an unpretentious plant with tiny, star-shaped scented flowers that persist for weeks in late spring and summer. With its attractive emerald-

GOOD COMPANIONS

Myrrhis odorata (1) (sweet Cicely), with its umbels of white flowers on tall stems, works well with the white spires of the foxglove *Digitalis purpurea* f. *albiflora* (2). Both are ideal in a shady corner.

The dark foliage and clear white daisy blooms of *Leucanthemum* × *superbum* 'Esther Read' (3) contrast in form with the delicate white spikes of *Delphinium* 'Clear Springs White' (4).

Anemone rivularis

Trifolium ochroleucon

green leaves, it makes good ground cover for woodland or for spaces under evergreen hedges. (See page 124.)

Another good, easy-to-grow plant is ***Anemone rivularis***, which has saucer-shaped white flowers with blue undersides. It flourishes in either sun or light shade, and the flowers grow on long, spreading stalks about 60cm (24in) long. ***Trifolium ochroleucon*** is an attractive clover reaching a similar height, with large, translucent cream flowerheads tinged with green.

Lilium regale

***Osteospermum* 'Whirlygig'** needs much more cosseting, as it is only half hardy and so does not survive if exposed to temperatures below 0°C (32°F). In frost-prone areas, therefore, it has to be lifted and brought into a frost-free environment in winter. However, its daisy-like flowerheads, about 5cm (2in) across, with petals just like teaspoons, are particularly eye-catching and, as they go on appearing from late spring until autumn, the effort is worthwhile.

Osteospermum 'Whirlygig' has a cheery charm very far removed from the grandeur of **lilies**, the aristocrats of the summer garden in many people's eyes. None produces blooms more beautiful than the pure white trumpets of ***Lilium candidum*** and the creamy-white ones of ***Lilium regale***.

PURPLE AND LAVENDER

When it comes to the violet shades of early summer, they range from the dark purples to the palest of lavenders, with numerous tones in between. Rich dark

Salvia × sylvestris 'Mainacht'

purples are found in ***Salvia* × *sylvestris* 'Mainacht'**♀ (see also page 159), which has thin spires of purple flowers and is effective in a wild planting of perennials and grasses, and the false indigo ***Baptisia australis***♀, whose dark purplish-blue, pea-like blooms appear in loose racemes on stems up to 1.2m (4ft) tall. (See Good Companions, opposite.)

Some of the prettiest of palest violets are found in the flowers of the **polemonium** clan, perennials that produce bell- or funnel-shaped flowers above finely divided, pinnate leaves. ***Polemonium caeruleum*** is a tall variety, with light blue flowers; those of ***Polemonium boreale*** vary from purple-blue to light blue. Low-growing ***Polemonium carneum*** has flowers in a variety of colours, from pale pink or yellow to dark purple and lavender, but the bell-shaped flowers of ***Polemonium* 'Lambrook Mauve'**♀ are always lilac-blue, growing on branching stems up to 45cm (18in) tall. While polemoniums make excellent border plants, the taller ones work just as well in a wildflower garden and *Polemonium caeruleum* looks good naturalized in grass.

Baptisia australis

Centaurea montana

Reliable perennial performers with brighter purple or violet flowers are numerous. One of the easiest to grow is ***Centaurea montana*** (knapweed), with its deep bluish-purple flowers with hints of red that appear consistently throughout summer; it can be effective

OTHER GROUND-COVER PLANTS *Artemisia schmidtiana* • *Lamium maculatum* 'Beacon Silver' •

in a wild planting or in a border. ***Stachys macrantha*** **'Superba'** is a fine plant for the front of a border, as it has striking pinkish-purple, hooded, two-lipped blooms carried in dense spikes and downy green leaves. The flower spikes, on 60cm (24in) stems, remain upright without support and appear for weeks from early summer to autumn. Hardy **tradescantias**, distinguished by their flowers of three triangular petals and three sepals, also make excellent border plants, and grow in either sun or light shade. ***Tradescantia*** **Andersoniana Group 'Concord Grape'** is a choice cultivar with rich purple flowers.

Scabious, with their pincushion flowerheads, are charming plants for a wildflower garden or border. ***Scabiosa caucasica*** is perhaps the most beautiful of all, and it has several excellent cultivars. Its large pale blue or lavender-blue flowerheads, 8cm (3in) across, grow on 45cm (18in) stems, and appear consistently from mid- to late summer. As well as looking good in a border, it makes an elegant container-grown plant. To fare well, scabious should be planted in full sun in well-drained, moderately fertile soil that is either neutral or alkaline.

Stachys macrantha 'Superba'

Tradescantia Andersoniana Group 'Concord Grape'

Scabiosa caucasica

Geranium pratense 'Plenum Violaceum'

Geraniums, also known as cranesbills, are very good, reliable, undemanding perennials with flowers in all the colours we associate with early summer: pinks, blues and white, as well as violets and purples. Taller species and cultivars are excellent plants for including in perennial plantings or as ground cover under shrubs and roses (see Good Companions, left). They do not mind being planted in sun or partial shade, and interweave happily among other plants in a border. Also, once flowering is over, they respond well to being cut hard back and, within a short time, produce fresh new leaves and, occasionally, more flowers.

Among the violet- and purple-flowered cranesbills, ***Geranium* × *magnificum***♡ produces lots of large, single blue flowers criss-crossed with darker violet-blue veins in densely packed cymes, and ***Geranium clarkei*** **'Kashmir Purple'** has single blooms in a rich lilac-blue with bright red veining and finely cut leaves. ***Geranium pratense*** **'Plenum Violaceum'**♡ (see also page 63), a delectable cultivar of the meadow

GOOD COMPANIONS

The mid- to lavender-blue *Geranium* 'Johnson's Blue'♡ (1) is a perfect companion for low-growing pale pink-flowered roses such as *Rosa* BONICA ('Meidomonac')♡ (2).

The indigo-blue *Baptisia australis*♡ (3) looks charming with *Rosa* 'Ballerina'♡ (4), which has mop-headed clusters of pale pink and white single flowers from summer to autumn.

Myosotis sylvatica • *Saponaria ocymoides* • *Saxifraga* × *urbium* • *Vinca minor* 'Azurea Flore Pleno' •

Geranium pratense 'Cluden Sapphire'

cranesbill, has fully double, violet flowers shaded with purple-blue in their centres, while ***Geranium pratense* 'Cluden Sapphire'**, a relatively tall cranesbill at 1m (40in) or more high, has a dense inflorescence of single, deep blue flowers from early summer to midsummer. ***Geranium himalayense*** has single blooms in violet-blue with white centres tinged red. They appear from early summer until late summer. ***Geranium sylvaticum* 'Mayflower'**♡, a choice cultivar of the wood cranesbill, has single flowers on 60cm (24in) stems in a soft blue with pink veins. It flowers best in dampish conditions, so may be included in a planting beside a pool or stream, or in a bog garden.

PINK FLOWERS

When thinking of colours for early summer, the pinks cannot be ignored. This is the time of year when they are at their most numerous, for as well as many pink-flowered perennials, most **roses** are at their best now. Descriptions of pink-flowered roses alone would fill many pages and so it is not possible to discuss them in detail. However, a short list of garden-worthy roses, arranged by colour, may be found on page 145.

Paeonia lactiflora 'Bowl of Beauty'

Peonies, with their showy flowers, add an air of glamour to any border in early and midsummer. There are shrubby tree peonies as well as herbaceous ones, and both kinds produce flowers in pink, white, red or yellow. Pink-flowered herbaceous peonies include ***Paeonia lactiflora* 'Sarah Bernhardt'**♡ (see Good Companions, page 135) and ***Paeonia lactiflora* 'Shirley Temple'**, both of which have blowsy double blooms packed with rose-pink petals. The

Paeonia lactiflora 'Sarah Bernhardt'

flowers of ***Paeonia lactiflora* 'Bowl of Beauty'**♡ resemble anemones, with reddish-pink petals and creamy-white centres; their centres are composed of many narrow petals packed together. Peonies may be included in shrub, mixed or herbaceous borders but, once planted, they should not be disturbed as they dislike being uprooted. Some have leaves that colour beautifully in autumn – a small compensation for their comparatively short flowering season.

Massed planting of peonies can look most effective, but teaming them with plants with spires of flowers emphasizes the plants' differing forms and flower shapes, particularly essential in single-colour plantings. ***Eremurus robustus***, with its imposing, foxtail-like racemes of

GOOD COMPANIONS

The buff-coloured plumes of *Macleaya microcarpa* (1) would make a good companion for apricot-pink plants, for example *Digitalis ferruginea*♡ (2).

The mauve-flowered *Dictamnus albus* var. *purpureus*♡ (3) is a perfect partner for cranesbills, such as the compact, pale pink *Geranium sanguineum* var. *striatum*♡ (4).

OTHER PINK-FLOWERED PERENNIALS *Campanula lactiflora* 'Loddon Anna' • *Erigeron* 'Charity' •

Rodgersia aesculifolia

Astilbe 'Venus'

pale pink flowers, would make a worthy companion for pink-flowered tree peonies or taller herbaceous ones. Its flower racemes are sometimes as long as 1.2m (4ft), growing on stems up to 3m (10ft) tall. ***Macleaya microcarpa*** (plume poppy) is a less imposing plant than *Eremurus robustus*, as its buff flowers are arranged in loose, plume-like panicles. They grow on 2m (6ft) stems. (See Good Companions, opposite.) The plumes of ***Macleaya microcarpa* 'Kelway's Coral Plume'**♡ are soft coral-pink. Macleaya is a fine plant but must be kept in check as it is invasive.

Rodgersia aesculifolia♡ is another plant with conspicuous inflorescences. It has large, fluffy pink or white panicles of tiny star-shaped flowers rising above leaves like those of a horse chestnut. It forms clumps up to 1.2m (4ft) tall.

Dictamnus albus var. *purpureus*

Astilbes are plume-like perennials that are ideal for semi-shade in moist soil. They look particularly effective en masse. ***Astilbe* 'Venus'** has feathery panicles of pinkish flowers.

Dictamnus albus (burning bush or dittany) is another imposing perennial with long, candle-like flower racemes. Its variant, ***Dictamnus albus* var. *purpureus***♡, has mauve flowers with purple veining on stems up to 90cm (3ft) tall, and it would make an excellent companion for bushy purple- or pink-flowered **cranesbills** (geraniums). (See Good Companions, opposite). Some pink-flowered cranesbills have good 'shock' value: the magenta ***Geranium psilostemon***♡ and ***Geranium* 'Ann Folkard'**♡ add drama to any planting, and ***Geranium maderense***♡, which can grow to 1.2m (4ft), has pinkish-magenta flowers and finely dissected leaves that add to its charms. The tender ***Geranium × riversleaianum* 'Russell Prichard'**♡, with its greyish foliage and rich magenta flowers produced over a long period, only grows up to 30cm (12in) and is a good 'spreader'.

Lychnis coronaria♡ is a grey-leaved perennial that bears pinkish-magenta rounded blooms on 90cm (3ft) stems; it is best suited to growing in a border, perhaps with other silver-leaved plants. Its relative ***Lychnis flos-jovis***♡ has less eye-catching, paler bluish-pink, white or red flowers, but is an excellent border perennial, with flowers on whitish stems that may grow to 60cm (24in).

Geranium maderense

Lychnis coronaria

YELLOW FLOWERS

Perhaps the most beautiful yellow blooms produced in early summer are the lemon-yellow blooms of the species peony ***Paeonia mlokosewitschii***. They

Incarvillea delavayi • *Liatris spicata* • *Persicaria bistorta* 'Superba' • *Rehmannia elata* • *Verbena* 'Sissinghurst' •

The star-shaped flowers of *Hemerocallis* 'Hyperion' with the tall spires of *Verbascum bombyciferum*.

are single, with oval petals that open to reveal a boss of pale yellow stamens. (See page 45.) The scented, double blooms of ***Paeonia lactiflora* 'Laura Dessert'**♀, which have creamy-white outer sepals and canary-yellow inner ones, are captivating too.

Most yellow-flowered daisies appear in late summer, but ***Argyranthemum* 'Jamaica Primrose'**♀ and ***Anthemis tinctoria* 'E.C. Buxton'** produce their daisy-like, yellow flowers in early and midsummer. In an all-yellow planting, they could provide a foil to ***Thalictrum lucidum***, with its fluffy flowerheads and ferny foliage. ***Achillea filipendulina* 'Gold Plate'**♀ (see page 154) has become more popular in recent years as its flattish, plate-like, golden yellow flowerheads mix well with grasses and other, smaller-flowered perennials.

Argyranthemum 'Jamaica Primrose'

Hemerocallis lilioasphodelus

Funnel-shaped, rounded, trumpet- or star-shaped flowers are features of **hemerocallis**, (daylilies, see page 69) and there are many garden-worthy cultivars with yellow flowers. But certain species, such as ***Hemerocallis lilioasphodelus***, with its lemon-yellow, star-shaped flowers, and ***Hemerocallis citrina***, with its pale greenish-yellow, star-shaped flowers, have enduring appeal. Among the cultivars, ***Hemerocallis* 'Hyperion'** and ***Hemerocallis* 'Marion Vaughn'**♀ are worth considering, as they have fragrant, lemon-yellow, star-shaped nocturnal flowers.

Anyone who grows **verbascums** (mulleins) will know that they produce tall spires of flowers. ***Verbascum* 'Gainsborough'**♀ has creamy-yellow flowers on 1.2m (4ft) stems and greyish-green leaves, and the taller ***Verbascum bombyciferum*** bears sulphur-yellow flowers on towering stems up to 1.8m (6ft) high. This verbascum also has attractive white-woolly, semi-evergreen leaves. **Phlomis** have decorative foliage as well as flowers, and ***Phlomis russeliana***♀ is a particularly attractive perennial, whose pale, soft yellow flowers are arranged in whorls around the 90cm (3ft) flowering stems. The winter seedheads are most attractive.

Thermopsis rhombifolia is another choice perennial, with charming, pale yellow, lupin-like flowers that also grow on 90cm (3ft) stems, but here the leaves are finely divided, hairy and distinctly silvery in colour.

A SHORT SELECTION OF RECOMMENDED ROSES

WHITE FLOWERS

Rosa 'Albéric Barbier' 🏆

Rosa 'Blanc Double de Coubert' 🏆

Rosa ICEBERG ('Korbin') 🏆

Rosa MARGARET MERRIL ('Harkuly') 🏆

Rosa 'Nevada' 🏆 (1)

Rosa 'Seagull' 🏆

YELLOW FLOWERS

Rosa 'Arthur Bell' 🏆

Rosa GOLDEN CELEBRATION ('Ausgold') 🏆 (2)

Rosa 'Golden Wings' 🏆

Rosa 'Goldfinch'

Rosa 'Grandpa Dickson'

Rosa 'Moonlight'

Rosa pimpinellifolia 'Dunwich Rose'

BLUISH-PINK FLOWERS

Rosa 'Celeste' 🏆

Rosa CONSTANCE SPRY ('Austance') 🏆

Rosa 'Fantin-Latour' 🏆

Rosa 'Königin von Dänemark' 🏆

Rosa MARY ROSE ('Ausmary') 🏆

Rosa 'Président de Sèze' 🏆 (3)

Rosa 'The Fairy' 🏆

APRICOT-PINK FLOWERS

Rosa 'Alchymist' (4)

Rosa BONICA ('Meidomonac') 🏆

Rosa 'Compassion' 🏆

Rosa 'Desprez à Fleurs Jaunes' 🏆

Rosa 'Gruss an Aachen'

Rosa 'Mrs Oakley Fisher' 🏆

Rosa × *odorata* 'Mutabilis' 🏆

RED FLOWERS

Rosa 'Crimson Shower' 🏆

Rosa 'Etoile de Hollande'

Rosa FRAGRANT CLOUD ('Tanellis')

Rosa 'Geranium' 🏆

Rosa TESS OF THE D'URBERVILLES ('Ausmove') (5)

Rosa 'Tuscany Superb' 🏆

Rosa 'Zigeunerknabe' 🏆

PURPLISH FLOWERS

Rosa 'Cardinal de Richelieu' 🏆

Rosa 'Madame Isaac Pereire' 🏆

Rosa 'Nuits de Young' 🏆

Rosa 'Roseraie de l'Haÿ' 🏆 (6) (see also page 69 and Good Companions, page 135)

Penstemons

Penstemon **'Burgundy'** has large, deep wine-purple flowers from midsummer to early or mid-autumn, on stems approximately 75cm (30in) high, and relatively large leaves.

Penstemon **'Andenken an Friedrich Hahn'**♀, also known as *Penstemon* 'Garnet', bears small, wine-crimson flowers from midsummer to mid-autumn and narrow leaves. Its flower spires reach about 75cm (30in).

Penstemons have become increasingly popular in recent years as gardeners have come to recognize the value of their elegant, foxglove-like flowers in a range of subtle and bright colours from white to dusky purple, and encompassing pinks, mauves and blues. Some have flowers with white throats, and others have blooms streaked with contrasting colours. The flowers may go on appearing week after week throughout summer, especially when they are deadheaded regularly.

There are about 250 species in the *Penstemon* genus, all of which are found in North and Central America. The genus includes deciduous, semi-evergreen and evergreen perennial species and sub-shrubs, and they are found in a variety of situations from open plains to alpine regions. While some of the species are garden-worthy plants, it is the arrival on the garden scene of some excellent cultivars that has led to them becoming such sought-after plants. The cultivars grow vigorously and flower prolifically, and some are semi-evergreen with leaves that persist throughout the winter months.

Penstemons produce their tubular flowers in racemes or panicles. Individual flowers are composed of two lips, the upper usually with two lobes, the lower with three. Some cultivars bear small leaves that are linear or lance-shaped, while others have larger, elliptic or ovate leaves.

The taller penstemons are superb perennials for borders, where they should be grown in sun or partial shade and in any good soil, as long as it is well drained. In areas where frost is prevalent in winter, it is a good idea to mulch the soil around them for protection. The shrubby and dwarf species must have full sun and prefer less fertile, very free-draining soil.

All of the penstemons described on these pages are perennial unless otherwise stated.

Penstemon **'Evelyn'** ♡ is a narrow-leaved penstemon, with small, pale pink flowers from midsummer to early or mid-autumn on stems up to 60cm (2ft) tall.

Penstemon **'Stapleford Gem'** ♡ has lilac to purple flowers with white throats from midsummer to early or mid-autumn, and dark leaves. It is about 90cm (3ft) high.

Penstemon **'Alice Hindley'** ♡ is a tall, large-leaved penstemon. Its large pale mauve flowers with white throats have purple tinges on the outside and are borne from midsummer to early or mid-autumn on stems up to 1m (40in) tall.

OTHER GOOD PENSTEMONS

Penstemon **'Apple Blossom'** ♡
Small pale pink and white flowers with white throats, from midsummer to early autumn; narrow leaves. Height 75cm (30in).

Penstemon isophyllus ♡
Evergreen sub-shrub with medium-sized, deep pink and red flowers, from early to late summer; lance-shaped leaves. Height 70cm (28in).

Penstemon **'King George V'**
Small flowers, bright red with red-veined white throats, from midsummer to early or mid-autumn; narrow leaves. Height 60cm (2ft).

Penstemon **'Sour Grapes'** ♡
Big, lilac-blue flowers, tinted purple, from midsummer to early or mid-autumn; large leaves. Height 90cm (3ft).

Penstemon **'White Bedder'** ♡
Large pure white flowers, from midsummer to early autumn; large leaves. Height 60cm (2ft).

Penstemon heterophyllus **'Catherine de la Mare'** ♡ is an evergreen sub-shrub, 30–50cm (12–20in) high, with medium-sized blue flowers in summer, and linear to lance-shaped leaves.

Penstemon barbatus (beardlip penstemon) is an erect variety, sometimes more than 1.2m (4ft) tall. It has pendent, narrow flowers, red with yellow 'beards', from early summer to early autumn.

Penstemon **'Raven'** ♡ (left) is an excellent border perennial, with deep purple flowers with white-veined throats, on stems about 1m (40in) high. The flowers bloom from early summer to mid-autumn.

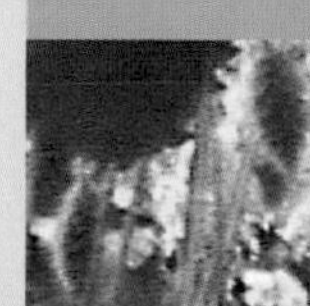

The colour of late summer: *Crocosmia* 'Lucifer' and *Lilium* Pink Perfection Group, with *Rosa glauca* and *Sambucus nigra*.

Late summer

However cool and wet the summer may be, there are days in late summer when the sun shines in all its glory, ripening fruit, and bringing a host of later-flowering perennials and shrubs into flower. On these dry, hot days the fresh, cool colours of early summer seem to melt away as an array of rich, warm hues start to appear. Late summer is the time when scintillating reds, oranges and yellows and some penetrating pinks, purples and blues hold sway.

Canna indica

In late summer, with so many vividly coloured perennials at their best, vibrant hot harmonies featuring reds, oranges and yellows can be breathtaking. But darker, more sumptuous and, perhaps, more mysterious colour schemes can also be made by adding coppers, bronzes, deep pinks, purples and blues to the mix. With such a rich palette to hand, gardeners can throw caution to the wind and make some of the boldest plantings of the year, remembering that vibrant-coloured schemes work best if they have lots of dark green foliage as well as flowers.

HOT REDS

When constructing hot plantings for late summer it would be hard to ignore plants with large, bright red flowers, such as the dramatic ***Dahlia* 'Bishop of Llandaff'**🏆 (see page 47), with its scarlet, semi-double blooms and almost black leaves; the elegant ***Crocosmia* 'Lucifer'**🏆, with its tomato-red flowers in arching sprays among pleated, sword-shaped leaves; and the stately ***Canna indica,*** which bears orange-scarlet, gladiolus-like blooms and has brownish-purple leaves. These plants have a weighty presence, so it is a good idea to contrast them with lots of foliage and plants with small flowers, such as potentillas, fuchsias or grasses. There are several **potentillas** with red flowers: the herbaceous perennial ***Potentilla* 'Gibson's Scarlet'**♡ (see also page 48) produces scarlet blooms; the shrubby ***Potentilla* 'Etna'** has semi-double, dark red blooms like velvet; and ***Potentilla fruticosa* 'Red Ace'** has attractive vermilion, saucer-shaped flowers with yellow-backed petals. Shrubby potentillas have the advantage of flowering for long periods from late spring to mid-autumn.

Fuchsias also bloom for a long time from summer to autumn. Semi-hardy kinds should be grown in pots and popped into borders when needed. ***Fuchsia* 'Mrs Popple'**♡ is one of the hardier cultivars, with single scarlet and violet flowers; bushy in habit, it grows up to 1m (40in), with a similar spread.

Potentilla 'Gibson's Scarlet'

In an all-red-planting, the perennial ***Lobelia tupa*** can be used to provide height, as its spires of brick-red, two-lipped flowers grow on 2m (6ft) stems. This Chilean lobelia will not survive a hard frost, so in cooler areas it should be lifted or mulched in winter. Its elongated flower spires would form a striking contrast to the rounded, shaggy-looking flowers of monardas. ***Monarda* 'Cambridge Scarlet'**♡ has scarlet flowers with brown calyces and ***Monarda* 'Mahogany'** has flowers in a deeper wine-red. The flowers of both cultivars grow on 90cm (3ft) stems. Monardas prefer moist, well-drained soil in sun or light shade.

With their bright, showy flowers that resemble small gladioli, the South African perennials **schizostylis** make fine companions for monardas at the front of a planting, but they do need sun. ***Schizostylis coccinea* 'Major'**♡ has scarlet flowers carried on 60cm (2ft) tall stems. Its cousins, ***Schizostylis* 'Viscountess Byng'** and ***Schizostylis* 'Sunrise'**♡, have pale pink and salmon-pink flowers respectively, and all three make excellent cut flowers.

Fuchsia 'Mrs Popple'

Schizostylis coccinea 'Major'

SMOKE BUSHES

Late summer is when smoke bushes (*Cotinus*) produce their small, inconspicuous flowers in light, airy panicles that resemble puffs of smoke. In addition to their highly decorative flowers, smoke bushes also have attractive rounded, purple or green leaves that turn glorious shades of orange and red in autumn. They are easy-to-grow shrubs, faring well in any moderately fertile, moist but well-drained soil, and may be grown in sun or light shade. However, the purple-leaved varieties, such as *Cotinus coggygria* 'Notcutt's Variety', with its deep-red leaves and pinkish flower panicles, perform best in sun. A particularly striking cultivar for autumn is *Cotinus coggygria* 'Royal Purple'♡ (above), whose dark wine-red foliage turns bright scarlet. The light green leaves of *Cotinus* 'Flame'♡, on the other hand, become orange-red or flame in autumn, and those of *Cotinus* 'Grace' (see pages 69, 162) go a deeper cardinal red. With their brilliant leaves, smoke bushes can be used either as specimens or as constituents of shrub borders. At The Courts, the National Trust's garden near Melksham in Wiltshire, cotinus form the centrepieces of the magnificent large late summer/autumn borders featuring reds, oranges, yellows and bronze foliage.

Tropaeolum speciosum

Where a red planting is backed by an evergreen hedge, it is fun to allow the attractive Chilean climber ***Tropaeolum speciosum***🏆, with its vermilion flowers and mid-green, palmate leaves, to tumble over it. However, to perform well this perennial nasturtium needs moist, humus-rich, neutral to acid soil, and its roots must be in cool shade.

Cirsium rivulare 'Atropurpureum'

DUSKY REDS

Reds with orange in their make-up, for instance scarlet, always command attention, while those with brown or violet in their composition are less eye-catching. However, their richness and sultry quality makes them very satisfying to use in plantings. These dusky reds are found in the flowers of plants such as ***Cirsium rivulare* 'Atropurpureum'** (see also page 103), with its dark, wine-red, thistle-like blooms, and ***Knautia macedonica*** and its cultivars, for example ***Knautia macedonica* 'Mars Midget'**, whose deep, purple-red flowers resemble small scabiouses. Perennials such as these, with small flowers in dark colours, not only have great charm but can be useful in schemes to provide dots or focuses of colour. Set amid larger, paler masses of colour, they highlight textures and enliven a planting. The same is also true of the much-admired Mexican perennial ***Cosmos atrosanguineus***, with its rich, velvety, brownish-red, saucer-shaped flowers that have a distinctive chocolate scent, borne on reddish-brown stems, 75cm (30in) long, amid dark green leaves. In cold areas, the tubers have to be lifted in winter and kept frost free.

If bright bluish-red, tall, fluffy panicles are needed for a late-summer planting, then you need look no further than ***Filipendula purpurea***🏆, which bears carmine flower plumes carried on purple stems to 1.2m (4ft) tall, or ***Filipendula rubra* 'Venusta'**🏆, which has rosy-red plumes that become paler with age. These perennials are easy to grow and fare especially well in damp conditions.

Eupatoriums also prefer moist soil, and are good for the back or middle of the border. ***Eupatorium purpureum* subsp. *maculatum* 'Atropurpureum'**🏆 has purplish-green leaves, deep pinkish-red, domed flowers on stems 2m (6ft) high and, in autumn, good seedheads.

Knautia macedonica 'Mars Midget'

PHYGELIUS

These late summer flowering, evergreen South African shrubs and sub-shrubs produce attractive tubular flowers in pink, magenta, red, yellow and orange. They look especially fine growing among perennials in borders or in front of a sunny wall. Excellent cultivars include *Phygelius* × *rectus* 'Winchester Fanfare' (above), with coral-red flowers, *Phygelius* × *rectus* 'Salmon Leap'🏆, with orange flowers, *Phygelius* × *rectus* 'Devil's Tears'🏆, with deep, reddish-pink flowers, *Phygelius* × *rectus* 'Moonraker', with creamy-yellow flowers, and *Phygelius aequalis* 'Yellow Trumpet'🏆, with light yellow flowers. As they are somewhat susceptible to cold weather, they should be mulched in winter in frost-prone areas.

MORE DUSKY PLANTS *Buddleja davidii* 'Black Knight' • *Dahlia* 'Mount Noddy' • *Imperata cylindrica* 'Rubra' •

Lilium henryi

Crocosmia × crocosmiiflora 'Jackanapes'

ORANGE-FLOWERED PLANTS

The range of orange-flowered plants for late summer offers a gardener the chance to create high drama by selecting large, showy flowers, such as **cannas, lilies, dahlias** and **kniphofias** (see page 152), or play it somewhat safer by choosing smaller-flowered plants such as **crocosmias, heleniums** and **potentillas**.

Cannas, with their paddle-shaped leaves and large, asymmetric, three-petalled flowers, are stars of late-summer plantings. The most glamorous are ***Canna* 'Striata'**🏆, with green leaves striped with yellow veins and bright orange flowers, and ***Canna* 'Wyoming'**🏆, which bears dark brownish-purple leaves and frilly orange flowers. There are many orange-flowered **lilies**, but ***Lilium henryi***🏆 (see Good Companions, right) is particularly elegant, producing its characteristic turk's cap blooms on tall stems of six or more well-spread flowers in late summer and early autumn. Another good orange lily is ***Lilium* African Queen Group**🏆, a vigorous grower with fragrant, trumpet-shaped flowers that grow on 2m (6ft) stems, appearing from midsummer onwards.

Crocosmias, or montbretias, do not have the grandeur of lilies or cannas, but they are undemanding plants that are useful for late-summer plantings, because their funnel-shaped flowers, which are carried on arching spikes, open over a long period. ***Crocosmia* × *crocosmiiflora* 'Jackanapes'** produces brilliant light and dark orange flowers on 60cm (2ft) stems, and ***Crocosmia* × *crocosmiiflora* 'Solfatare'**🏆 has flowers that are apricot tinged with yellow.

Daisy-flowered perennials are always popular, and some of the best flower in late summer. Among the best orange-flowered ones is ***Helenium* 'Moerheim Beauty'**🏆, which has flowerheads composed of burnt orange petals and dark brown centres. The flowers grow on branching stems up to 90cm (3ft) tall and stay for weeks. There are also other handsome heleniums with red, yellow and bronze flowers. All make excellent border plants, suitable for growing in sunny spots. ***Helenium* 'Blütentisch'**🏆 has rich yellow flowers flecked with brown, ***Helenium* 'Butterpat'**🏆 has butter-yellow flowers, and ***Helenium* 'Bruno'** has rusty-red blooms.

Dahlias were out of fashion for a long time but now many are being grown again, especially those in rich, deep and exciting, vibrant colours. ***Dahlia* 'David Howard'**🏆 is a stunning cultivar, whose flowers are crowded with apricot-orange petals that are darker in the centre. It grows on 75cm (30in) stems and has dark green leaves tinged with black. (*Continued on page 153.*)

GOOD COMPANIONS

The striking orange, turk's cap flowers of *Lilium henryi*🏆 (1) stand out beautifully among the golden, tufted spikelets of grasses, such as those of *Stipa gigantea*🏆 (2) (see also page 67).

The deep red flowers of *Penstemon* 'Port Wine'🏆 (3) (see also page 49) look very striking set against the bronze-chocolate foliage of *Eupatorium rugosum* 'Chocolate'🏆 (4).

Lysimachia atropurpurea 'Beaujolais' • *Penstemon* 'Raven' • *Phlox paniculata* 'Amethyst' • *Potentilla atrosanguinea* •

Kniphofias

Red-hot pokers, or kniphofias, are statuesque plants with torch-like flowerheads carried on rigid stems above grass- or strap-like leaves; they are much loved by bees. The species, both evergreen and deciduous, are denizens of tropical and southern Africa, but as they have been extensively hybridized there are numerous elegant and interesting cultivars. Their small flowers are tubular or cylindrical, in colours varying from red and orange to yellow, cream, white and greenish white, and they are grouped together in long racemes – these are the characteristic torches. The torches vary enormously in shape and size; they may be long and thin, short and rounded, tapering, bulbous or straight-sided, and in every size, from 5 to 40cm (2–16in). Some are two-toned in shades of red and yellow. The majority bloom in late summer or autumn, although some flower from late spring and early summer.

The orange-red flowerheads of *Kniphofia rooperi* are borne on robust stems, 1.2m (4ft) tall. They later turn to orange-yellow.

Red-hot pokers add an aura of drama wherever they are planted, in groups in large plantings or individually in meadow-style plantings. They thrive in sun or partial shade, in any good, humus-rich and well-drained soil. Young plants are vulnerable in their first winter, so should be mulched.

Kniphofia **'Erecta'** has coral flowers that turn upwards once the buds have opened; it reaches 90cm (3ft) high.

Kniphofia **'Victoria'**, which is one of the taller cultivars at up to 1.8m (6ft) high, bears a lemon-yellow flower spike.

Kniphofia **'Royal Standard'**♡, the classic, up to 1m (40in) tall, has pale yellow buds and red flowers.

OTHER GOOD KNIPHOFIAS

***Kniphofia* 'Bees' Sunset'**♡ has yellowish-orange flowers; 90cm (3ft) high.

***Kniphofia* 'Green Jade'** is evergreen, with pale creamy-green flowers that fade to white; 1.5m (5ft) high.

***Kniphofia* 'Little Maid'** has white flowers that are yellow in bud; 60cm (2ft) high. (See also page 44.)

***Kniphofia* 'Percy's Pride'** has canary-yellow flowers, green in bud; 1.2m (4ft) high.

Kniphofia thomsonii* var. *thomsonii has fewer flowers than most varieties on each 'poker', in coral or yellow-orange; 90cm (3ft) high.

Dahlia 'Nargold'

Achillea 'Walther Funcke'

***Dahlia* 'Nargold'** (see also page 65) is a spiky-looking dahlia with pinkish-orange, double flowers with slightly pointed petals. In an all-orange planting, its rounded shape would contrast well with the thick, upright flower spikes of the exotic red ginger lily ***Hedychium coccineum* 'Tara'**♡, which produces racemes of pale orange flowers with darker stamens and styles. The flowers grow on stems that may reach 1.5 (5ft) in ideal conditions, but are usually much shorter. This ginger lily withstands temperatures down to about –5°C (23°F) but, like all ginger lilies, needs protection from cold winds. Ginger lilies like any good, well-drained soil, and are happy in sun or partial shade.

The flattened, disc-like flowerheads of **yarrows** are great foils for ginger lilies, grasses and tall flower spires. Two particularly attractive orange cultivars are ***Achillea* 'Terracotta'** (see page 47) and ***Achillea* 'Walther Funcke'**.

Helianthus 'Loddon Gold'

Rudbeckia fulgida

YELLOW-FLOWERED PERENNIALS

While we associate spring with an explosion of yellows, late summer is also a yellow season, as this is when many daisy-like, yellow-flowered perennials bloom. None are more imposing than annual sunflowers, with their large flowerheads that resemble miniature suns. Today, thanks to plant breeders, there are also annual sunflowers with orange, red, brown and bronze flowers, but for those who prefer to grow perennials, there are some excellent cultivars, such as ***Helianthus* 'Lemon Queen'**♡, whose flowers have lemon-yellow petals and darker centres; the flowers, which appear in large numbers from late summer to mid-autumn, grow on 1.7m (5½ft) stems above dark green, heavily veined leaves, and may not need staking. ***Helianthus* 'Loddon Gold'**♡ has fully double, rich golden yellow flowers on 1.5m (5ft) stems.

Many late-summer, daisy-flowered perennials are natives of North, Central and South America but have become denizens of European gardens. In addition to helianthus, **rudbeckias**, **heleniums**, **heliopsis** and **echinaceas** have all become firm favourites with British gardeners. ***Rudbeckia laciniata* 'Herbstsonne'**♡ has attractive flowers with sunny yellow petals that curve backwards and green centres gathered into a dome; the flowers grow on 2m (6ft) stems. ***Rudbeckia fulgida*** (black-eyed Susan) and its cultivars are always popular, such as ***Rudbeckia fulgida* var. *sullivantii* 'Goldsturm'**♡, which has golden flowers with blackish-brown centres borne on 60cm (2ft) stems. The flowerheads of the double-flowered ***Rudbeckia laciniata* 'Goldquelle'**♡ are packed with lemon-yellow petals and grow on stems 90cm (3ft) high.

The daisies of **heliopsis** (ox-eyes) resemble those of sunflowers, and their solitary blooms, which are normally yellow, are carried on stiff, branching stems. ***Heliopsis helianthoides* var. *scabra* 'Sommersonne'** bears single or semi-double flowers with brown centres and dark gold-yellow petals that may be tinged with orange-yellow; the stems are 90cm (3ft) high. ***Heliopsis helianthoides* var. *scabra* 'Light of Loddon'**♡ has semi-double, bright

Heliopsis helianthoides var. *scabra* 'Sommersonne'

YELLOW-FLOWERED SHRUBS

While it is yellow-flowered perennials that steal the show in late summer, there are some shrubs with yellow flowers that are worth growing as well. ***Potentilla fruticosa* 'Primrose Beauty'**🏆 (1) is a great standby, as it has greyish-green leaves and pale primrose flowers. Like potentillas, shrubby hypericums can be relied upon to provide flowers over a long period. ***Hypericum* 'Hidcote'**🏆 (2) has cup-shaped flowers and is a dense evergreen that grows up to 1.2m (4ft); ***Hypericum* × *inodorum* 'Elstead'**, a deciduous cultivar, has small, star-shaped flowers followed by large pinkish-red fruits; ***Hypericum calycinum*** (Rose of Sharon) has bright yellow flowers and dark green leaves and makes attractive ground cover in shady sites, as it only grows up to 40cm (16in).

A warm wall or a sunny, sheltered spot is needed to grow ***Cytisus battandieri***🏆 (3) successfully. This late summer flowering deciduous broom has decorative silvery-grey leaves and candles of bright yellow flowers with a strong pineapple scent. A mature specimen can reach 5 x 5m (15 x 15ft).

Achillea filipendulina 'Gold Plate'

yellow flowers with domed, yellow centres, on 1.1m (3½ft) branched stems. The leaves are a darker green than most cultivars'. ***Heliopsis helianthoides* var. *scabra* 'Incomparabilis'** has double orange-yellow flowerheads.

Inulas also have yellow flowerheads, but their daisies are flat with narrow petals. ***Inula magnifica*** has bright yellow flowerheads on 1.8m (6ft) stems, and those of ***Inula hookeri*** are a paler yellow on shorter stems, 75cm (30in) high. All these daisies look enchanting planted among grasses and other perennials whose flowers have very different shapes. In an all-yellow planting, **evening primroses** and **yarrows** would make attractive companions for them. ***Oenothera fruticosa*** is an evening primrose with deep yellow, saucer-shaped flowers that appear during daylight from late spring through to late summer, and ***Achillea filipendulina* 'Gold Plate'**🏆 and ***Achillea* 'Moonshine'**🏆 both have the characteristic, disc-like flowerheads of the yarrow clan, in dark gold and pale yellow respectively.

Euphorbia schillingii🏆 (see Good Companions, page 127), ***Euphorbia sikkimensis***🏆, ***Alchemilla mollis***🏆, and its much smaller relative ***Alchemilla conjuncta***, all produce light and airy clusters of yellow flowers into late summer and are perfect for growing among daisies and other perennials at the front of plantings.

For scent, grow the late summer flowering lily ***Lilium* Golden Splendor Group**🏆, which has large, trumpet-shaped flowers held aloft on sturdy 2m (6ft) stems. This lily is a very stately plant, as is ***Angelica archangelica***, an umbellifer, like a huge cow-parsley, with greenish-yellow flowers supported by thick stems, also 2m (6ft) tall. This perennial dies after flowering, so many grow it as a biennial. (See page 100.)

Alchemilla mollis

BLUE-FLOWERED SHRUBS *Caryopteris* × *clandonensis* • *Ceanothus* × *delileanus* 'Gloire de Versailles' •

Geranium wallichianum 'Buxton's Variety'

Echinops ritro

Eryngium bourgatii Graham Stuart Thomas's selection

Agapanthus 'Blue Giant'

BLUE-FLOWERED PLANTS

Some blue-flowered perennials flower for long periods in late summer. The beautiful deep blue- and white-flowered ***Geranium wallichianum* 'Buxton's Variety'**♡, and ***Geranium* ROZANNE ('Gerwat')**, with its purplish-blue flowers, both flower for long periods, and the undemanding ***Echinops bannaticus*** and ***Echinops ritro*** (globe thistle) display their drumstick flowerheads in greyish blue and steel-blue respectively for weeks in late summer. Attractive as these are, it is the pinhead flowers of **eryngiums**, with their decorative spiny bracts and rosettes of basal leaves, that are even more eye-catching. The degree of blueness of their flowers and bracts varies: ***Eryngium giganteum***♡ (Miss Willmott's Ghost, see page 57) has silver bracts surrounding a core of steel-blue flowers, while in ***Eryngium* × *oliverianum***♡ the flowers and bracts are both silvery blue. ***Eryngium alpinum***♡ has similarly coloured flowers and bracts to *Eryngium* × *oliverianum*♡, but its bracts are finely divided and soft to the touch. ***Eryngium* × *tripartitum***♡ produces very much smaller, lavender-blue flowers with fine, linear, greyish-blue bracts, and ***Eryngium bourgatii* Graham Stuart Thomas's selection** has veined foliage and silver-blue flowers and bracts, carried on 45cm (18in) stems (the other eryngiums grow up to 90cm/3ft). Eryngiums keep their colour when dried, and make good companions for the lavender-blue, cloud-like flower panicles of ***Limonium latifolium*** (sea lavender), which appear in late summer on branching, wiry stems. Most geraniums, eryngiums and limoniums are medium-sized plants, so are best placed in the front or middle of a planting scheme. In contrast, ***Cynara cardunculus***♡ (cardoon) is a giant perennial with large, silvered, lobed leaves and thistle-like, violet-blue flowerheads that grow on stems 1.8m (6ft) tall in late summer. With its architectural lines and stature, it makes a fine specimen or focal point for a large planting. (See page 57.)

Intensely blue flowers, for example those of ***Salvia patens***♡ and ***Salvia uliginosa***♡ are always welcome in a garden in late summer. The Australian perennial ***Parahebe perfoliata***♡ also has rich blue flowers that appear at this time of year; tiny and saucer-shaped, they are carried in spikes on 75cm (30in) stems and nestle among its glaucous, rounded leaves. As it has a cascading habit, this is a perfect plant for tumbling over walls or for planting in a gravel bed. It prefers full sun in well-drained, poor to moderately fertile soil.

Agapanthus, indisputably one of the stars of the late-summer garden, also need sun to flourish, but require more fertile, well-drained soil to produce their spherical clusters of bell-shaped or tubular, blue or white flowers. Some have pale blue flowers, others rich blue, but the species ***Agapanthus inapertus*** has the darkest, midnight-blue blooms. There are many stunning deciduous agapanthus cultivars available, for example ***Agapanthus* 'Blue Giant'** and ***Agapanthus* 'Midnight Blue'**, all of which are hardier than evergreen kinds such as ***Agapanthus africanus***♡. Agapanthus grow particularly well in pots but the less hardy ones should be overwintered indoors.

Ceratostigma willmottianum • *Hibiscus syriacus* 'Oiseau Bleu' • *Perovskia* 'Blue Spire' •

PINK-FLOWERED PLANTS

The pinks of late summer are not as numerous as those of early summer, but there are some first-rate perennials, shrubs and bulbs among them. **Astrantias** are perennials with an understated but elegant charm. Their first flush of pincushion-like flowerheads comes in early to midsummer, but they perform right through to the end of

Astrantia 'Hadspen Blood'

summer. ***Astrantia maxima***🏆 has pointed, rich pink bracts surrounding slightly paler pink tiny flowers. Its flower clusters grow on 60cm (2ft) stems above mid-green, deeply lobed leaves. Its cousin ***Astrantia major*** grows up to 60cm (2ft) and has whitish-pink bracts that form a collar for the green or pink purple flowers. (See pages 54, 70.) ***Astrantia* 'Hadspen Blood'** has deep red flowerheads, and ***Astrantia major* subsp. *involucrata* 'Shaggy'** is distinguished by having especially elongated bracts. Astrantias, with their small, rounded flowerheads, make good foils for plants with spiky flowers, such as those of **liatris**, which have tubular flowers tightly packed into spires. These North American perennials are unusual in that their flower spikes open from the top downwards. ***Liatris spicata*** (see page 74) has bluish-pink or white flowers, but its cultivars may be white, purple, or bluish purple.

Physostegias (obedient plants) are also North American perennials from moist, sunny sites; the 'obedient' sobriquet refers to the flowers' property of remaining in a new position if they are moved on the stalks. ***Physostegia virginiana*** has deep purple, lilac-pink or white flowers carried in small, pointed spires; ***Physostegia virginiana* 'Vivid'**🏆 is a striking cultivar with purplish-pink flowers carried on 60cm (2ft) stems. **Linarias** are grown for their snapdragon-like flowers in a range of colours and ***Linaria purpurea*** produces slender spires of violet-purple flowers from early summer to early autumn; its popular cultivar ***Linaria purpurea* 'Canon Went'** has pale pink flowers. Both physostegias and linarias make good companions for daisies and, in a pink planting, these could be the flowers of ***Echinacea purpurea*** (see Good Companions, below, and page 75), with purplish-pink petals and

Echinacea purpurea 'Rubinstern'

golden brown, domed centres, on stems up to 1m (40in) high. It has given rise to some excellent cultivars, such as the deep pink to carmine-red ***Echinacea purpurea* 'Rubinstern'**🏆.

Chelones also flower in late summer and have two-lipped, pink, white or purple flowers. A dark pink species is ***Chelone obliqua***, which is borne on strong 60cm (2ft) stems. Both chelones and echinaceas are good partners for the popular ***Verbena bonariensis***🏆, a perennial from South America with lilac or purple flowers that appear over a long period from midsummer to early autumn; the flowers are in little domed clusters and are carried on long, thin stems that can reach 2m (6ft) tall. (See Good Companions, below.)

GOOD COMPANIONS

The showy, tubular dark pink or purple flowers of *Chelone obliqua* (1) are shown off to great effect when combined with the lighter, lilac-purple flowerheads of *Verbena bonariensis*🏆 (2).

Linaria purpurea (3), with its erect spires of purple, snapdragon-like flowers, is an excellent foil to the solitary, daisy-like, purplish-pink flowers of *Echinacea purpurea* (4) (see also page 75).

PINK-FLOWERED SUMMER BULBS *Crinum* × *powellii* • *Colchicum alpinum* • *Lilium speciosum* •

There are some striking pink-flowered shrubs for late summer that can be used to add interest and height to large plantings. ***Abelia* × *grandiflora*** ♀ and its cultivars flower over a very long period, and their leaves colour well too. **Hibiscus** flower for weeks at the end of summer and add a touch of the exotic to the garden. ***Hibiscus syriacus* 'Woodbridge'** ♀ has clear, rich pink flowers with darker centres, and grows slowly into a mature specimen of 3 x 2m (10 x 6ft). The **indigoferas** also come from exotic climes, and ***Indigofera heterantha*** ♀ is an elegant shrub with deep purplish-pink, pea-like flowers that appear from early summer to early autumn. It looks marvellous growing among perennials, and makes a pretty backdrop for later-flowering violet or purple-flowered clematis such as ***Clematis* 'Etoile Violette'** ♀.

Abelia × *grandiflora*

Hibiscus syriacus 'Woodbridge'

Escallonia 'Iveyi'

Romneya coulteri

Chamerion angustifolium 'Album'

WHITE-FLOWERED PLANTS

Anyone looking for white-flowered plants for late summer will not be disappointed, as there are some gems among them: trees as beautiful as **eucryphias**, with their white, saucer-shaped, fragrant flowers, and ***Catalpa bignonioides*** ♀, with its candle-like inflorescences; and elegant shrubs, such as the evergreen ***Escallonia* 'Iveyi'** ♀ (see also page 61) and ***Luma apiculata*** ♀, with its peeling brown and cream bark and cup-shaped flowers. There are also some splendid yuccas, including ***Yucca gloriosa*** ♀, ***Yucca flaccida* 'Ivory'** ♀ and ***Yucca whipplei***, all of which produce their towers of flowers above dramatic, sword-like leaves in late summer. In total contrast, ***Romneya coulteri*** ♀ (tree poppy) has an ethereal beauty, with cup-shaped flowers that look as though they are made from tissue paper and finely divided, greyish-green leaves.

Among the perennials, the white willow herb ***Chamerion angustifolium* 'Album'** (formerly called *Epilobium angustifolium* f. *album*), with its spires of saucer-shaped flowers, is a beautiful plant for a large planting where its wandering ways can be accommodated. Another useful plant is ***Eupatorium rugosum***, a North American perennial that produces clusters of flowers, looking like cotton wool, over a long period from midsummer to early autumn. ***Sanguisorba canadensis*** (Canadian burnet) produces spiky, bottlebrush-like flowerheads on stems 1.8m (6ft) high, while ***Lysimachia clethroides*** ♀ (Asian loosestrife), with a somewhat rampant habit, is a shorter plant with flowers arranged in curving spires that resemble shepherds' crooks. Its cousin ***Lysimachia ephemerum***, which is much better behaved, produces thin spires of flowers on 1m (40in) stems in midsummer. These loosestrifes should be grown in moist, humus-rich but well-drained soil that does not dry out at all.

Tulbaghia violacea • *Tulbaghia violacea* 'Silver Lace' • *Tritonia disticha* subsp. *rubrolucens* •

Salvias

Culinary sage will, no doubt, be familiar to many readers, but there are lots of other kinds of sage (*Salvia*) that are well worth growing too. Salvias have brilliantly coloured flowers in reds, blues, purples, pinks, cream and white, and are highly valuable to gardeners, as they grow happily in various situations from sunny borders to dappled woodland and wild-style meadow plantings. There are about 900 species in the genus, which includes annuals, biennials, herbaceous and evergreen perennials and shrubs. Most flower in summer or autumn, but there are also salvias that flower in spring and even winter.

The leaves and stems of salvias may be hairy, woolly or silver, and many species are aromatic. Leaf shapes vary, but a characteristic of all species is that their tubular, bell- or funnel-shaped flowers open out into two lips at the tip. The flowers' upper lip is hooded and upright, and the lower one, with two lobes, is flatter. While most species produce colourful flowers, some also have colourful, leaf-like bracts. Some species produce flowers in clusters known as panicles, and others in whorls around the flowering stems. The hardy salvias should be grown in light, moderately fertile, humus-rich, moist but well-drained soil. Those with silver or distinctly hairy leaves need full sun and sharp drainage and require protection from cold winds and from excessive wet in winter.

Annual sages, or perennials grown as annuals, for instance *Salvia splendens* and its cultivars, have brilliant clear colours and so bring a dazzling quality to borders and containers. The more tender species and cultivars, for example *Salvia* × *jamensis* 'La Luna', which has creamy-yellow flowers but is not always frost-hardy, fare well when grown in pots. The hardy annual *Salvia viridis* (clary) has pink, purple and white bracts, and there are some excellent cultivars with even more pronounced bract colours that make excellent cut and dried flowers.

Salvia sclarea **var.** ***turkestanica*** **white-bracted** is a biennial whose white flowers appear from spring to summer. It grows to 1m (40in). (See also page 55.)

Salvia lavandulifolia, known as lavender sage or Spanish sage, as it is the only sage used in cooking in Spain, is a perennial with blue-violet flowers in summer and grey to white, furry leaves. (See also page 53.)

Salvia farinacea 'Victoria' ♀ (mealy sage), a perennial that is usually grown as an annual, has whitish stems and deep blue flowers carried in long, tapering but densely packed spikes on 60cm (2ft) stems from summer to autumn. Its leaves are glossy, mid-green and lance-shaped.

OTHER GOOD SALVIAS

Salvia argentea ♀ is an attractive biennial or short-lived perennial that is worth growing for its leaves alone; they grow in rosettes and are woolly and distinctly silvered. Its white or pale pink flowers, on 90cm (3ft) stems, appear in midsummer and late summer.

Salvia fulgens ♀ (syn. *Salvia cardinalis*) is a woody perennial or sub-shrub that produces bright red flowers in short spikes in summer. The lower lips of the flowers are particularly downy. The flowers grow on 1m (40in) stems.

***Salvia guaranitica* 'Blue Enigma'** ♀ is a sub-shrub or perennial that produces fragrant, rich royal-blue flowers with striking green calyces, arranged in spikes on 1.5m (5ft) stems, from late summer through to late autumn.

***Salvia involucrata* 'Bethellii'** ♀ is a perennial with rich crimson flowers in late summer and mid-autumn. The dark green leaves are velvety and hairy, and the flowers grow on 1.5m (5ft) stems.

Salvia microphylla* var. *microphylla is an evergreen shrub or shrubby perennial with soft green leaves and cherry-red flowers, which appear in autumn and grow in racemes on 1.2m (4ft) stems.

Salvia patens ♀ is a perennial with hairy, mid-green leaves and pure blue flowers in loosely arranged racemes on stems up to 60cm (2ft) tall. The flowers appear from midsummer to mid-autumn. ***Salvia patens* 'Cambridge Blue'** has paler blue flowers than the species.

***Salvia pratensis* Haematodes Group** ♀ is a short-lived perennial that produces rosettes of dark green, wavy-margined leaves, from which its bluish-violet flowers with paler throats and hairy upper lips emerge. The flowers grow on 90cm (3ft) stems in early summer and midsummer.

Salvia uliginosa ♀ (bog sage), a perennial sage, produces short racemes of clear, mid-blue flowers on thin, branching stems up to 1.5m (5ft) tall, from late summer to mid-autumn. It needs moist soil and full sun.

Salvia nemorosa 'Ostfriesland' ♀ is a neat, clump-forming perennial. From summer to autumn it carries densely packed, deep blue-purple flowerheads on erect, branching stems, 45cm (18in) high.

Salvia × *sylvestris* 'Mainacht' ♀ is an erect, branching perennial with large, dark indigo-blue flowers in long, tapering spires, on stems up to 70cm (28in) tall. The flowers appear from early summer to midsummer. (See also page 140.)

The glorious autumn foliage of the Japanese maple *Acer japonicum* 'Vitifolium'.

Autumn

Trees weighed down by fruit, early morning mist hovering above the landscape, cobwebs festooning hedges and a chill in the air confirm that summer is drawing to a close and autumn is under way. Nature may be pulling in its horns with temperatures falling and days shortening, but gardens are glorious, with muted yellows, browns and beiges interspersed with stunning reds and oranges. Inevitably, the drama will come to an end, so enjoy it while you can.

Autumn is when trees show off their swansong finery, and shrubs smothered with berries take centre stage. There are perennials and bulbs that start blooming now, but most colour in the garden is supplied by late summer flowering perennials that go on producing flowers well into autumn, and by ornamental grasses (see pages 170–71). Autumn may be the season of decay, but it is also the most brilliant season in the garden.

AUTUMN REDS

The reds of autumn are numerous, but none are more glorious than those of the leaves of ***Acer rubrum*** (red or scarlet maple) and its cultivars. This maple is a native of eastern North America, and is one of the trees that contributes to the breathtaking autumn colour of the woods in New England. Good cultivars include ***Acer rubrum***

Acer rubrum 'Schlesingeri'

'Schlesingeri', with foliage that turns dark red in early autumn; ***Acer rubrum* 'Scanlon'**♀, which produces orange-red autumn leaves; and ***Acer rubrum* 'October Glory'**♀, which has shiny leaves that turn a rich red shade in early autumn. These striking maples can reach 15–20m (50–70ft) tall, with a spread of 5–10m (15–30ft), so a large garden is needed to accommodate them.

In contrast, ***Acer palmatum*** and its cultivars are well suited to small spaces. ***Acer palmatum* 'Bloodgood'**♀ is a choice cultivar with beautiful dark red, deeply incised leaves that become rich bluish red in autumn. It seldom grows larger than 5 x 5m (15 x 15ft) and so would make a good specimen for a small garden, if sheltered from cold winds. (See also page 49.) Another elegant Japanese maple with dark red leaves in autumn is ***Acer japonicum* 'Vitifolium'**♀, a spreading tree that reaches 10 x 10m (30 x 30ft), with big, fan-shaped leaves.

Acers do not hold the patent for fine red foliage in autumn. ***Liquidambar styraciflua*** (sweet gum), a largish tree of about 25 x 12m (80 x 40ft), has leaves that turn bright red, orange and purple, and there are cultivars with other permutations of autumn colour. Liquidambars grow and colour best in acid or neutral soil in full sun. Acid soil is also needed to grow ***Quercus coccinea*** (scarlet oak) successfully. This North American oak is a rounded tree, similar in size to *Liquidambar styraciflua*. Its shiny dark green leaves have whiskered lobes and turn scarlet in autumn; those of its cultivar ***Quercus coccinea* 'Splendens'**♀ become darker and richer than the species in autumn.

Nyssa sylvatica♀ (black gum or tupelo) is another elegant, large tree that is splendid for a large garden. It comes into its own in autumn, when the leaves turn gorgeous shades of red, orange and gold.

Acer palmatum 'Bloodgood'

Quercus coccinea 'Splendens'

Liquidambar styraciflua

Nyssa sylvatica

While oaks, liquidambars and black gums are beautiful trees for larger gardens, ***Sorbus aucuparia*** (mountain ash) is suitable for planting in smaller gardens, as it seldom grows taller than 12 x 6m (40 x 20ft); its leaves turn red or yellow after its reddish-orange berries ripen. ***Sorbus commixta*** is a particularly dramatic feature in autumn, as its pinnate leaves, 25cm (10in) long, turn rich red, then yellow and purple, and its bright red berries are produced in great numbers. Likewise, crab apples often produce their fruits in large numbers, some of which are gleaming red. Among the most eye-catching are those found on ***Malus pumila* 'Cowichan'**, which produces round, deep bluish-red fruit, about 4cm (1½in) in diameter; ***Malus* × *robusta* 'Red Sentinel'**♀, which has smaller dark red rounded fruit; and ***Malus* 'John Downie'**♀, whose egg-shaped scarlet and orange fruits make excellent crab-apple jelly.

Sorbus commixta

Malus 'John Downie'

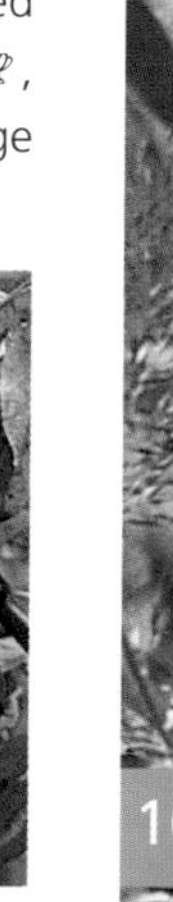

There are also some shrubs that are worth growing for their red autumn leaves alone. ***Euonymus alatus***♡ has dark green leaves that turn a breathtaking rich dark red in autumn. This euonymus is a bushy, dense shrub that is rarely taller than 2 x 3m (6 x 10ft), whereas ***Euonymus europaeus* 'Red Cascade'**♡ is a larger, more spreading shrub. It has scalloped leaves that turn red in autumn, providing an eye-catching backdrop for its dazzling deep pink fruits with their bright orange seed arils. ***Euonymus latifolius*** has finely scalloped leaves that turn crimson in late autumn, and pendent red fruits with prominent wings and orange seed arils. As it grows to 3 x 3m (10 x 10ft), this handsome euonymus is ideal for a large shrub border.

A large border or a woodland setting is the perfect place for the larger **cotoneasters**, many of which produce striking berries. ***Cotoneaster frigidus* 'Cornubia'**♡, a semi-evergreen shrub, is particularly handsome, producing masses of scarlet berries in large clusters and dark green leaves; left to its own devices, it reaches 6 x 6m (20 x 20ft). Cotoneasters are easy to grow, and there are cultivars to suit every taste.

Berberis are also very adaptable plants, and some cultivars have good autumn colour, for example ***Berberis thunbergii* f. *atropurpurea* 'Dart's Red Lady'**, with very dark reddish-purple leaves that turn bright red in autumn. **Smoke bushes** are also excellent for autumn colour, for example the bushy shrub ***Cotinus* 'Grace'**, which turns bright, translucent red in late autumn. (See also pages 69, 149.)

Cotinus 'Grace'

RED CLIMBERS FOR AUTUMN

One of autumn's pleasures is watching climbers, such as *Parthenocissus tricuspidata*♡ (Boston ivy) (1) and *Parthenocissus quinquefolia*♡ (Virginia creeper) acquire their magnificent autumn colours. Despite its common name, Boston ivy is a native of China, Japan and Korea, and its bright green, 20cm (8in) long, lobed leaves turn scarlet to purple in autumn. Its cultivar *Parthenocissus tricuspidata* 'Veitchii' is more restrained than the species, and its leaves become a dark, sultry reddish purple before they fall.

Rich red is the colour of the leaves of the Virginia creeper in autumn. Characteristically, they are 12cm (5in) long and composed of five ovate leaflets with toothed edges. Even more spellbinding autumn colour is found in the large, textured leaves of the vine *Vitis coignetiae*♡ (2). They are heart-shaped, 30cm (12in) long, dark green with felted undersides, and have attractively roughened upper surfaces caused by the indentations of the veins. When they turn bright orange-red in autumn they are a magnificent sight, especially if this climber is allowed to reach its full height of 15m (50ft). *Vitis vinifera* 'Purpurea'♡, which climbs to 7m (22ft), has more discreet charms, as its 15cm (6in) lobed leaves are plum-coloured but turn dark purple in autumn.

Sedums are very welcome in late summer and autumn, as their disc-like flowerheads are decorative and some, such as ***Sedum spectabile***♡, attract bees and butterflies. One fine cultivar is ***Sedum telephium* subsp. *maximum* 'Atropurpureum'**♡, with dark purple leaves and stems and bluish-red flowerheads or cymes (see Good Companions, opposite).

Handsome as this perennial is, for sheer shock value it can't compete with the moisture-loving perennial ***Darmera peltata***♡. This plant undergoes a metamorphosis when its huge, rounded and lobed, dark green leaves, carried on 2m (6ft) stems, turn bright red in autumn. It looks spectacular growing beside a stream or pond.

Sedum telephium subsp. *maximum* 'Atropurpureum'

TREES WITH RED, YELLOW AND ORANGE AUTUMN LEAVES *Acer circinatum* • *Aesculus flava* •

ORANGE LEAVES AND FRUIT

While there are numerous trees whose autumn leaf colour is principally red, those with orange leaves are few and far between. However, the maple ***Acer triflorum***🏆 carries mid-green leaves that become discernibly orange in autumn, and ***Acer saccharinum*** (silver maple) has orange leaves with hints of red and yellow. *Acer triflorum* grows to 10 x 8m (30 x 25ft) and *Acer saccharum* reaches 20 x 12m (70 x 40ft).

Perhaps the most spectacular orange autumn leaves belong to ***Sorbus sargentiana***🏆. They are pinnate, 35cm (14in) long, and turn bright orange. This sorbus also has other attractive features in autumn, as this is when its crimson, sticky winter buds appear. This tree grows up to 10 x 10m (30 x 30ft) and performs best in acid or neutral soil.

Orange fruits are less common than red, but there are trees and shrubs that produce them, although they are likely to be tinged with red or yellow. Some

Sorbus sargentiana

crab apples produce orange fruit, namely ***Malus × zumi* var. *calocarpa* 'Professor Sprenger'** (in dark orange-red), ***Malus tschonoskii***🏆 (yellowish-green flushed with red) and ***Malus* 'Butterball'** (orange-yellow). Other good plants include ***Cotoneaster simonsii***🏆, with egg-shaped, orange fruit borne in autumn, and ***Pyracantha* 'Golden Charmer'**🏆 and ***Pyracantha* 'Golden Dome'**, which produce orange-red and orange-yellow berries respectively.

Attractive as all these fruits are, perhaps none is as show-stopping as

Malus × zumi var. *calocarpa* 'Professor Sprenger'

Pyracantha 'Golden Charmer'

Physalis alkekengi

those of the popular, though invasive, perennial ***Physalis alkekengi***🏆, known as Chinese lantern. With its bright orange or scarlet berries, encased in papery orange-red bracts or 'lanterns', this cottage-garden favourite needs no introduction, and the colour of its lanterns makes it an excellent candidate for an autumn planting scheme. (See Good Companions, left, and page 46.)

GOOD COMPANIONS

The bright orange berries and bracts of *Physalis alkekengi*🏆 (Chinese lantern) (1) complement the purple-leaved *Sedum telephium* subsp. *maximum* 'Atropurpureum'🏆 (2) and the grass *Panicum virgatum* 'Heavy Metal' (3) (see also page 171), with its leaves that turn purple in autumn and plumes that turn orange in winter.

Pink-flowered Japanese anemones, such as *Anemone hupehensis* var. *japonica* 'Prinz Heinrich'🏆 (4), associate well with *Actaea simplex* Atropurpurea Group (5), a bugbane with thin spires of white flowers.

Cercidiphyllum japonicum • *Parrotia persica* • *Rhus typhina* 'Dissecta' • *Sorbus* 'Joseph Rock' • *Zelkova serrata* •

Acer cappadocicum

Ginkgo biloba

AUTUMN YELLOWS

There are some glorious yellows to be enjoyed in autumn in the form of leaves, berries, fruits and flowers. Moreover, numerous ornamental grasses have flower spikelets that turn yellow as they ripen (see pages 170–71).

Especially fine yellow autumn leaves are found on the two trees ***Acer cappadocicum*** (Caucasian maple) and ***Ginkgo biloba***♀ (maidenhair tree). *Acer cappadocicum* is a spreading tree that grows up to 20 x 15m (70 x 50ft) and has broadly ovate, light green leaves that become bright yellow before they fall. *Ginkgo biloba* has beautiful fan-shaped, yellowish-green leaves, 12cm (5in) across, that turn golden yellow in autumn. Ginkgos are large and columnar in habit, and make good landscape trees.

Some of the best yellow berries of the season are produced by ***Cotoneaster salicifolius* 'Rothschildianus'**♀, an evergreen cotoneaster with narrow, lance-shaped, pale green leaves, that grows to 5 x 5m (15 x 15ft). It carries spherical, golden yellow berries that are produced for weeks in large clusters. The deciduous ***Cotoneaster frigidus* 'Fructu Luteo'** bears creamy-yellow berries and dull green leaves with wavy edges. It needs room to spread, as it grows into a large shrub, 10 x 10m (30 x 30ft) when mature.

Much less space is needed for ***Viburnum opulus*** **'Xanthocarpum'**♀, although this appealing cultivar of the guelder rose is quite a vigorous shrub. It has attractive, maple-like leaves and, in autumn, produces clusters of fleshy, glowing yellow berries.

Yellow crab apples, which resemble small golden eggs, are produced by ***Malus* × *zumi* var. *calocarpa* 'Golden Hornet'**♀. They brighten the autumn garden and last for weeks after the leaves have fallen. This crab apple grows into a rounded tree, about 10 x 8m (30 x 25ft) when mature.

Malus × zumi var. *calocarpa* 'Golden Hornet'

Cotoneaster salicifolius 'Rothschildianus'

If yellow flowers are required, there are some beautiful shrubs that start blooming in autumn and flower into winter. **Mahonias** produce sweetly scented yellow flowers, for example ***Mahonia* × *media* 'Buckland'**♀, which has bright yellow flowers in long, arching racemes, and ***Mahonia* × *media* 'Charity'**, which has similarly coloured flowers. Its racemes are upright when they first appear but spread as they mature. These mahonia hybrids, hardier than some of the species, are useful evergreens for winter colour. Though vigorous and large if left unpruned, they can be successfully cut back in spring if they become too tall and leggy. (See also pages 177–78.)

Witch hazels make truly excellent specimen shrubs for a winter garden, as they produce decorative, spider-like, fragrant flowers that appear on the shrubs' bare branches in winter. ***Hamamelis virginiana***, although not the showiest of the family, has yellow flowers that start appearing in autumn at the same time as its leaves turn yellow; it grows quite slowly and is best left unpruned. (See also pages 177–79.)

The narrow, rich dark green leaves and pretty flowers of the beguiling small bulb ***Sternbergia lutea*** appear simultaneously in autumn. The flowers

Mahonia × media 'Charity'

MORE BERRIES FOR AUTUMN *Arbutus × andrachnoides* • *Cotoneaster salicifolius* 'Exburyensis' •

resemble rich yolk-yellow goblets on 15cm (6in) stems. This bulb is perfect for growing in a sunny rock garden or at the front of a border that has free-draining, moderately fertile soil.

Callicarpa bodinieri var. *giraldii* 'Profusion'

BLUES AND VIOLETS

Late summer flowering shrubs with blue or purplish-blue flowers, such as ***Perovskia*** **'Blue Spire'**♀, ***Caryopteris*** **×** ***clandonensis*** **'First Choice'**♀ and ***Ceratostigma willmottianum***♀, as well as blue- or purple-flowered perennials, such as ***Salvia patens***♀, ***Salvia uliginosa***♀, and ***Aster*** **×** ***frikartii*** **'Mönch'**♀, continue to flower well into autumn. However, there are some plants that only start producing flowers now. ***Ceanothus*** **'Autumnal Blue'**♀, an evergreen Californian lilac, flowers profusely in autumn. It has deep sky-blue flowers that stand out against its glossy, bright green leaves and grows to 10m (30ft) when mature.

Caryopteris × *clandonensis* 'First Choice'

Aster × *frikartii* 'Mönch'

Ceratostigma willmottianum

Aconitum carmichaelii

Aconitum carmichaelii is a good early autumn flowering perennial, with leathery, dark green, lobed leaves and upright, densely packed spikes, which are sometimes up to 60cm (2ft) long, of blue or violet, hooded flowers carried high above the leaves, on tall stems. This monkshood has some very attractive cultivars, such as ***Aconitum carmichaelii*** **'Arendsii'**♀, which has rich blue flowers on branching stems, and the lavender-blue ***Aconitum carmichaelii*** **Wilsonii Group 'Kelmscott'**♀. Monkshoods like partial shade in moist, fertile soil.

Shade is also preferred by ***Liriope muscari***♀, an evergreen, autumn-flowering perennial from China and Japan, but it needs acid soil that is light and moderately fertile. It has strap-like leaves, up to 30cm (12in) long, in rich dark green, and tiny rounded mauve or violet flowers packed into short, thick spikes on 30cm (12in) stems. Liriopes make excellent ground cover under shrubs and trees. The flowers are long-lasting, and large drifts are a lovely sight.

Autumn is when the deciduous shrub ***Callicarpa bodinieri*** **var.** ***giraldii*** **'Profusion'** looks its best, as this is when its clusters of unusual violet, bead-like berries appear. They give a new dimension to this somewhat bland shrub, with its rather dull leaves and little pink flowers in summer. This plant grows happily in sun or partial shade in a good, fertile, well-drained soil, and a mature specimen can reach 3 x 2.5m (10 x 8ft).

Gentians could never be described as bland, as most of them have quite large and very distinctive flowers in beautiful deep blues. ***Gentiana sino-ornata***♀ is an autumn-flowering species with trumpet-shaped flowers, deep blue around their rims but striped inside with deep purplish blue and outside with greenish cream. Its flowers grow on 7cm

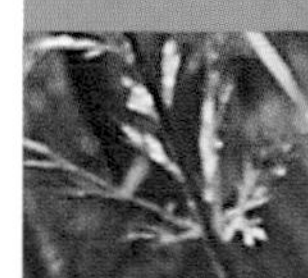

Gaultheria mucronata • *Hippophae rhamnoides* • *Rosa rugosa* • *Sorbus commixta* 'Embley' • *Viburnum opulus* •

(3in) stems amid slender dark green leaves. **Gentiana septemfida**🏆 also flowers in autumn, and has bright or purplish-blue, narrow, bell-shaped flowers on 15–20cm (6–8in) stems. The blooms are striped with darker blue and have white throats. Gentians can be tricky, normally needing lime-free soil that is well drained but never dries out. Like most gentians, *Gentiana sino-ornata* needs protection from hot sun, while *Gentiana septemfida* prefers sun.

When it comes to blue-flowered bulbs for autumn we turn to **crocuses**, which typically flower when the ground becomes damper after rain. ***Crocus speciosus***🏆, which naturalizes well in grass, and ***Crocus pulchellus***🏆 produce violet-blue and lilac-blue flowers respectively, and the blooms are prettily veined. ***Crocus sativus*** (saffron crocus) produces dark lilac flowers with dark purple veins; it does not set seed so has to be increased by division.

Camellia sasanqua 'Narumigata'

Anemone × *hybrida* 'Honorine Jobert'

AUTUMN WHITES

White is not normally associated with autumn, but ***Sorbus cashmiriana***🏆 and ***Sorbus prattii*** both bear round white berries, and ***Symphoricarpos albus*** (snowberry) also produces fleshy white berries at this time. The latter is really a plant for the wild garden, forming dense thickets with its running roots. It has the advantage of being extremely hardy and tolerant of poor soil conditions, but, unlike some of its more compact and refined relatives, it is not attention-grabbing.

Sorbus cashmiriana

Symphoricarpos albus

Sasanqua camellias produce flowers in autumn and, with their glossy, dark green leaves and waxy, cup-shaped blooms, have all the glamour that most snowberries lack. ***Camellia sasanqua* 'Narumigata'**🏆 has beautiful, single white, fragrant flowers, 4cm (1½in) across, tinged with pink. Generally, camellias must be grown in acid soil that is moist and humus-rich, in positions sheltered from cold winds. Sasanqua camellias, unlike other types, will grow in sun once established. In colder areas, this camellia would make a lovely specimen for a large container.

Just as lovely in their own way, and considerably less fussy about their growing conditions, are the **Japanese anemones**. They produce their flowers over a long period in late summer and into autumn, but none are prettier than the single white blooms of ***Anemone* × *hybrida* 'Honorine Jobert'**🏆, whose flowers are 9cm (3½in) across and grow on wafting 1m (40in) stems set above its mid-green basal leaves. In addition to white, there are also pink Japanese anemones (see opposite).

MORE FLOWERING PLANTS FOR AUTUMN *Aster* 'Coombe Fishacre' • *Colchicum byzantinum* •

AUTUMN PINKS

The perennial and bulb fraternities contribute most of the pinks of autumn. There are hundreds of cultivars of **chrysanthemums, Michaelmas daisies** and **asters** in every tone of pink, so it is worth seeking out specialist growers when selecting them. One fine cultivar is ***Aster novae-angliae* 'Pink Victor'**, a sturdy, clump-forming New England aster that produces sprays of pink flowers with yellow centres between late summer and mid-autumn.

Among the **Japanese anemone** clan, there are now numerous cultivars with both pale and dark pink, single, semi-double and double flowers. ***Anemone hupehensis* var. *japonica* 'Prinz Heinrich'**🏆 and ***Anemone hupehensis* 'Hadspen Abundance'**🏆 are fine single varieties with darker pink flowers, and ***Anemone* × *hybrida* 'Königin Charlotte'**🏆 has semi-double, rich pink flowers, while those of ***Anemone* × *hybrida* 'September Charm'**🏆 are single and pale pink. Japanese anemones such as these grow on stems from 60 to 100cm (24–40in) tall. (See Good Companions, page 163.)

We tend to think of bulbs as flowering in spring, but there are some that bloom in autumn and, of these, some have pink flowers. Nerines are bulbs from southern Africa, with wavy-margined, lily-like flowers that appear

Aster novae-angliae 'Pink Victor'

Nerine bowdenii

Anemone hupehensis var. *japonica* 'Prinz Heinrich'

in autumn with, or before, their strap-shaped leaves. ***Nerine bowdenii***🏆 has exotic-looking, funnel-shaped, shocking pink flowers grouped on 45cm (18in) stems and is one of the hardiest nerine species. It thrives if grown in front of a sunny, warm wall in well-drained soil.

Amaryllis belladonna🏆 is another southern African, autumn-flowering bulb that has blowsy, showy flowers resembling large-flowered lilies. The flowers are funnel-shaped, usually in a rich rosy pink, and are scented. They are arranged in umbels with six or more blooms in each, and are carried on sturdy, upright stems, 60cm (2ft) tall. *Amaryllis belladonna* may be grown in front of a warm wall, and thrives best in moderately fertile, well-drained soil. It can only withstand temperatures down

Amaryllis belladonna

to about –5°C (23°F), so it must be grown inside in colder areas.

There are **colchicums** (autumn crocus or naked ladies) that flower in late summer, winter and spring, as well as the more numerous autumn-flowering ones. Their flowers are similar to those of crocuses, but usually taller, in pink, lilac and white, and most open long before the leaves, hence the reference to nakedness in their common name. ***Colchicum speciosum*** has pinkish-mauve, goblet-shaped flowers, with yellow anthers. There is also a beautiful white form. ***Colchicum* 'Waterlily'**🏆 has double, pinkish-lilac blooms and ***Colchicum autumnale*** (meadow saffron) bears goblet-shaped, lavender-pink flowers, and some cultivars have white. All these colchicums should be planted in full sun. They can sometimes be successfully naturalized in grass.

Colchicum autumnale

Fuchsia 'Mrs Popple' • *Indigofera heterantha* • *Kniphofia* 'Prince Igor' • *Salvia uliginosa* • *Schizostylis coccinea* 'Major' •

Cyclamen

Cyclamen grow from tubers and come from a variety of habitats, from the Mediterranean region to Iran in the east and Somalia in the south. They bear elegant, nodding flowers, between 8mm and 2.5cm (⅜ and 1in) long, on stems 5–15cm (2–6in) high, depending on the species. The flowers have five twisted petals, which curl back on themselves to reveal the openings of their perianth tubes. These tiny openings look like little rounded mouths, and are often highly coloured. Some flowers' petals are white, others are shades of pink, and some are carmine-red. Their leaves are rounded, triangular or heart-shaped, some with distinctive silver and grey mottling and marbling; the leaves of autumn-flowering cyclamen remain through winter into spring.

There are cyclamen flowers for every season of the year. After flowering is over, most species' flower stalks coil on the soil surface to release the seeds. The cyclamen sold around Christmas time are cultivars of *Cyclamen persicum* that have larger and more varied colours than the species. Hardy species cyclamen may be grown in raised beds, rock gardens or borders, and some fare well naturalized under tall trees.

CULTIVATION DETAILS

The various species have different growing requirements.

Cyclamen cilicium, Cyclamen purpurascens, Cyclamen repandum – Plant tubers in light shade about 3–5cm (1–2in) deep, in any good soil that is well drained and enriched with compost, or in an alpine house or bulb frame in loam-based compost mixed with grit and leaf mould.

Cyclamen coum, Cyclamen hederifolium – Plant tubers about 3–5cm (1–2in) deep, in any good soil that is well drained and enriched with compost. Grow in light shade, in positions that are dry and warm in summer.

Cyclamen graecum – Thrives best if it is grown in containers, in a loam-based compost with added grit and leaf mould.

Cyclamen pseudibericum – Plant tubers about 2.5cm (1in) deep or at the soil surface, in loam-based compost mixed with sharp sand and leaf mould.

Cyclamen hederifolium ♕ (above) has large, flat tubers and produces attractive flowers, sometimes faintly perfumed, mostly in shades of pink but some white, with deep red blotches around the mouth. The flowers appear in mid- to late autumn, before the heart-shaped leaves emerge. The foliage is dark green and patterned with purple undersides.

AUTUMN-FLOWERING CYCLAMEN

Cyclamen cilicium ♕ produces flowers in white or pink, with carmine staining around the mouth. They appear in autumn, at the same time as the leaves. The foliage is mid-green, rounded or heart-shaped, with distinct and attractive silver patterning.

Cyclamen graecum has flowers in various pinks and carmine-red, with maroon marks around the mouth. The flowers appear in autumn, just before the leaves, which are deep green and heart-shaped and patterned with silver and pale green.

WINTER- AND SPRING-FLOWERING CYCLAMEN

Cyclamen pseudibericum ♕ bears fragrant, magenta-red flowers, darker at the mouths with white rims, from winter to spring. The foliage, which is borne at the same time as the flowers, is heart-shaped in a silvery dark green, and may be lightly or heavily mottled with silvery grey or silvery green.

Cyclamen repandum produces fragrant, slender bright pink flowers together with the dark green, heart-shaped or triangular leaves in mid- to late spring.

SUMMER-FLOWERING CYCLAMEN

Cyclamen purpurascens ♕ has strongly scented, pale and dark carmine flowers, with broad mouths, borne at the same time as the leaves in midsummer and late summer. The dark green, rounded or heart-shaped leaves have purplish-red undersides and are generally evergreen. Sometimes there is faint mottling on their upper surfaces.

Cyclamen coum ♕ (left) produces flowers in a variety of colours, mostly shades of pink but including white and deep carmine-red, with carmine stains around the mouth. The flowers appear in winter and early spring, at the same time as the handsome rounded, dark green leaves, which show variations in their markings. (See also page 51.)

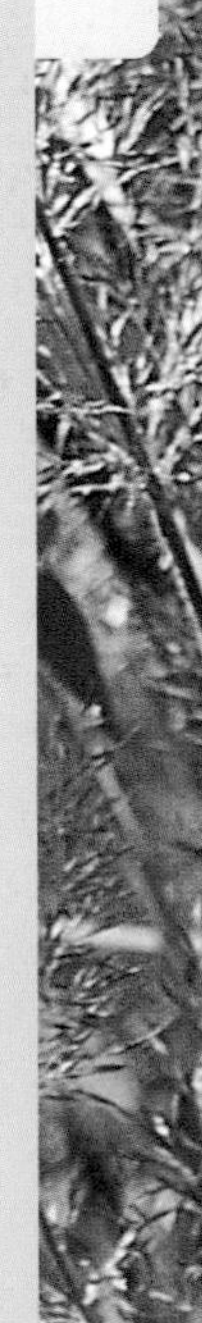

PLANT PROFILE

Ornamental grasses

***Miscanthus sinensis* 'Morning Light'** is a clump-forming deciduous grass with panicles of pale grey, silky spikelets tinted pink in early autumn on 1.2m (4ft) stems. The graceful, arching foliage is finely textured green and cream. (See also page 74.)

We are surrounded by native grasses but it is only in fairly recent times that they have become the must-have plants for many gardeners, who have recognized they are easily cultivated, reliable plants with a long season of interest.

Grasses are always elegant and bring movement into any planting of which they are a part. Their leaf and flower colours are subtle and so they are useful for all kinds of schemes, but perhaps look best when planted with those perennials that flower in late summer and autumn. Echinaceas, heleniums and rudbeckias with daisy-like flowerheads complement them well, and grasses provide a perfect foil for those perennials with large composite flowerheads carried on stiff stems, such as eupatoriums, achilleas, sedums and verbenas.

Other suitable companions for grasses include pincushion-flowered perennials, such as astrantias, sanguisorbas and knautias. Dotting these throughout a grass planting produces dark spots of colour in the neutral colours of the grasses' flowers and foliage.

Most grasses are happy growing in average garden soils and prefer open, sunny sites. Some with blue leaves thrive in very dry conditions, for example *Festuca* 'Elijah Blue', and many sedges and rushes tolerate very damp conditions. Sedges also tolerate some shade.

***Panicum virgatum* 'Heavy Metal'** has deciduous, blue-grey upright leaves, 60cm (2ft) long, that turn yellow in autumn and light brown in winter. It has broad panicles, 50cm (20in) long, of tiny, purple-green spikelets on 1m (40in) stems in autumn. (See Good Companions, page 163.)

Stipa tenuissima produces dense tufts of erect, bright green, deciduous leaves. Throughout summer it bears panicles of feathery, greenish-white spikelets on 60cm (2ft) stems. In autumn the spikelets become straw-coloured. (See also page 43.)

***Calamagrostis* × *acutiflora* 'Overdam'** is a striking, deciduous perennial grass that has mid-green linear leaves with cream margins. The leaves fade in autumn to pink flushed with white, and complement the pinkish-brown plumes of flowers that first appear between mid- and late summer. The seedheads last well through the winter.

***Miscanthus* 'Yakushima Dwarf'** is a tufted, mound-forming grass, up to 1m (40in) high, that is ideal for the front of a border. The foliage is pale green with white midribs, and small pinkish-buff, fluffy plumes emerge from the centre of the clump from late summer on; the plumes fade to silver with age and persist on plants well into winter.

OTHER GOOD GRASSES

Briza media This common quaking grass is a short-lived perennial with blue-green leaves and delicate purple and green flowerheads that dance in the breeze. The flowerheads, on 60–90cm (2–3ft) stems, turn buff in autumn.

Carex buchananii 🏆 Evergreen sedge with arching, copper-bronze leaves characteristically curled at the tips. Brown flower spikes, 3cm (1¼in) long, appear on bending 50cm (20in) stems in midsummer and remain until late summer.

***Deschampsia cespitosa* 'Goldschleier'** Evergreen grass with arching dark green leaves, 60cm (2ft) long, and a cloud of airy, silver-tinted purple flowerheads from early to late summer on 2m (6ft) stems. The flowers change colour as they age, so in autumn are bright silvery yellow.

***Molinia caerulea* subsp. *caerulea* 'Moorflamme'** Deciduous perennial with mid-green leaves that have purple hints in autumn. Narrow, dense flowerheads are produced from spring to autumn on erect 45cm (18in) stems. These dark purple spikelets turn orange in winter.

The red stems of *Cornus alba* 'Sibirica' with the variegated foliage of *Carex oshimensis* 'Evergold'.

Winter

A beech hedge retains its coppery leaves, which filter the low winter sun.

Winter can be cold and frosty but, all too often, it is characterized by dreary grey days, wind and rain. Faced with this unprepossessing picture, it is tempting to retreat indoors until the first shoots of spring appear, but to do so is to miss the great pleasure a garden in winter can give.

To be attractive in winter, a garden needs an underlying structure of hard landscaping and evergreen trees, hedges and shrubs. As most evergreens have dark green leaves, this is the principal colour of the winter garden, but alongside it there are many other beautiful colours. We find black, brown, grey, silver and white in the bark of trees and shrubs; rust and coppery-brown in the retained leaves of **beech** (*Fagus*) and **hornbeam** (*Carpinus*); bright yellow in the flowers of some shrubs, such as **mahonias** (see page 177); and various beiges, fawns and dull yellows in the skeletons of uncut perennials. There are also brighter hues in the garden during this time: **viburnums**, **hellebores**, **winter-flowering cherries** (*Prunus*) and **camellias** (see pages 180–81), as well as **cyclamen** (see pages 168–69), have flowers in a variety of pinks and purples, and there are **witch hazels** (*Hamamelis,* see pages 177–79) with flowers in yellow, orange and red. Some **willows** (*Salix*) and **dogwoods** (*Cornus*) have vivid red and gold winter stems (see page 181), and there are some ***Rubus*** species with pure white stems (see page 176). Moreover, with climate change bringing about milder winters, many plants are flowering in winter that, in the past, would have ceased to flower in late summer or autumn, or that wouldn't have started flowering until spring. In my garden, hellebores flower from early autumn to late spring, and ***Brunnera macrophylla*** 🏆 (see page 62) seems to be forever in flower.

SMALL GARDENS

Green may be the pre-eminent colour of winter, but in a small garden there may not be room to accommodate a number of larger evergreen shrubs, trees or hedges. The solution can be to grow small evergreens in containers, or to plant ones that occupy very little space. Among the most elegant plants to grow in containers are topiaries of ***Buxus sempervirens*** (box) or hollies, such as the variegated ***Ilex aquifolium* 'Ferox Argentea'** (hedgehog holly, see also page 77) or ***Ilex cornuta***. A pair of junipers, such as ***Juniperus scopulorum* 'Skyrocket'**, grown as sentinels beside a path or a flight of steps, also gives a smaller garden style. This conifer has greyish-green, pointed leaves that lie flat against its branches, and it grows into a tall, slim, pencil-shaped tree. Moreover, it grows slowly to 5m (15ft) but never spreads more than 50–60cm (20–24in).

The evergreen flowering currant ***Ribes laurifolium*** is another shrub that deserves a place in a smaller garden, as it is happy growing in partial shade, produces leathery, rich green, scalloped leaves, 8cm (3in) long, and its male and female, lime-green, dangling flower clusters appear in late winter and early spring. It is a low-spreading shrub, and looks truly enchanting surrounded by hellebores with greenish-white flowers.

The **sarcococcas** (Christmas or sweet box) are also excellent for small gardens. They have the advantage of growing well in shade – even deep, dry shade – and are decorative in winter, when most produce their deliciously scented, tiny petalless flowers. ***Sarcococca confusa*** has dark green leaves and fragrant white flowers followed by black fruit; it makes a small, compact bush. Its smaller relative ***Sarcococca hookeriana* var. *humilis*** spreads to cover an area of over 1m (40in) but never gets taller than 60cm (24in), making it a good ground-cover plant. It has dark green leaves and scented white flowers tinged with pink, followed by bluish-black berries. As it is so low-growing and shade-tolerant, it is a useful shrub for enclosed urban gardens that are perennially in shade. ***Sarcococca hookeriana* var. *digyna*** (see page 61) is a taller, more upright species, growing to about 1.5m (5ft), with slender, dark green leaves, and cream and pink flowers followed by attractive bluish-black fruit. ***Sarcococca hookeriana* var. *digyna* 'Purple Stem'** has young shoots that are reddish-purple when young, and pink flowers. (See Good Companions, below.)

Ilex cornuta

Ilex aquifolium 'Ferox Argentea'

Ribes laurifolium

Sarcococca hookeriana var. *digyna* 'Purple Stem'

GOOD COMPANIONS

The pink-flowered *Sarcococca hookeriana* var. *digyna* 'Purple Stem' (1) combines well with purplish *Helleborus* × *hybridus* (2). Later in the season, the sarcococca's reddish-purple stems are highlighted by similarly coloured tulips, such as *Tulipa* 'Attila' (3).

Ilex aquifolium 'Handsworth New Silver'

VARIEGATED SHRUBS

Evergreen shrubs with variegated leaves can add greatly to a winter garden, although it is wise not to plant too many very close together. There are, of course, many **hollies** with variegated foliage, but a truly splendid garden cultivar is ***Ilex aquifolium* 'Handsworth New Silver'** ♀. It is a female holly, and its most attractive features are the shiny mid-green leaves with clearly defined cream borders. The leaves are spiny and grow on dark purple stems. This holly also produces vivid scarlet berries and grows into a large, dense bush with an upright habit.

The evergreen shrub ***Osmanthus heterophyllus* 'Aureomarginatus'** is similar to a holly, as it has spiny, dark green leaves with a bright yellow border. Like holly, it looks marvellous in winter. The fragrant, tubular white flowers appear in late summer, followed by black berries in autumn. It matures into a large shrub, and is happy growing in sun or partial shade. The great advantage of this plant is that it doesn't resent being clipped, so makes a good hedge or topiary.

Osmanthus heterophyllus 'Aureomarginatus'

A much less showy but elegant shrub for winter is the variegated ***Prunus lusitanica* 'Variegata'** (Portugal laurel), whose leaves have a fine line of cream around their rims. They are a dark, glossy green, and grow on bright red

Prunus lusitanica 'Variegata'

SPECIMEN CONIFERS FOR LARGER GARDENS

Coniferous trees are not at the top of everyone's 'favourite plants' list, but there are some beautiful ones that make admirable specimens for larger gardens.

Pinus wallichiana ♀ (Bhutan pine) (1) is an unusual pine that grows into a broad, rounded tree with greyish-green or bluish-green needles. As the needles age they droop, and so the tree looks elegant and elongated. It grows to 35 x 12m (120 x 40ft) and tolerates low levels of lime.

Picea breweriana ♀ (Brewer spruce) (2) is another striking conifer with spreading, level branches from which smaller and more slender branches dangle. It has flattened, glossy, deep green needles, with white undersides, arranged radially around the smaller branches. This spruce grows slowly into a columnar tree, 15 x 4m (50 x 12ft).

Beautiful as these two conifers are, neither has quite the grandeur of the blue Atlas cedar, *Cedrus atlantica* Glauca Group ♀ (3). It has silvery, fissured bark and sharply pointed, silvery young leaves, which become a distinct greyish blue as they mature. They are carried on curving, spreading branches that give mature specimens their typical conical outline. When mature, this plant reaches 40 x 10m (130 x 30ft).

Abies concolor 'Argentea' (4) is a silver fir that would grace any large garden. Its needle-like leaves point upwards and outwards on the branches. As it grows, it loses its conical shape and becomes columnar, finally reaching about 25 x 5m (80 x 15ft).

MORE PLANTS WITH STRIKING STEMS AND BARK *Acer capillipes* • *Cornus sericea* 'Flaviramea' •

Vinca major 'Variegata'

stems. Unlike the species, variegated Portugal laurel grows slowly and so is a good choice for a small garden; it can also be clipped for topiary.

In all gardens, there are places where ground-cover plants are needed, and there are variegated shrubs that can perform this function admirably. The prostrate ***Euonymus fortunei*** cultivars, such as ***Euonymus fortunei* 'Emerald 'n' Gold'**🏆, are perfect candidates. This euonymus has bright green leaves with wide gold margins, tinged with pink in winter, and it never gets taller than about 60cm (2ft), although it spreads over 90cm (3ft); its variegations are more obvious when it is grown in sun. Greater periwinkle has a tendency to be invasive, but it makes good ground cover for larger spaces, as it thrives in all but the driest of soils. ***Vinca major* 'Variegata'**🏆 is guaranteed to brighten the darkest of corners on a winter's day. Its lance-shaped, shiny dark green leaves are margined with a band of cream and are carried on arching stems that trail along the ground and take root here and there.

WHITE OR SILVER BARK

Winter gives us the opportunity to enjoy the bark of deciduous trees and shrubs and some, especially the white or silver ones, are beautiful when seen against a blue winter sky. **Birches** (*Betula*) have some of the most attractive white and silver bark (see box, below), but none is more beautiful than that of the evergreen ***Eucalyptus dalrympleana***🏆, which is silky smooth in a luminous creamy white. ***Eucalyptus pauciflora* subsp. *niphophila***🏆 has less arresting, greyish-white or pale tan bark. However, it becomes very eye-catching in late summer, when it sheds in patches and reveals areas of new bark that are bronze, yellow or green. Both of these eucalyptus grow into tall trees, about 20 x 8m (70 x 25ft) when mature, so they need a spacious garden to look their best.

Eucalyptus pauciflora subsp. *niphophila*

DECORATIVE BIRCH BARK

Birches have some of the loveliest coloured barks and, as these trees are deciduous, they are revealed in all their glory in winter.

Betula papyrifera (paper or canoe birch) has white outer bark that peels in thin layers to reveal its new bark in pale tan beneath, while *Betula utilis* var. *jacquemontii* (see pages 41, 54) is a white-barked form of the Himalayan birch. There are a number of good refined selections available, including *Betula utilis* var. *jacquemontii* 'Doorenbos'🏆, *Betula utilis* var. *jacquemontii* 'Grayswood Ghost'🏆, *Betula utilis* var. *jacquemontii* 'Jermyns'🏆 (1) and *Betula utilis* var. *jacquemontii* 'Silver Shadow'🏆, all of which have luminously white bark that shines in winter.

Betula albosinensis🏆 (Chinese red birch) has beautiful orange-brown bark; as it ages, it peels to reveal young cream bark covered with a whitish glaucous bloom. *Betula albosinensis* var. *septentrionalis*🏆 (2) is a selection of the species, with pinkish-cream bark that peels to reveal mahogany-coloured new bark. *Betula nigra* (river or black birch) (3) has reddish-brown young bark that peels so much that it appears to be rough and shaggy. As this birch ages, its bark becomes dark grey and fissured. *Betula ermanii* (Erman's birch) (4) has peeling bark that is whitish cream, tinged with pink and cream.

To bring out the wonderful colours of these barks, some nurserymen recommend scrubbing them with clean water in spring and autumn. Birches look lovely as either multi-stemmed or single-stemmed specimens.

Rubus cockburnianus 'Goldenvale'

Viburnum farreri

Acer pensylvanicum

The shrubby ornamental brambles require little space and some, for instance ***Rubus biflorus*** ♕, ***Rubus cockburnianus* 'Goldenvale'** and ***Rubus thibetanus*** ♕, bring an ethereal quality to a winter garden, as they have gleaming white young stems. To achieve the best effects, bushes should be pruned to the ground each spring. Some snake-bark maples, such as ***Acer davidii, Acer pensylvanicum*** ♕ and ***Acer tegmentosum***, also have white striations in their bark.

Lonicera × *purpusii* 'Winter Beauty'

WHITE FLOWERS

There is nothing quite like finding flowers in bloom on cold, grey winter mornings for lifting the spirits. Some **viburnums** sport white flowers in winter, for example the handsome evergreen ***Viburnum tinus*** and the lovely deciduous ***Viburnum farreri*** ♕. The minute flowers of *Viburnum tinus* are unscented, but their domed clusters are produced over a long period from late winter to spring, among long, dark green leaves. The tiny, tubular white or pink-tinted flowers of *Viburnum farreri* are lightly scented, and packed densely into clusters on its bare stems. Both these viburnums mature to become large shrubs.

Some winter-flowering honeysuckles have an intense, sweet scent that lingers in the air for months. ***Lonicera* × *purpusii* 'Winter Beauty'** ♕ is a superb shrubby honeysuckle that has tiny, creamy-white, highly scented flowers with gold anthers that go on appearing for at least three months from early winter through to early spring. Its semi-evergreen, ovate leaves are dark green, and it grows up to 2 x 2.5m (6 x 8ft). (See Good Companions, below.)

GOOD COMPANIONS

The honeysuckle *Lonicera* × *purpusii* 'Winter Beauty' ♕ (1) looks wonderful in winter, but is rather uninteresting for the rest of the year. To disguise this, plant a clematis to grow through it, for example the summer-flowering, blue-flowered *Clematis* 'Prince Charles' ♕ (2). In winter it looks charming underplanted with pale blue-flowered pulmonarias, such as *Pulmonaria longifolia* (3).

MORE FLOWERS FOR WINTER *Camellia sasanqua* 'Crimson King' • *Cornus mas* • *Eranthis pinnatifida* •

I cannot imagine owning a garden and not growing **snowdrops**. They are an endless source of pleasure at the gloomiest time of the year, and they are so easy to grow. There are numerous cultivars, but there is much to be said for only growing the common snowdrop, ***Galanthus nivalis*** 🏆, and allowing it to seed itself so it makes drifts in grass or under tall trees. To prolong the season, you just need to plant some of the later-flowering kinds. Snowdrops hybridize easily, so to keep them 'pure' plant them at a distance from each other.

GOOD SNOWDROPS

***Galanthus* 'Atkinsii'** 🏆 (1) Large, early flowers on robust plants that make good clumps. Ideal for the back of a border, where emerging spring foliage can conceal the snowdrop's long leaves as they fade.

***Galanthus* 'Magnet'** 🏆 (2) Long, slender flower stems that make the flowers move with the slightest breeze. A reliable snowdrop cultivar that has been grown for over 100 years.

***Galanthus nivalis* 'Viridapice'** (3) Markings on the outer tepals give this snowdrop its name, which means green-tipped. Popular for its distinctive small flowers on a tallish plant.

***Galanthus* 'S. Arnott'** 🏆 (4) A fine, large and vigorous cultivar well worth growing for its plump, classic snowdrop blooms and faint honey-like fragrance. Makes good, tall clumps.

Acacia dealbata

YELLOW FLOWERS

While white flowers and stems in winter never pall, plants sporting yellow flowers bring a cheerful zest to a garden. Some of the brightest belong to shrubs such as **acacias**, **witch hazels** (*Hamamelis*) and **mahonias**. Acacias are often overlooked in the quest for winter colour, perhaps because they are tender or only half hardy, but they have charming round, fluffy flowers that are often scented. ***Acacia dealbata*** 🏆 and ***Acacia baileyana*** 🏆 are half-hardy species, so must be grown against a warm wall in frosty areas. Their bright, sunny yellow flowerheads, which resemble small footballs, are collected together in clusters and appear among the leaves from winter to spring. *Acacia dealbata* has ferny, glaucous, hairy leaves and scented blooms, while *Acacia baileyana* has silvery-grey, fern-like leaves and unscented flowers. These acacias are large shrubs, or small trees, and both require a neutral or acid, moderately fertile soil.

Witch hazels also require an acid or neutral soil, and also produce flowers in winter. However, unlike acacias, their spidery flowers can withstand frost and all of them are fragrant. Those with yellow flowers (all those described being 3cm/1¼in across) include ***Hamamelis* × *intermedia* 'Arnold Promise'** 🏆, which has rich yellow flowers, ***Hamamelis mollis*** 🏆 (see Good Companions, page 178), with golden yellow, strongly scented blooms, and ***Hamamelis* × *intermedia* 'Pallida'** 🏆, in pale yellow. The flowers of witch hazels appear from midwinter to late winter, and these slow-growing shrubs make excellent specimens for lawns or centrepieces for small gardens devoted to winter-flowering plants. Mature specimens are approximately 3 x 2m (10 x 6ft).

Hamamelis × intermedia 'Pallida'

Mahonias are popular evergreen shrubs, celebrated for their striking, glossy, dark green, spiny-edged leaves and bright yellow flowers borne in late autumn, winter or spring (see pages 125, 164 and 178), some of which are scented. ***Mahonia* × *media* 'Winter**

Galanthus alpinus var. *alpinus* • *Iris reticulata* • *Iris unguicularis* 'Mary Barnard' • *Prunus* × *subhirtella* 'Autumnalis' •

Mahonia × media 'Winter Sun'

Stachyurus praecox

Sun'♀ is an erect mahonia with bright yellow, very fragrant flowers from late autumn to late winter, and dark green, holly-like leaves.

Much less widely grown than mahonias are **stachyurus**, choice deciduous and semi-evergreen shrubs that also bear attractive yellow flowers in winter (see also page 113). ***Stachyurus chinensis*** has 10–12cm (4–5in) racemes of tiny, bell-shaped, pale yellow flowers dangling from the stems, and ***Stachyurus praecox***♀ has slightly shorter racemes of lemon-yellow or greenish flowers. The flowers appear in late winter and spring, before the mid-green leaves open. These pretty shrubs reach 2 x 3m (6 x 10ft) when mature. They will flourish in either sun or light shade, in fertile, humus-rich, well-drained soil, but it must be neutral or acid.

Jasminum nudiflorum♀ (winter jasmine) is a marvellous plant to have growing in a garden in winter. Although deciduous, its cheery yellow flowers, on dark green, arching or climbing stems, bring a splash of colour throughout the season, flowering even when trained against a north-facing wall.

Despite their small size, the bright yellow flowers of ***Eranthis hyemalis***♀ (winter aconites) have immense charm and cheer up the dullest of days. They grow from small tubers, and their buttercup-like flowers are carried above a collar or ruff of rich green leaves from midwinter to late winter. Aconites thrive best in alkaline soil that is fertile and humus-rich and does not dry out in summer. They are happy growing in either sun or dappled shade, and may be naturalized in grass or planted beneath shrubs or trees. (See also page 115 and Good Companions, left.)

GOOD COMPANIONS

Yellow-flowered witch hazels, such as *Hamamelis mollis*♀ (1), look effective underplanted with smaller daffodils, such as *Narcissus pseudonarcissus*♀ (2) or *Narcissus* 'Jack Snipe'♀.

The yellow-flowering *Eranthis hyemalis*♀ (3) (winter aconites) make good companions for the evergreen creeping perennial *Asarum europaeum* (4), which has kidney-shaped, shiny dark green leaves.

WINTER REDS AND ORANGES

Bright red berries on **holly** bushes (*Ilex*) are another of winter's joys, but for those who want to ring the changes, there are other shrubs whose berries are also present throughout the season. ***Cotoneaster lacteus***♀ bears scarlet berries that show up well against the dark leaves and persist until midwinter. It is evergreen, medium-sized and makes an excellent hedge if clipped regularly. ***Cotoneaster conspicuus*** **'Decorus'**♀ is a low-spreader with stems that grow outwards more than upwards, making it good for a bank. It has dark green leaves

MORE GOOD BERRIES *Berberis wilsoniae* • *Cotoneaster frigidus* 'Cornubia' • *Crataegus* × *lavalleei* 'Carrierei' •

Cotoneaster conspicuus 'Decorus'

Nandina domestica 'Fire Power'

and bears copious small, shiny red berries that remain on the bush well into winter. There are also some female **skimmias** whose berries are an attractive winter feature, for example several ***Skimmia japonica*** cultivars. The male clone ***Skimmia japonica* 'Rubella'**🏆, although it does not fruit, has striking red flower buds.

Another source of red in winter is found in leaves. The evergreen perennial ***Bergenia* 'Sunningdale'** has large round, thick leathery foliage, which turns to a rich copper colour at the beginning of the season, especially on plants grown in full sun; the leaves provide a sumptuous background for the magenta flowers when they emerge in early spring.

Nandina domestica* 'Fire Power'**🏆 is a dwarf evergreen that carries dramatic, bright red leaves throughout the year. Reaching 45 x 60cm (18 x 24in), it makes a stunning addition to the front of a red-themed border, and looks good with an evergreen shrub with red berries, or one with winter flowers, for example the strawberry tree ***Arbutus* × *andrachnoides🏆 (see Good Companions, below). The latter has attractive peeling, reddish-brown bark, glossy, lance-shaped leaves and tiny, pitcher-shaped flowers that go on appearing from autumn to spring. The flowers are creamy white, with red tinges, and hang from the stems in clusters or panicles.

GOOD COMPANIONS

The red-tinged leaves of *Nandina domestica* 'Fire Power'🏆 (1) make it a dramatic planting partner for the creamy-white, red-tinged flowers of *Arbutus* × *andrachnoides*🏆 (2).

With its striking, deep red winter shoots, *Hamamelis* × *intermedia* 'Diane'🏆 (3) looks marvellous surrounded by bushes of *Cornus alba* 'Sibirica'🏆 (4) (see also page 172).

Hamamelis 'Jelena'

Witch hazel flowers are a valuable asset in winter, for example those of ***Hamamelis* × *intermedia* 'Diane'**🏆, which are dark, rich red, and appear on the bare stems from midwinter to late winter (see Good Companions, left). The leaves of witch hazels are also a feature in autumn, turning brilliant hues. One of the most brightly coloured cultivars is ***Hamamelis* 'Jelena'**🏆, which has copper-orange flowers in early winter and midwinter, and gorgeous autumn tints in red and orange. The flowers of both witch hazels described are about 3cm (1¼in) across.

Ilex aquifolium 'J.C. van Tol' • *Malus* × *scheideckeri* 'Red Jade' • *Pyracantha* 'Orange Charmer' •

For striking bark, ***Acer griseum*** (paper-bark maple) is outstanding. It is a rich burnished orange, peels prolifically, and is revealed in all its glory in the winter months. This maple also has attractive dark green leaves and grows slowly into a spreading, medium-sized tree, 10 x 10m (30 x 30ft). Its leaves turn orange-red or scarlet in autumn, but it is the unique orange, peeling bark that makes this maple such a wonderful treasure. (See page 47.)

Prunus × *subhirtella* 'Autumnalis Rosea'

Camellia 'Nicky Crisp'

PINK FLOWERS

For those who prefer pinks to orange-reds in winter, there are trees, shrubs and perennials that fit the bill. The pretty winter-flowering cherry ***Prunus* × *subhirtella* 'Autumnalis'** has great charm and value, as its flowers start appearing in autumn, just when many gardens need a lift. They go on appearing intermittently throughout winter but are susceptible to frost; however, new flowers appear every time the temperature rises. They are semi-double, whitish pink and bowl-shaped, and 2cm (¾in) across. The flowers of the lovely cultivar ***Prunus* × *subhirtella* 'Autumnalis Rosea'** are similar but in a rosy pink. These cherries grow into spreading trees, 8 x 8m (25 x 25ft) when mature, and have dark green leaves that are bronze when young and turn yellow in autumn.

Most **camellias** start to flower from early winter onwards. The varieties of

Viburnum × *bodnantense* 'Dawn'

Camellia sasanqua (see page 166) are the first to bloom, from autumn onwards, followed by the hybrids of ***Camellia japonica*** (see page 78) and ***Camellia* × *williamsii***. ***Camellia* 'Nicky Crisp'** is a compact, slow-growing, rounded shrub that has large, semi-double, lavender-pink flowers from

Helleborus × *hybridus*

late winter to mid-spring. Camellias are best planted in a sheltered position, avoiding the early morning sun, which can damage frosted blooms. If *Camellia* 'Nicky Crisp' proves hard to find, ***Camellia* 'Inspiration'** makes a good alternative (see page 78).

The bright pink, heavily scented flowers of ***Viburnum* × *bodnantense* 'Dawn'** are hard to miss. They are tiny, carried in densely packed clusters, either along the bare branches or at the branch tips, in midwinter. The flowers are a rosy pink when young, but they fade to white flushed with pink. A mature specimen is 3 x 2m (10 x 6ft).

It is not surprising that hellebores have become the 'must have' winter-flowering perennials for many people, as their cup- or saucer-shaped flowers, in white, cream, pink, purple, green and white are exceptionally beautiful. The 15 hellebore species vary enormously: for example, ***Helleborus cyclophyllus*** has yellowish-green, saucer-shaped flowers on 30cm (12in) high stems, ***Helleborus foetidus*** (stinking hellebore, see page 94) has bell-shaped green flowers on taller stems, about 50cm (20in) high, ***Helleborus niger*** (Christmas rose) has attractive saucer-shaped, white or whitish-pink flowers and ***Helleborus purpurascens*** has cup-shaped flowers in a range of colours from purple to

DECORATIVE SEEDHEADS FOR WINTER *Calamagrostis* × *acutiflora* 'Karl Foerster' • *Dipsacus fullonum* •

PLANT PROFILE

Winter-flowering daphnes

Daphnes are among the aristocrats of the shrub world, as they have delightfully scented flowers, handsome leaves, and attractive prostrate, rounded or upright forms of growth. Some have the added bonus of producing pink, purple or white flowers in winter, at a time of year when little else is in flower. Daphne flowers are tubular with four lobes, and they are found singly or in short racemes or clusters. The leaves of the species described here are about 8–12cm (3–5in) long.

Daphnes may be grown in any good soil as long as it is well drained and well nourished, but they thrive best in soils that are slightly alkaline to slightly acid. They are happy to be grown in sun or partial shade, but always benefit from having their roots mulched, as this keeps them cool.

Daphne odora is an evergreen species that originates in China and Japan. It grows into a rounded shape, with glossy, leathery leaves and clusters of fragrant, deep purple, pink and white flowers. It eventually grows to 1.5 x 1.5m (5 x 5ft).

Daphne bholua has an upright habit and deciduous or evergreen, leathery, dark green leaves. The flowers are white flushed with purplish pink. Carried in clusters, they appear in late winter. This beautiful daphne reaches 2–4 x 1.5m (6–12 x 5ft).

Daphne bholua 'Jacqueline Postill' 🏆 is an evergreen cultivar with especially fragrant flowers that are purplish pink on their outer surfaces and white inside.

Daphne mezereum is an upright shrub, growing to 1.2 x 1m (4 x 3ft) when mature. It is deciduous, with pale greyish-green leaves and fragrant flowers in a deep purplish pink blooming in late winter and early spring on bare stems. Its berries are poisonous. This daphne is somewhat disease-prone.

Daphne mezereum f. _alba_ differs from *Daphne mezereum* in having creamy-white flowers.

Daphne odora 'Aureomarginata' 🏆 has similarly sized and shaped leaves to the species, but here they are embellished with a narrow band of pale yellow around the margins. Also, its flowers are purple with reddish tinges and they have paler pink or creamy-white insides.

slate-grey, with tinges of pink and purple, and light green insides. Because hellebores reproduce wantonly, there are innumerable hybrids available listed as ***Helleborus* × *hybridus*** in a range of wonderfully subtle colours that will enhance any garden. (See also pages 38, 42, 114, 173.) Furthermore, there are various spotted kinds, and breeders have bred some with double flowers. If you are happy to allow your hellebores to breed randomly, and plant hybrids in a mixture of colours in close proximity, you will be rewarded with a colour selection all of your own.

ORNAMENTAL STEMS

Some of the brightest winter stems are found on cultivars of the white willow, *Salix alba*. They are bright yellow in *Salix alba* subsp. *vitellina* 🏆 (1) and orange-red in *Salix alba* subsp. *vitellina* 'Britzensis' 🏆 (see page 48). Young stems display the best colour, so cut back these willows in early spring, once every two or three years, to two or three buds from the base, to encourage new growth. Grow them in deep, moist, well-drained soil in full sun.

Some cornuses also have attractively coloured winter stems. Especially eye-catching are those of *Cornus alba* 'Sibirica' 🏆 (see pages 172, 179), which are bright coral-red; *Cornus alba* 'Kesselringii' (see page 38), which are dark purple; *Cornus sericea* 'Flaviramea' 🏆, with yellow, green-tinged stems; and *Cornus sanguinea* 'Winter Beauty' (2), with shoots that are a blaze of red and bright orange-yellow in winter.

Author's choice:
favourite colour planting groups

Throughout the book there are plants with flowers and foliage in a wide range of colours. I have tried to select those that have been tried and tested and proved their worth. Here, I have grouped some of these into harmonious schemes, covering all the seasons; some are suitable for sunny sites, others for shade. All are easy to grow and should give you a basis on which to build your own, more elaborate schemes.

GREEN AND WHITE FOR SPRING (SUN)

Tulipa 'White Triumphator' 🏆 (page 54) Bulb; elongated white flowers on tall stems, in late spring.

Anemone nemorosa 🏆 (page 96) Perennial; creeping, low-growing ground cover, with white flowers and pretty, ferny leaves.

Buxus sempervirens 'Suffruticosa' 🏆 (page 77) Compact, slow-growing shrub; small, glossy dark green leaves.

Pulmonaria 'Sissinghurst White' 🏆 (page 114) Evergreen perennial; white-spotted leaves, white flowers in early spring; good ground cover.

Osmanthus delavayi 🏆 (page 123) Rounded evergreen shrub; dark green leaves, scented white flowers in mid- to late spring.

BLUE AND YELLOW FOR SPRING (SHADE)

Pulmonaria 'Blue Ensign' (page 115) Perennial; unspotted dark green leaves, rich blue flowers in early to mid-spring.

Erythronium 'Pagoda' 🏆 (page 45) Low-growing perennial; leaves deep green with bronze spots, sulphur-yellow turk's cap flowers in mid-spring.

Omphalodes cappadocica 'Starry Eyes' 🏆 (page 127) Perennial; tiny white-edged, azure-blue flowers amid bright green leaves; ground cover.

Brunnera macrophylla 🏆 (page 62) Perennial; long-lasting bright blue, forget-me-not flowers and large leaves; useful for ground cover.

Fatsia japonica 'Variegata' 🏆 (page 78) Medium to large evergreen shrub; big, dark green, cream-margined leaves, creamy-white flowers in autumn.

BLUE, LIME AND WHITE FOR EARLY SUMMER (SUN)

Anchusa azurea 'Loddon Royalist' 🏆 (page 134) Perennial; bright blue flowers on tall, sturdy stems, hairy mid- to dark green leaves.

Alchemilla mollis 🏆 (page 154) Low-growing perennial; froth of tiny, lime-green flowers, pretty leaves that hold dew and raindrops.

Veronica spicata subsp. *incana* (page 135) Perennial; dark blue flower spikes, silver leaves; for the front of a border.

Exochorda macrantha 'The Bride' 🏆 (page 123) Deciduous shrub; cup-shaped white flowers; will not tolerate shallow, chalky soil.

Philadelphus 'Virginal' (page 138) Deciduous shrub; very fragrant double white flowers.

PINK, VIOLET, BLUE AND SILVER FOR MIDSUMMER (SUN)

Paeonia lactiflora 'Sarah Bernhardt' 🏆 (page 142) Herbaceous peony; large double, rose-pink, scented flowers margined silver.

Artemisia 'Powis Castle' 🏆 (page 56) Perennial; forms a dense clump of finely cut, feathery silver-grey leaves.

Baptisia australis 🏆 (page 140) Perennial; dark blue flowers on erect stems, dark green leaves.

Geranium pratense 'Plenum Violaceum' 🏆 (page 141) Perennial; dark violet-blue double flowers, attractive leaves.

Rosa 'Roseraie de l'Haÿ 🏆 (page 145) Dense, vigorous Rugosa rose with flat, double rich-red flowers from early summer to autumn.

RED, YELLOW AND ORANGE FOR SUMMER (PARTIAL SHADE)

Penstemon 'Andenken an Friedrich Hahn' ♀ (page 146) Perennial; spires of wine-red, bell-shaped flowers.

Lilium henryi ♀ (page 151) Bulb; deep orange turk's cap flowers in clusters of up to ten blooms.

Rodgersia aesculifolia ♀ (page 143) Perennial; large horse-chestnut-like, crinkled leaves, star-shaped pink or white flowers in loose clusters.

Ligularia dentata 'Britt-Marie Crawford' (page 66) Perennial; dark orange flowers on tall stems and red-brown leaves.

Rheum palmatum 'Atrosanguineum' ♀ (page 65) Perennial; impressive red-veined leaves on thick stems, with tall spires of deep pink flowers.

Acer palmatum 'Bloodgood' ♀ (page 161) Decorative tree; red-purple, finely cut leaves that turn rich red in autumn.

BRONZE, PURPLE AND BLUE FOR LATE SUMMER (SUN)

Agapanthus 'Blue Giant' (page 155) Perennial; spherical clusters of rich blue, bell-shaped flowers on tall stems, strap-like leaves.

Eryngium bourgatii Graham Stuart Thomas's selection (page 155) Perennial; spiny silver-veined, leaves, blue thimble-like flowers with spiky bracts.

Miscanthus sinensis 'Morning Light' ♀ (page 170) Grass; narrow arching leaves with white margins and maroon or purple flower spikelets.

Heuchera 'Plum Pudding' (page 67) Low-growing evergreen perennial; large, ruffled deep-purple leaves mottled silver, delicate white flowers.

Penstemon 'Port Wine' ♀ (page 49) Perennial; dark claret-red flowers with white throats, semi-evergreen leaves.

Cotinus 'Grace' (page 162) Large deciduous shrub; wine-coloured leaves turn red in autumn. Smoke-like clusters of flowers.

ORANGE, GOLD AND BEIGE FOR SUMMER/AUTUMN (SUN)

Achillea filipendulina 'Gold Plate' ♀ (page 154) Perennial; golden, flat flowerheads, ferny leaves.

Stipa tenuissima (page 171) Grass; bright green, narrow rolled leaves, buff-coloured flower spikes.

Kniphofia rooperi (page 152) Evergreen perennial; bulbous candles of orange-red flowers on tall stems, broad, arching, strap-like leaves.

Stipa gigantea ♀ (page 67) Evergreen or semi-evergreen grass; tall, delicate flower spikelets turn golden when ripe.

Heliopsis helianthoides var. *scabra* 'Sommersonne' (page 153) Perennial; golden-yellow single or semi-double daisies.

Acer cappadocicum (page 164) Deciduous tree; bright green, lobed leaves turn dark yellow or gold in autumn.

CREAM, PINK, SILVER AND GREEN FOR WINTER

Ilex aquifolium 'Handsworth New Silver' ♀ (page 174) Large evergreen holly; green, prickly leaves with cream margins. Purple stems, red berries.

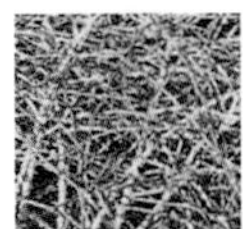

Rubus cockburnianus 'Goldenvale' ♀ (page 176) Medium-sized deciduous shrub; yellow leaves; prickly, arching stems with white bloom in winter.

Helleborus × hybridus (page 173) Perennial; saucer-shaped flowers, leathery, dark green, lobed leaves. Flower colours vary.

Sarcococca hookeriana var. *digyna* 'Purple Stem' ♀ (page 173) Evergreen shrub; dark green leaves, very fragrant white flowers in winter.

Daphne odora (page 181) Evergreen shrub; dark green leathery leaves, very fragrant, purplish-pink flowers.

Betula utilis var. *jacquemontii* (page 54) Elegant deciduous tree; brilliant white bark, dark green leaves. There are numerous selections available.

Index

Page numbers with suffix 'b' indicate plants listed across bottom of page. Suffix 'i' refers to illustrations.

A
Abbott, Marylyn 17, 103
Abelia × grandiflora 157i
Abies concolor 'Argentea' 174i
Abutilon vitifolium 53
Acacia
A. baileyana 177
A. dealbata 114b, 177i
Acanthus
A. mollis 70
A. spinosus 43, 70, 89
Acer
A. capillipes 95i, 174b
A. cappadocicum 164i, 183i
A. circinatum 162b
A. davidii 95, 176
A. griseum 46, 47i, 180
A. japonicum 104; *A.j.* 'Vitifolium' 160i, 161
A. negundo var. *violaceum* 72i
A. palmatum 104, 161; *A.p.* 'Bloodgood' 49, 161i, 183i; *A.p.* 'Fireglow' 49i
A. pensylvanicum 176i
A. rubrum 49, 160–1; *A.r.* 'October Glory' 161; *A.r.* 'Scanlon' 161; *A.r.* 'Schlesingeri' 160i–161
A. saccharinum 163
A. tegmentosum 176
A. triflorum 163
Achillea
A. filipendulina 'Gold Plate 144, 154i, 183i
A. millefolium 'Cerise Queen' 49
A. 'Moonshine' 32i, 154
A. 'Terracotta' 47i, 153
A. 'Walther Funcke' 47, 153i
Aconitum
A. carmichaelii 165i; *A.c.* 'Arendsii' 41, 49, 165; *A.c.* 'Spark's Variety' 63i; *A.c.* Wilsonii Group 'Kelmscott' 165
A. 'Ivorine' 138i
Actaea simplex 97
A.s. Atropurpurea Group 163i; *A.s.*A.G. 'James Compton' 39
Actinidia kolomikta 126b
Aeonium 'Zwartkop' 39
Aesculus flava 162b
Agapanthus 109i, 155
A. africanus 155
A. 'Blue Giant' 20i, 155i, 183i
A. Headbourne hybrids 41i
A. inapertus 155
A. 'Midnight Blue' 155
Agave americana 56i, 57, 84, 108
AGM (Award of Garden Merit) 7
Ajuga reptans 41, 115
A.r. 'Atropurpurea' 115i
Akebia quinata 126b
Alcea rosea 13i, 76i
A.r. 'Black Beauty' 38
A.r. 'Nigra' 38, 39i
Alchemilla
A. conjuncta 154
A. mollis 19i, 43, 97, 154i, 182i
Alisma plantago-aquatica 99
Allingham, Helen 89
Allium 21i, 33i, 68i
A. caeruleum 41
A. cernuum 51
A. cristophii 53
A. 'Globemaster' 52i, 53
A. hollandicum 41i, 89i; *A.h.* 'Purple Sensation' 53
A. moly 45
A. 'Mount Everest' 42i
A. nigrum 89i
Alstroemeria aurea 19i, 46i, 47
Amaryllis belladonna 167i
Amelanchier
A.× grandiflora 'Ballerina' 33
A. lamarckii 25i, 85
Amomyrtus luma 123
Amsonia
A. orientalis 137
A. tabernaemontana 41, 137
Anchusa azurea 'Loddon Royalist' 41, 134i, 135i, 182i
Anemone
A. blanda 40i, 116; *A.b.* blue-flowered 115i; *A.b.* 'Radar' 49
A. hupehensis: A.h. 'Hadspen Abundance' 51, 167; *A.h.* var. *japonica* 51, 167; *A.h.v.j.* 'Prinz Heinrich' 163i, 167i
A.× hybrida 51; *A.× h.* 'Honorine Jobert' 166i; *A.× h.* 'Königin Charlotte' 167; *A.× h.* 'September Charm' 167
A.× lipsiensis 126
A. nemorosa 54, 85, 96i, 97, 107, 124b, 182i
A. ranunculoides 126
A. rivularis 140i
Angelica
A. archangelica 70, 100i, 154
A. gigas 49, 70i
Anthemis
A. punctata subsp. *cupaniana* 55, 57, 138
A. tinctoria 'E.C. Buxton' 44, 144
Anthriscus sylvestris 'Ravenswing' 28i, 39, 71i, 75
Aquilegia 89
A. chrysantha 'Yellow Queen' 20
A. vulgaris 138b; *A.v.* var. *stellata* 'Black Barlow' 39, 79
Arbutus
A.× andrachnoides 164b, 179i
A. unedo 93
architectural plants
for foliage 65
for pots 84
silver/grey 57
Argyranthemum 'Jamaica Primrose' 144i
Arley Hall, Cheshire 88
Artemisia 89–90
A. absinthium 89
A. lactiflora 55
A. ludoviciana: A.l. 'Silver Queen' 56i, 79i; *A.l.* 'Valerie Finnis' 56i, 57
A. 'Powis Castle' 56i, 57, 109, 182i
A. schmidtiana 140b; *A.s.* 'Nana' 39, 57
A. stelleriana 'Boughton Silver' 56i
Arts & Crafts Movement 16
Arum italicum subsp. *italicum* 'Marmoratum' 40, 45, 97, 124i
Asarum
A. europaeum 43, 73, 85, 178i
A. splendens 124b
Asphodeline lutea 126
Asphodelus albus 124i
Asplenium scolopendrium 'Crispum' 73i
Astelia chathamica 57, 85
Aster
A. amellus 'King George' 53
A. 'Coombe Fishacre' 166b
A. divaricatus 54
A. frikartii 'Mönch' 165i
A. novae-angliae 'Pink Victor' 167i
Astilbe 'Venus' 143i
Astrantia 70, 156
A. 'Hadspen Blood' 28i, 49, 70, 156i
A. major 43, 55, 156; *A.m. alba* 54i; *A.m.* 'Claret' 70i; *A.m.* subsp. *involucrata* 'Shaggy' 156
A. maxima 51, 156
Athyrium
A. filix-femina 43
A. niponicum var. *pictum* 57
Atriplex halimus 93
Aucuba japonica
A.j. 'Crotonifolia' 83
A.j. 'Nana Rotundifolia' 82–3
author's choice 182–3
autumn
colour 160–171
favourite planting groups 183
autumn crocus see *Colchicum*
Award of Garden Merit (AGM) 7
azaleas 132–3
Azara microphylla 116b

B
bamboo, black-stemmed see *Phyllostachys nigra*
bamboos 21, 39, 77, 78–9
banana see *Musa*
Baptisia australis 41, 53, 140i, 141i, 182i
bark, decorative 174–5b, 175–6
Barrington Court, Somerset 27, 88
Barry, Charles 15
bay laurel see *Laurus nobilis*
bedding plants, history of 15–16
Berberis
B. 'Goldilocks' 116b
B. thunbergii: B.t. f. *atropurpurea* 66; *B.t.* f. *atropurpurea* 'Dart's Red Lady' 162; *B.t.* 'Atropurpurea Nana' 49
B. wilsoniae 178b
Bergenia
B. cordifolia 129
B. 'Morgenröte' 129
B. 'Rosi Klose' 127i, 129i
B. 'Sunningdale' 179
berries 164–5b, 178–9b
Betula 175
B. albosinensis 175; *B.a.* var. *septentrionalis* 175i
B. ermanii 175i
B. nigra 175i
B. papyrifera 175
B. utilis var. *jacquemontii* 41i, 54i, 175, 183i; *B.u.v.j.* 'Doorenbos' 175; *B.u.v.j.* 'Grayswood Ghost' 175; *B.u.v.j.* 'Jermyns' 175i; *B.u.v.j.* 'Silver Shadow' 175
Bhutan pine see *Pinus wallichiana*
Bidens aurea 'Hannay's Lemon Drop' 67
birch see *Betula*
Birket Foster, Myles 89
Black gum see *Nyssa sylvatica*
black plants 38–9, 52, 79
tulips 131
Black Tulip, The 38
bladdernut see *Staphylea*
Blechnum pennamarina 73
blue-eyed Mary see *Omphalodes verna*
blue plants 40–1
autumn-flowering 165–6
calming harmonies of 60–3
rhododendrons/azaleas 133
spring-flowering 115–16, 127
summer-flowering 134–7, 155
for sunny sites 63
tulips 131
boggy ground see water gardens
borders
country-garden 88–9
maintaining 88
monochrome 28–9
rejuvenating 43
Boston ivy see *Parthenocissus tricuspidata*

botanical Latin 22–3
boundary planting 33–5, 103–4
Bourton House, Gloucestershire 77
Bowood House, Wiltshire 14–15i
box see *Buxus*
Bradley-Hole, Christopher 103
Brewer spruce see *Picea breweriana*
Bridgeman, Charles 13
Briza media 171
broom see *Cytisus*
Brown, Lancelot (Capability) 13
Brunnera macrophylla 44, 62i, 172, 182i
B.m. 'Dawson's White' 127
B.m. 'Hadspen Cream' 40
B.m. 'Jack Frost' 127i
Buddleja davidii 'Black Knight' 150b
bugbane see *Actaea*
bugle see *Ajuga*
bulbs, spring 91, 92, 112–13
burning bush see *Dictamnus albus*
Butomus umbellatus 99
Buxus sempervirens 12i, 19i, 84
B.s. 'Suffruticosa' 43, 79, 182i

C
Calamagrostis × *acutiflora*
C. × *a.* 'Karl Foerster' 47, 75i, 88, 180
C. × *a.* 'Overdam' 43, 171i
California lilac see *Ceanothus*
Callicarpa bodinieri var. *giraldii* 'Profusion' 53, 165i
Caltha palustris 45, 100, 126
C.p. 'Flore Pleno' 126
C.p. var. *palustris* 126
Camassia 62
C. cusickii 41; *C.c.* 'Zwanenburg' 62
Camellia 78
C. 'Inspiration' 78i, 180
C. japonica 78, 180; *C.j.* 'Adolphe Audusson' 78i; *C.j.* 'Lavinia Maggi' 78i
C. 'Nicky Crisp' 180i
C. sasanqua 176b, 180; *C.s.* 'Narumigata 166i
C. × *williamsii* 180
Campanula
C. alliariifolia 54
C. cochlearifolia 41, 137
C. glomerata 'Superba' 20
C. lactiflora: C.l. 'Loddon Anna' 142b; *C.l.* 'Prichard's Variety' 137i
C. persicifolia 'Telham Beauty' 135
C. 'Samantha' 137i
candelabra primulas 80i
Canna 151
C. 'Assault' 49
C. 'Endeavour' 49
C. indica 41, 98, 148i
C. 'Rosemond Coles' 46, 49, 67
C. 'Striata' 47, 151
C. TROPICANNA ('Phasion') 65i, 67i
C. 'Wyoming' 46, 67, 151
Cardamine pratensis 90i
Cardiocrinum giganteum 97
cardoon see *Cynara cardunculus*
Carex
C. buchananii 171
C. elata 'Aurea' 19i, 45i, 109
C. oshimensis 'Evergold' 109, 172i
Carpenteria californica 55
carpet bedding 15
Caryopteris × *clandonensis* 154i
C. × *c.* 'First Choice' 165i
Catalpa bignonioides 157
catmint see *Nepeta*
Ceanothus 69
C. arboreus 'Trewithen Blue' 136i
C. 'Autumnal Blue' 69, 165
C. 'Blue Mound' 20i, 136i
C. 'Cascade' 136
C. 'Concha' 69i, 136i
C. × *delileanus* 'Gloire de Versailles' 154b
C. impressus 126b, 136
C. thyrsiflorus 'Skylark' 69, 136i
plant profile 136
Cedrus atlantica Glauca Group (blue Atlas cedar) 174i
Centaurea montana 40, 65i, 138b, 140i
Centranthus ruber 93i
C.r. var. *coccineus* 49
Centurea montana 'Carnea' 51
Cephalaria gigantea 44
Ceratostigma willmottianum 41, 155b, 165i
Cercidiphyllum
C. japonicum 163b
C. magnificum 85
Cerinthe major 'Purpurascens' 28i
Chaenomeles 117
C. speciosa: C.s. 'Moerloosei' 117i; *C.s.* 'Nivalis' 114i
C. × *superba: C.* × *s.* 'Crimson and Gold' 48i, 117i; *C.* × *s.* 'Knap Hill Scarlet' 117; *C.* × *s.* 'Nicoline' 48, 117; *C.* × *s.* 'Pink Lady' 117
Chamaerops humilis 84i
Chamerion angustifolium 55i
C.a. 'Album' 157i
Chanel, Coco 38
Chatto, Beth 95
Chelone 156
C. obliqua 156i
cherries see *Prunus*
chicory see *Cichorium intybus*
Chimonanthus praecox var. *luteus* 114b
Chinese lantern see *Physalis alkekengi*
Chionodoxa 92i
C. forbesii 41, 115
Choisya ternata 93, 123
C.t. SUNDANCE ('Lich') 44, 65
Christchurch Meadows, Oxford 91
Cichorium intybus 137
Cirsium rivulare 'Atropurpureum' 8–9i, 103i, 150i
Cistus × *obtusifolius* 'Thrive' 138i
Clematis
C. 'Abundance' 49
C. alpina 128; *C.a.* 'Pamela Jackman' 128
C. armandii 127b
C. 'Bill MacKenzie' 45
C. cirrhosa var. *balearica* 45i
C. 'Columbine' 126
C. 'Constance' 126
C. 'Etoile Violette' 157
C. 'Frankie' 126
C. 'Jackmanii Superba' 52i, 53
C. 'Jacqueline du Pré' 128
C. 'Jan Lindmark' 128
C. macropetala 128i; *C.m.* 'Bluebird' 128i
C. 'Markham's Pink' 128
C. montana 128; *C.m.* var. *rubens* 'Tetrarose' 79i, 128
C. 'Prince Charles' 176i
C. rehderiana 45
C. 'White Swan' 128
C. 'Willy' 128
plant profile 128
climbers
autumn reds 162
clematis, early-flowering 128
for late spring 126–7b
coccineus (scarlet), origin of 23
Code des Couleurs 22
Colchicum
C. alpinum 156b
C. autumnale 51, 167i
C. byzantinum 166b
C. speciosum 167
C. 'Waterlily' 167
Colour for Adventurous Gardeners 31
colour charts 22
Colour by Design 29
colour theory 18–21
colour wheel 18–19i, 20
Colour in Your Garden 28
colours
in botanical Latin 23
contrasting/complementary 20
in garden design through the ages 11–17
harmonies 19, 53, 60–3
and light, impact of 24–5
in past/present gardens 26–31
saturation/tone 21
and scale/distance 32–5
see also black; blue; green; orange; pink; purple/violet; red; silver/grey; white; yellow
Colutea × *media* 47
conifers, specimen 174
Consolida ajacis 40
containers/pots 84, 106–9
architectural plants for 84
choosing 107
plants for 108–9
topiary in 84
Convallaria majalis 124b
Cordyline australis
C.a. 'Torbay Dazzler' 82i
C.a. 'Torbay Red' 109i
Cornus
C. alba: C.a. 'Aurea' 65; *C.a.* 'Elegantissima' 55; *C.a.* 'Kesselringii' 38i, 39, 181; *C.a.* 'Sibirica' 172i, 179i, 181
C. canadensis 55, 85
C. controversa 'Variegata' 42i, 55, 72–3, 137
C. 'Eddie's White Wonder' 55i
C. florida 123
C. kousa var. *chinensis* 'China Girl' 85
C. mas 176b
C. 'Norman Hadden' 123i
C. sanguinea 'Winter Beauty' 181i
C. sericea 'Flaviramea' 174b, 181
white varieties 55
Cortaderia 88
Corydalis
C. flexuosa: C.f. 'Père David' 90i; *C.f.* 'Purple Leaf' 62i
C. lutea 34i, 45
Corylopsis 113
C. glabrescens 113
C. pauciflora 113i
C. sinensis 44i, 113
Cosmos
C. atrosanguineus 150
C. bipinnatus 51
Cotinus 21i, 69, 149
C. coggygria: C.c. 'Notcutts Variety' 149; *C.c.* 'Royal Purple' 149i; *C.c.* Rubrifolius Group 66i
C. 'Flame' 69, 149
C. 'Grace' 69i, 149, 162i, 183i
Cotoneaster
C. conspicuus 'Decorus' 178–9i
C. frigidus: C.f. 'Cornubia' 162, 178b; *C.f.* 'Fructu Luteo' 164
C. lacteus 178
C. salicifolius: C.s. 'Exburyensis' 164b; *C.s.* 'Rothschildianus' 164i
C. simonsii 163
cottage gardens 89–90, 138–9b
cotton grass see *Eriophorum angustifolium*
country gardens 86–91
The Courts, Wiltshire 149
crab apple see *Malus*
Crambe
C. cordifolia 54i, 138i
C. maritima 93i
cranesbill see *Geranium*
Crataegus 93
C. × *lavalleei* 'Carrierei' 178b
Creating Small Gardens 33
Crinum × *powellii* 156b
Crocosmia 151

C. × *crocosmiiflora:*
C. × *c.* 'Citronella' 67;
C. × *c.* 'Jackanapes' 19i, 71, 151i; *C.* × *c.* 'Lucifer' 19, 49, 67; *C.* × *c.* 'Solfatare' 47, 151
C. 'Lucifer' 148i
C. masoniorum 67; *C.m.* 'Rowallane Yellow' 71i
Crocus 91, 114
C. biflorus 'Miss Vain' 114
C. chrysanthus: C.c. 'Blue Pearl' 115i; *C.c.* 'Snow Bunting' 114i
C. flavus subsp. *flavus* 47
C. × *luteus* 'Golden Yellow' 45
C. pulchellus 166
C. sativus 166
C. sieberi: C.s. 'Albus' 114, 115i; *C.s.* 'Bowles White' 114
C. speciosus 166
C. tommasinianus 116i; *C.t.* 'Ruby Giant' 116i; *C.t.* 'Whitewell Purple' 116
C. vernus subsp. *albiflorus* 'Jeanne d'Arc' 114
crown imperial see *Fritillaria imperialis*
Cupressus macrocarpa 92
Cyclamen
C. cilicium 168, 169
C. coum 51i, 94, 117, 168–9i; *C.c.* subsp. *caucasicum* 'Album' 73
C. graecum 168, 169
C. hederifolium 34i, 51, 168, 169i
C. persicum 168
C. pseudibericum 168, 169
C. purpurascens 168, 169
C. repandum 168, 169
plant profile 168–9
Cynara cardunculus 21, 39, 57i, 88, 155
Cytisus
C. battandieri 154i
C. × *beanii* 125
C. decumbens 125
C. 'Firefly' 125
C. 'Golden Sunlight' 125
C. × *praecox* 125;
C. × *p.* 'Allgold' 125;
C. × *p.* 'Warminster' 125i
C. scoparius 'Cornish Cream' 125

D
daffodil see *Narcissus*
Dahlia 65
D. 'Bishop of Llandaff' 47i, 48, 148
D. 'David Howard' 151
D. 'Ellen Huston' 47
D. 'Glow Orange' 65i
D. 'Moonfire' 65i
D. 'Mount Noddy' 150b
D. 'Nargold' 65i, 153i
D. 'Scarlet Comet' 49
D. 'Zorro' 49
Daphne 129, 181
D. arbuscula 129
D. bholua 181; *D.b.* 'Jacqueline Postill' 115b, 181
D. × *burkwoodii* 'Somerset' 129
D. laureola 97, 116b
D. mezereum 181; *D.m.* f. *alba* 181
D. odora 181, 183i; *D.o.* 'Aureomarginata' 181
D. petraea 'Grandiflora' 129
D. pontica 97i
D. tangutica 129; *D.t.* Retusa Group 129i
D. 'Valerie Hillier' 129
winter-flowering varieties 181
Darmera peltata 43, 162
Davidia involucrata 55, 137i
daylilies see Hemerocallis
deadnettles see *Lamium*
Delphinium 71
D. × *bellamosum* 135
D. 'Blue Jay' 40
D. 'Blue Nile' 40, 49, 71, 135
D. 'Bluebird' 63
D. 'Clear Springs White' 139i
D. 'Cliveden Beauty' 40
D. elatum hybrid 70i
D. 'Faust' 71
D. grandiflorum 'Blue Butterfly' 40i, 135
D. 'Kestrel' 135i
D. 'Lord Butler' 53
D. 'Oliver' 135i
D. tatsienense 40
Deschampsia cespitosa 'Goldschleier' 171
Dianthus barbatus 'Nigrescens Group' 48
Diascia rigescens 50i, 51
Dicentra
D. spectabilis: D.s. 'Alba' 54, 90, 139i; *D.s.* 'Gold Heart' 44
D. 'Stuart Boothman' 96i
Dicksonia antarctica 30i, 73
Dictamnus albus 139i
D.a. var. *purpureus* 142i, 143i
Dierama pulcherrimum 75i
Digitalis 97
D. davisiana 71
D. ferruginea 71i, 96i, 142i
D. × *mertonensis* 50i
D. purpurea 50, 87, 138b; *D.p.* f. *albiflora* 54, 139i
Dipsacus fullonum 180
dog's-tooth violet see *Erythronium*
dogwood see *Cornus*
Doronicum × *excelsum* 'Harpur Crewe' 45, 126i
Douglas, David 22
Drimys winteri 115b
dry shade 85
Dryopteris affinis 73
Dumbarton Oaks, Washington DC 105
Dutch garden styles 12–13
dyes/pigments 23

E
Echeveria 104
E. elegans 41
E. secunda var. *glauca* 57
Echinacea
E. purpurea 75i, 156i; *E.p.* 'Rubinstern' 156i
Echinops
E. bannaticus 155
E. ritro 155i
Echium pinana 41
elder see *Sambucus*
Elaeagnus
E. × *ebbingei* 'Gilt Edge' 82
E. 'Quicksilver' 56i, 57
Elizabethan gardens 11–12
Endsleigh, Devon 14
Epilobium angustifolium 157
Epimedium 124
E. grandiflorum 'White Queen' 124
E. × *perralchicum* 41
E. pubigerum 124
E. × *versicolor* 'Sulphureum' 34i, 90i
E. × *youngianum* 'Niveum' 54, 124
Eranthis 91, 94
E. hyemalis 45, 115i, 178i
E. pinnatifida 176b
Eremurus
E. × *isabellinus* 'Cleopatra' 71
E. robustus 142–3
E. stenophyllus 71i
Erica carnea 'King George' 51
Erigeron 'Charity' 142b
Eriophorum angustifolium 100
Eryngium 108i, 155
E. alpinum 155
E. bourgatii 183i; *E.b.* Graham Stuart Thomas's selection 155i
E. giganteum 57i, 155, 180b
E. maritimum 93i
E. × *oliverianum* 41, 155
E. × *tripartitum* 155
Erythronium 124
E. californicum 94i, 124; *E.c.* 'White Beauty' 124
E. dens-canis 51
E. oregonum 124
E. 'Pagoda' 45i, 182i
Escallonia 93
E. 'Iveyi' 55, 61i, 157i
Eschscholzias 93i
espalier trees 84
Eucalyptus pauciflora subsp. *niphophila* 175
Eucomis bicolor 42i
Eucryphia 157
Euonymus
E. alatus 49, 162
E. europaeus 'Red Cascade' 162
E. fortunei 93; *E.f.* 'Emerald 'n' gold' 32i; *E.f.* 'Silver Queen' 125i
E. latifolius 162
Eupatorium 150
E. purpureum 51; *E.p.* subsp. *maculatum* 'Atropurpureum' 150
E. rugosum 38, 157; *E.r.* 'Chocolate' 151i
Euphorbia 21i
E. amygdaloides var. *robbiae* 126
E. cyparissias 126
E. dulcis 'Chameleon' 66
E. griffithii 'Dixter' 46
E. myrsinites 126
E. palustris 43, 66, 100
E. polychroma 66i, 126i
E. schillingii 34i, 43, 127i, 154
E. seguieriana 126
E. sikkimensis 154
evening primrose see *Oenothera*
Exochorda × *macrantha* 'The Bride' 55, 97, 123i, 182i
exotic plantings 30–1

F
fairies' thimbles see *Campanula cochlearifolia*
Farrand, Beatrix 105
Fatsia japonica 43, 78i, 83i
F.j. 'Variegata' 34i, 182i
Feate of Gardening, The 11
fences/railings 61, 104–5
ferns 43, 73
Festuca
F. glauca 109; *F.g.* 'Blaufuchs' 41; *F.g.* 'Elijah Blue' 170
feverfew 34i, 138i
Filipendula
F. purpurea 150
F. rubra 'Venusta' 150
F. ulmaria 89, 99
flax see *Linum narbonense*
flowering quince 117
see also *Chaenomeles*
flowering rush see *Butomus umbellatus*
foliage, dramatic 65, 100–1
forget-me-not see *Myosotis* 40, 87, 89i, 127
formal planting ideas 79
Forsythia 113
F. × *intermedia* 97i; *F.* × *i.* 'Weekend' 113i
F. suspensa 113
Fothergilla major 123i
foxglove see *Digitalis*
foxtail lily see *Eremurus*
fragrant plants, spring 114–15b
French garden styles 12–13
Fritillaria 129
F. acmopetala 129
F. imperialis 129; *F.i.* 'Maxima Lutea' 45; *F.i.* 'Rubra Maxima' 46i, 66i
F. meleagris 91i, 129
F. michailovskyi 129i
F. pallidiflora 129i
F. persica 129;
F.p. 'Adiyaman' 129

F. pontica 129
F. raddeana 129
Fuchsia 'Mrs Popple' 149i, 167b

G
Galanthus 87, 91, 97, 177
G. alpinus var. *alpinus* 177b
G. 'Atkinsii' 177i
G. elwesii 55
G. 'Magnet' 114, 177i
G. nivalis 177; *G.n.* 'Viridapice' 177i
G. 'S. Arnott' 114, 177i
Galega officinalis 139b
Galium odoratum 97, 124i, 139–40
Galtonia
G. candicans 39
G. viridiflora 43
Gardener, Jon 11
Garrya elliptica 43, 82
Gaultheria mucronata 165b
G.m. 'Mulberry Wine' 53
Gaura lindheimeri 55
Gentiana
G. acaulis 127
G. septemfida 166
G. sino-ornata 165
G. verna 41, 127
Geranium 63, 141–2, 143
G. 'Ann Folkard' 51, 143
G. (Cinereum Group) 'Ballerina' 50i, 51, 53
G. clarkei: G.c. 'Kashmir Purple' 141; *G.c.* 'Kashmir White' 54, 138i
G. himalayense 142; *G.h.* 'Gravetye' 70–1
G. 'Johnson's Blue' 141i
G. macrorrhizum 97
G. maderense 143i
G. × *magnificum* 141
G. phaeum 97; *G.p.* var. *phaeum* 'Samobor' 39
G. pratense: G.p. 'Cluden Sapphire' 142i; *G.p.* 'Mrs Kendall Clark' 53; *G.p.* 'Plenum Violaceum' 53, 63i, 141i–142, 182i
G. psilostemon 43, 49, 51, 89, 89i, 143
G. renardii 138
G. × *riversleaianum* 'Russell Prichard' 143
G. ROZANNE ('Gerwat') 155
G. sanguineum var. *striatum* 142i
G. sylvaticum: G.s. 'Album' 138; *G.s.* 'Mayflower' 142
G. wallichianum 'Buxton's Variety' 155i
Gerard, John 12
Geum
G. 'Borisii' 46
G. coccineum 43
G. 'Mrs J. Bradshaw' 49
giant lily see *Cardiocrinum giganteum*
giant scabious see *Cephalaria gigantea*
Gillenia trifoliata 138i
ginger lily see *Hedychium coccineum*
Ginkgo biloba 164i
Gladiolus byzantinus 51
Glebe House Museum, Connecticut, USA 27
globe thistle see *Echinops*
globeflower see *Trollius*
grasses, ornamental
for containers 109
plant profile 170–1
Gravetye Manor, West Sussex 16
Great Dixter, East Sussex 19, 31i
green 42–3, 76
flowers 42, 43, 131
in historic gardens 11, 12i–13, 14
grey/silver plants 56–7, 79, 175
Griselinia littoralis 92i
ground-cover plants 140–1b
Gunnera
G. magellanica 100
G. manicata 43, 98i, 100, 101i
Gypsophila paniculata 'Bristol Fairy' 54, 138

H
Hadspen Garden, Somerset 17, 20, 29i
Hakonechloa macra 87
H.m. 'Alboaurea' 109
Hamamelis 177
H. × *intermedia: H.* × *i.* 'Arnold Promise' 177; *H.* × *i.* 'Diane' 179i; *H.* × *i.* 'Jelena' 85, 179i; *H.* × *i.* 'Pallida' 45, 177i
H. mollis 177, 178i
H. virginiana 164
Hamilton, Charles 14
Hampton Court 11, 12, 13
handkerchief tree see *Davidia involucrata*
hard landscaping 102–5
fences and features 61, 104–5
walls and floors 103–4
harmonies 19, 53, 60–3
hawthorn 93
Hebe pinguifolia 'Pagei' 57i
Hedera 96
H. colchica 'Sulphur Heart' 45i
H. helix 39; *H.h.* 'Goldchild' 45; *H.h.* 'Parsley Crested' 82
hedges 61, 77
Hedychium
H. coccineum 'Tara' 47, 153
H. densiflorum 'Assam Orange' 83
Helenium
H. 'Blütentisch' 151
H. 'Bruno' 151
H. 'Butterpat' 45, 151
H. 'Chipperfield Orange' 67
H. 'Moerheim Beauty' 46, 47, 151
H. 'The Bishop' 67i
H. 'Waldtraut' 28i, 47i
Helianthemum 'Henfield Brilliant' 47
Helianthus
H. annuus 45
H. 'Lemon Queen' 153
H. 'Loddon Gold' 153i
Helichrysum italicum 57
Helictotrichon sempervirens 41, 57, 104, 109
Heliopsis helianthoides var. *scabra* 20i
H.h.v.s. 'Incomparabilis' 154
H.h.v.s. 'Light of Loddon' 153–4
H.h.v.s. 'Sommersonne' 153i, 183i
Helleborus
H. argutifolius 43
H. cyclophyllus 180
H. foetidus 94i, 96, 180
H. × *hybridus* 38i, 42i, 43, 97, 114i, 117, 173i, 180i–181, 183i
H. niger 180
H. orientalis 'Hillier Hybrid Green' 43
H. purpurascens 180–1
Hemerocallis 69, 144
H. 'American Revolution' 69
H. 'Anzac' 71i
H. 'Bella Lugosi' 69
H. citrina 144
H. 'Dominic' 69
H. fulva 'Flore Pleno' 69i
H. 'Hyperion' 144i
H. 'Indian Paintbrush' 47
H. lilioasphodelus 20i, 93, 144i
H. 'Marion Vaughn' 144
H. 'Missenden' 69
H. 'Starling' 69
Hermodactylus tuberosus 39
Hesperis
H. matronalis 8–9i, 89i, 139; *H.m.* var. *albiflora* 'Alba Plena' 55, 139
Hestercombe House, Somerset 17
Het Loo Palace, Holland 12i
Heuchera 21i
H. EBONY AND IVORY ('E and I') 47
H. 'Key Lime Pie' 42i, 43
H. 'Mint Frost' 79
H. 'Plum Pudding' 67i, 183i
Hibberd, Shirley 16, 28–9
Hibiscus syriacus
H.s. 'Oiseau Bleu' 155b
H.s. 'Woodbridge' 157i
Hicks, David 76, 107
Hidcote, Gloucestershire 17, 77
Hillier Gardens, Sir Harold, Hampshire 95i
Hippophae rhamnoides 57, 85, 165b
history of colour 11–17
Hobhouse, Penelope 28
Holcus mollis 'Albovariegatus' 109
holly see *Ilex*
hollyhock see *Alcea rosea*
honesty see *Lunaria annua*
Hosta
container-growing 108
H. 'Fragrant Blue' 41i
H. 'Frances Williams' 125i
H. 'Halcyon' 40
H. sieboldiana var. *elegans* 41, 43, 127i
H. 'Sum and Substance' 98
Hyacinthoides non-scripta 40, 96i, 125b
Hyacinthus orientalis 'Midnight Mystique' 39
Hydrangea 62
H. anomala subsp. *petiolaris* 127b
H. serrata 'Bluebird' 62i
Hypericum 89
H. calycinum 154
H. 'Hidcote' 154i
H. × *inodorum* 'Elstead' 154
Hyssopus officinalis 90

I
Ilex 77, 93, 97
I. × *altaclerensis* 77
I. aquifolium 77; *I.a.* 'Ferox Argentea' 77i, 173i; *I.a.* 'Handsworth New Silver' 77, 174i, 183i; *I.a.* 'Silver Queen' 77, 82; *I.a.*'J.C. van Tol' 43, 97, 179b
I. cornuta 173i
I. latifolia 43
Iford Manor, Wiltshire 91
Imperata cylindrica 'Rubra' 151b
Incarvillea delavayi 143b
Indigofera 157
I. heterantha 53, 157, 167b
Inula 154
I. hookeri 154
I. magnifica 45, 154
Ipheion 116
I. uniflorum 'Wisley Blue' 116i
Iris
I. 'Blackout' 52
I. chrysographes 'Black Knight' 38
I. 'Dusky Challenger' 52
I. ensata 100i
I. foetidissima 96
I. japonica 'Variegata' 53
I. pseudacorus 45
I. reticulata 177b
I. sibirica 63; *I.s.* 'Annemarie Troeger' 63i; *I.s.* 'Caesar's Brother' 53; *I.s.* 'Ego' 40i, 41; *I.s.* 'Ruffled Velvet' 53; *I.s.* 'Sparkling Rosé' 63
I. 'Study in Black' 39i
I. unguicularis 116i; *I.u.* 'Mary Barnard' 116, 177b

J
Japanese anemone see *Anemone* × *hybrida*
Japanese gardens 72–3i

Japanese laurel see *Aucuba japonica*
Japanese maple see *Acer japonicum*
Jarman, Derek 93
Jasminum nudiflorum 82, 117b, 178
Jekyll, Gertrude 16–17, 26–9, 106
Johnston, Lawrence 17
jungle-style planting 30–1, 82–3
Juniperus scopulorum 'Skyrocket' 173

K
Kent, William 13–14
Kerria japonica 'Golden Guinea' 45
Kingston Maurward, Dorset 88
Klein, Carol 29
Knautia macedonica 'Mars Midget' 150i
Kniphofia
K. 'Bees' Sunset' 152
K. 'Erecta' 152i
K. 'Green Jade' 43, 152
K. 'Little Maid' 44i, 45, 152
K. 'Percy's Pride' 152
K. 'Prince Igor' 48–9, 167b
K. rooperi 152i, 183i
K. 'Royal Standard' 46i, 47, 152i
K. thomsonii var. *thomsonii* 152
K. uvaria 'Nobilis' 47
K. 'Victoria' 152i
plant profile 152

L
lady's mantle see *Alchemilla mollis*
Lamium 96
L. maculatum 'Beacon Silver' 127i, 129i, 140b
landscape gardening 13–14
landscaping, hard 102–5
fences and features 61, 104–5
walls and floors 103–4
Lapageria rosea 83i
large gardens 35
specimen conifers for 174
Larix 95
larkspur see *Consolida ajacis*
Latin, botanical 22–3
Laurus nobilis 77
Lavandula 90, 93
L. angustifolia 'Hidcote' 52i, 53
L.× intermedia 'Grosso' 77, 78i
Leucanthemum x *superbum* 'Esther Read' 139i
Leucojum aestivum 124i, 125
L.a. 'Gravetye Giant' 55
Leucothoe SCARLETTA ('Zeblid') 49i
Lewis, Pam 17
Liatris 156
L. spicata 74i, 143b, 156
light, impact on colour 24–5
Ligularia
L. dentata 'Britt-Marie Crawford' 66i, 67, 183i
L. 'Desdemona' 98
L. 'The Rocket' 66i, 67
L. 'Zepter' 98i
Ligustrum
L. delavayanum 84i
L. ovalifolium 61
L. quihoui 85
L. 'Vicaryi' 97
Lilium
L. African Queen Group 151
L. candidum 54, 140
L. 'Fire King' 47
L. Golden Splendor Group 154
L. henryi 151i, 183i
L. martagon 91; *L.m.* var. *album* 96i
L. 'Pink Perfection' 148
L. regale 140i
L. speciosum 156b
lily, giant see *Cardiocrinum giganteum*
Limonium latifolium 155
Linaria 156
L. purpurea 156i; *L.p.* 'Canon Went' 156
Linum
L. grandiflorum 40
L. narbonense 137
Liquidambar styraciflua 161i
Liriope muscari 'Variegata' 85i, 165
Little Court, Hampshire 98i
Lloyd, Christopher 19, 31
Lobelia
L. 'Cherry Ripe' 49
L. tupa 149
Long Barn, Kent 17
Lonicera
L. fragrantissima 115b
L. japonica 'Halliana' 127
L. pileata 85, 97
L.× purpusii 'Winter Beauty' 176i
loosestrife see *Lysimachia*
Lotus hirsutus 108
love-in-a-mist see *Nigella*
Luma apiculata 157, 175b
Lunaria annua 96i
Lutyens, Edwin 17
Lychnis
L. chalcedonica 48
L. coronaria 51, 143i
L. flos-jovis 143
Lysichiton americanus 45, 101i, 113–14
Lysimachia
L. atropurpurea 'Beaujolais' 151b
L. ciliata 'Purpurea' 39
L. clethroides 38–9
L. ephemerum 157

M
Macleaya microcarpa 'Kelway's Coral Plume' 142i, 143
Magdalen College, Oxford 91
Magnolia 118–19
M.× brooklynensis 'Yellow Bird' 45, 45i
M. campbellii 119i
M. 'Elizabeth' 113i
M. 'Galaxy' 119
M. 'Heaven Scent' 19
M.× loebneri 'Leonard Messel' 118i
M.× soulangeana 118i; *M.× s.* 'Lennei' 51
M. stellata 55, 114i; *M.s.* 'Centennial' 119i
M. 'Susan' 119i
M. wilsonii 95i, 119
plant profile 118–19
Mahonia 177–8
M. aquifolium 125i
M.× media: M.× m. 'Buckland' 164; *M.× m.* 'Charity' 164i; *M.× m.* 'Lionel Fortescue' 115b; *M.× m.* 'Winter Sun' 178i
M. stellata 118
maidenhair tree see *Ginkgo biloba*
Malus
M. 'Butterball' 163
M. 'John Downie' 161i
M. pumila 'Cowichan' 161
M.× robusta 'Red Sentinel' 161
M.× scheideckeri 'Red Jade' 179b
M. sieboldii 123
M. toringo 123; *M.t.* subsp. *sargentii* 95, 123
M. transitoria 123
M. tschonoskii 163
M. × *zumi* var. *calocarpa: M.× z.v.c.* 'Golden Hornet' 164i; *M.× z.v.c.* 'Professor Sprenger' 163i
Malva 89
maple see *Acer*
marsh marigold see *Caltha palustris*
Matteuccia struthiopteris 43i, 73i, 95i
mauve plants see purple/violet
meadow rue see *Thalictrum*
meadow saffron see *Colchicum autumnale*
meadowsweet see *Filipendula ulmaria*
Meconopsis
M. cambrica 45, 47
M.× sheldonii 41, 58i
Melianthus major 43, 65, 109
Mentha suaveolens 108
Mertensia virginica 40, 127
Mesembryanthemum 93i
Mexican orange blossom see *Choisya ternata*
Milium effusum 'Aureum' 34i65, 67, 109
mind-your-own-business see *Soleirola soleirolii*
minimalist planting 83
Miscanthus
M. sinensis: M.s. 'Morning Light' 74i, 170i, 183i; *M.s.* 'Silberfeder' 180b; *M.s.* 'Yakushima Dwarf' 171i
mock orange see *Philadelphus*
Molinia caerulea
M.c. subsp. *arundinacea* 'Karl Foerster' 99
M.c. subsp. *caerulea* 'Moorflamme' 171
Mollet, André 12
Monarda 75, 149
M. 'Cambridge Scarlet' 149
M. 'Croftway Pink' 74i, 75
M. 'Mahogany' 149
M. 'Schneewittchen' 54
Monet's Garden, Giverny 91i
monkshood see *Aconitum*
monochrome borders 28–9
montbretia see *Crocosmia*
moods
calming 60–3
dramatic 68–71
exciting/vibrant 64–7
sophisticated 76–9
subtle 72–5
mountain ash see *Sorbus*
mullein see *Verbascum*
Munstead Wood, Surrey 27
Musa
M. 'Dwarf Cavendish' 83
M. lasiocarpa 83i
Muscari 79, 92i, 109i
M. armeniacum 'Valerie Finnis' 19, 116i
Myosotidium hortensia 137
Myosotis 40, 87, 89i, 127
M. scorpioides 141b
Myrrhis odorata 139i
Myrtus lechleriana 123

N
names, botanical 22–3
Nandina domestica 'Fire Power' 179i
Narcissus 120–1
dwarf/miniature varieties 120–1
N. 'Baby Moon' 121
N. 'Canaliculatus' 121i
N. cyclamineus 110i, 112i, 121
N. 'Fairy Chimes' 121
N. 'February Gold' 112, 115i, 120i
N. 'Hawera' 116i, 120i
N. 'Jack Snipe' 121
N. 'Jenny' 112
N. 'Jetfire' 121i
N. jonquilla 121
N. 'Minnow' 121i
N. minor 112
N. 'Mite' 121
N. pseudonarcissus 91, 121, 121i, 178i
N. 'Small Talk' 121
N. 'Sundial' 121
N. 'Surfside' 127i
N. tazetta 121
N. 'Tête-à-tête' 121
N. 'Thalia' 120i
N. 'Topolino' 91
N. triandrus 121

naturalistic plantings 16, 30, 86–7
water gardens 98–100
navelwort see *Omphalodes*
Nepeta
N. × *faassenii* 63
N. 'Six Hills Giant' 63i, 139b
Nerine bowdenii 167i
Nesfield, William Andrews 15
Nicolson, Harold 17
Nicotiana
N. 'Lime Green' 43i, 138i
N. sylvestris 34i
Nigella 40
N. damascena 'Miss Jekyll' 41i
Nymphoides peltata 100
Nyssa sylvatica 161i

O
oak see *Quercus*
obedient plants see *Physostegia*
Observations on Modern Gardening 14
Oehme, Wolfgang 43
Oenothera 93
O. fruticosa 154
Olea europaea 56, 104
Omphalodes
O. cappadocica 41i, 127; *O.c.* 'Parisian Skies' 127; *O.c.* 'Starry Eyes' 127i, 182i
O. verna 127
Onopordum 89i
O. nervosum 57i
Ophiopogon planiscapus 'Nigrescens' 36i, 39i, 78i, 79
orange plants 46–7
autumn leaves/fruit 163
rhododendrons 132
summer-flowering 151–3
tulips 131
winter-flowering 178–80
Origanum 34i, 51
O. laevigatum 'Herrenhausen' 51, 74i
Osmanthus
O. delavayi 123i, 182i
O. heterophyllus 'Aureomarginatus' 174i
Osmunda regalis 73i
Osteospermum 'Whirlygig' 140
Oudolf, Piet 30, 43, 87
ox-eyes see *Heliopsis*
Oxalis oregana 125b

P
Paeonia 142
P. lactiflora: *P.l.* 'Bowl of Beauty' 142i; *P.l.* 'Laura Dessert' 144; *P.l.* 'Sarah Bernhardt' 135i, 142i, 182i; *P.l.* 'Shirley Temple' 142; *P.l.* 'White Wings' 138
P. mlokosewitschii 44, 45i, 143–4
P. officinalis 'Rubra Plena' 139b
Painshill Park, Surrey 14
Panicum virgatum 'Heavy Metal' 163i, 171i
Papaver 91i, 93
P. orientale 70; *P.o.* 'Allegro' 42–3; *P.o.* 'Black and White' 39; *P.o.* 'Cedric Morris' 51; *P.o.* 'Garden Glory' 70i; *P.o.* Goliath Group 'Beauty of Livermere' 48, 49i, 70; *P.o.* 'Ladybird' 49; *P.o.* 'Patty's Plum' 28i, 57, 70; *P.o.* 'Türkenlouis' 48
P. rupifragum 24i
P. somniferum 181b; *P.s.* 'Black Paeony' 6–7i, 70; *P.s.* Peony Flowered Mixed 70i
Paradisi in Sole, Paradisus Terrestris 13, 22
Parahebe perfoliata 155
Paris polyphylla 43
Parkinson, John 13, 22, 42
Parrotia persica 163b
parterres 14–15
Parthenocissus
P. quinquefolia 162
P. tricuspidata 162i; *P.t.* 'Veitchii' 162
Passiflora 93
Paulownia tomentosa 66
Pearson, Dan 87
Pennisetum orientale 109, 181b
Penstemon
P. 'Alice Hindley' 53i, 79i, 147i
P. 'Andenken an Friedrich Hahn' 146i, 183i
P. 'Apple Blossom' 147
P. barbatus 147i
P. 'Burgundy' 146i
P. 'Evelyn' 147i
P. 'Garnet' 146
P. heterophyllus 'Catherine de la Mare' 147i
P. isophyllus 147
P. 'King George V' 147
P. 'Port Wine' 49i, 151i, 183i
P. 'Purple Bedder' 53
P. 'Raven' 147i, 151b
P. 'Sour Grapes' 147
P. 'Stapleford Gem' 53, 147i
P. 'White Bedder' 79, 147
plant profile 146–7
periwinkle see *Vinca*
Perovskia 'Blue Spire' 63, 155b, 165
Persicaria
P. amplexicaulis 87
P. bistorta 'Superba' 143b
Petasites japonicus var. *giganteus* 109
Philadelphus 62, 137–8
P. 'Beauclerk' 138
P. 'Belle Etoile' 62i
P. 'Buckley's Quill' 138
P. 'Burfordensis' 138
P. coronarius 'Aureus' 97
P. 'Manteau d'Hermine' 62i, 138
P. 'Virginal' 55, 138i, 182i
Phillyrea
P. angustifolia 77
P. latifolia 61i, 93
Phlomis 144
P. russeliana 45, 144, 181b
Phlox paniculata 53i, 75i
P.p. 'Amethyst' 151b
P.p. 'Eva Cullum' 75
P.p. 'Mother of Pearl' 51
P.p. 'Norah Leigh' 75
Phormium 101
P. cookianum subsp. *hookeri*: *P.c.s.h.* 'Cream Delight' 67; *P.c.s.h.* 'Tricolor' 101
P. 'Sundowner' 101
Phygelius 150
P. aequalis 'Yellow Trumpet' 150
P. × *rectus*: *P.* × *r.* 'Devil's Tears' 150; *P.* × *r.* 'Moonraker' 150; *P.* × *r.* 'Salmon Leap' 150; *P.* × *r.* 'Winchester Fanfare' 150i
Phyllostachys nigra 21, 39
Physalis alkekengi 46i, 163i
Physocarpus opulifolius 'Diabolo' 39
Physostegia 156
P. virginiana 156; *P.v.* 'Vivid' 156
Picea breweriana 174i
Pieris japonica 123
P.j. 'Scarlett O'Hara' 123
pink-flowered plants 50–1
autumn-flowering 167
rhododendrons/azaleas 133
roses 50, 145
spring-flowering 117, 129
summer-flowering 142–3, 156–7
tulips 131
winter-flowering 180–1
Pinus
P. mugo 92
P. sylvestris 95i
P. wallichiana 174i
Pittosporum tenuifolium 'Tom Thumb' 39i
plant names 22–3
Plant Names Explained 23
plant profiles
ceanothus 136
clematis, early-flowering 128
cyclamen 168–9
daphne, winter-flowering 181
grasses, ornamental 170–1
kniphofias 152
magnolias 118–19
penstemons 146–7
rhododendrons and azaleas 132–3
salvias 158–9
tulips 130–1
pleached hedges 77
Pleioblastus
P. auricomus 77
P. pygmaeus 'Distichus' 77
P. variegatus 77, 79i
P. viridistriatus 65, 67
Pliny the Younger 11
plume poppy see *Macleaya microcarpa*
Polemonium 140
P. boreale 140
P. caeruleum 139b, 140
P. carneum 140
P. 'Lambrook Mauve' 53, 140
Polygonatum × *hybridum* 54, 62, 125i
P. × *h.* 'Striatum' 125i
Polypodium interjectum 'Cornubiense' 43
Polystichum setiferum 43
ponds see water gardens
Pope, Nori and Sandra 17, 20, 29
poppies see *Papaver*
Populus
P. alba 93
P. tremula 93
Portugal laurel see *Prunus lusitanica*
Potentilla 149
P. atrosanguinea 49, 151b
P. 'Etna' 149
P. fruticosa: *P.f.* 'Elizabeth 32i, *P.f.* 'Primrose Beauty' 154i; *P.f.* 'Red Ace' 49, 149
P. 'Gibson's Scarlet' 48i, 49, 149i
P. 'William Rollison' 47
pots/containers 106–9
architectural plants for 84
choosing 107
plants for 108–9
topiary in 84
prairie planting 30
primroses 87, 89, 90, 107
Primula 80i, 87
P. florindae 100i, 101i
Prior Park, Bath 13i
Prospect Cottage, Dungeness 93
Prunus
P. avium 'Plena'
P. glandulosa 'Alba Plena' 123
P. incisa 114
P. lusitanica 43, 61, 77; *P.l.* 'Variegata' 82i, 174i–175
P. mume 'Beni-chidori' 117b
P. padus 'Watereri' 61
P. serrula 175b
P.' Shirotae'
P. × *subhirtella*: *P.* × *s.* 'Autumnalis' 177b, 180; *P.* × *s.* 'Autumnalis Rosea' 180i
P. 'Taihaku' 122i
small, white-flowered varieties 123
Pulmonaria 97, 115
P. 'Blue Ensign' 41, 62i, 115i, 116i, 182i
P. longifolia 176i
P. 'Mawson's Blue' 115
P. saccharata 'Leopard' 127i
P. 'Sissinghurst White' 54, 114i, 182i
purple dyes 23
purple/violet plants 52–3
autumn-flowering 165–6
rhododendrons/azaleas 133
roses, recommended 145
spring-flowering 115–16
summer-flowering 140–2

tulips 131
Pyracantha
P. 'Golden Charmer' 163i
P. 'Golden Dome' 163
P. 'Orange Charmer' 179b
P. 'Orange Glow' 21
Pyrus salicifolia 'Pendula' 56, 57

Q
Quercus 22–3, 95
Q. coccinea 161; *Q.c.* 'Splendens' 161i
Q. ilex 92
quince, flowering see *Chaenomeles*

R
railings/fences 61, 104–5
Ranunculus
R. aconitifolius 124i
R. ficaria 'Brazen Hussy' 38
red plants 48–9
autumn colour 160–2
climbers, autumn 162
dusky reds 150
hot reds 148–50
rhododendrons/azaleas 133
roses, recommended 145
spring-flowering 48, 117
summer-flowering 148–50, 152
tulips 131
winter-flowering 178–80
Rehmannia elata 143b
Repton, Humphry 14
Rheum palmatum 101i
R.p. 'Ace of Hearts' 98
R.p. 'Atrosanguineum' 65i, 101, 183i
Rhodochiton atrosanguineus 39
Rhododendron
plant profile 132–3
R. 'Blue Danube' 133
R. Blue Diamond Group 133
R. calophytum 133
R. 'Colonel Coen' 133i
R. 'Cynthia' 133
R. 'Cunningham's White' 132
R. 'Fireball' 133
R. 'Homebush' 133
R. 'Horizon Monarch' 133i
R. 'Hotei' 133
R. 'Irene Koster' 132i
R. Loderi Group 51i, 132i
R. luteum 133
R. 'Mrs Furnivall' 133
R. 'Peste's Fire Light' 132i
R. 'Polar Bear' 132
R. 'Purple Splendour' 53
R. 'Scarlet Wonder' 53
R. 'Silver Slipper' 132
R. 'The Hon. Jean Marie de Montague' 133i
Rhus typhina 'Dissecta' 104, 163b
Ribes
R. laurifolium 173i
R. sanguineum 85i; *R.s.* 'Pulborough Scarlet' 117b
Robinia pseudoacacia 'Frisia' 44i
Robinson, William 16–17
Rodgersia 100–1, 139
R. aesculifolia 139, 143i, 183i
R. pinnata 'Superba' 101
R. podophylla 43, 65i, 101i, 139
Rodmarton Manor, Gloucestershire 88
Roman gardens 10i, 11
Romneya coulteri 157i
Rosa 11i, 50, 69, 145
R. 'Albéric Barbier' 145
R. 'Albertine' 50, 82i
R. 'Alchymist' 145i
R. 'Arthur Bell' 145
R. 'Ballerina' 50i, 141i
R. banksiae 'Lutea' 127b
R. 'Blanc Double de Coubert' 145
R. BONICA ('Meidomonac') 141i, 145
R. canina 50
R. 'Cardinal de Richelieu' 145
R. 'Celeste' 145
R. × *centifolia* 'Cristata' 50
R. 'Charles de Mills' 49, 50
R. 'Compassion' 145
R. CONSTANCE SPRY ('Austance') 89i, 145
R. 'Crimson Shower' 145
R. 'Desprez à Fleurs Jaunes' 145
R. 'Duchesse de Montebello' 50
R. 'Etoile de Hollande' 145
R. 'Fantin-Latour' 145
R. FRAGRANT CLOUD ('Tanellis') 145
R. 'Frensham' 49
R. 'Geranium' 145
R. glauca 57, 148i
R. 'Gloire de Dijon' 47
R. GOLDEN CELEBRATION ('Ausgold') 145i
R. 'Golden Wings' 145
R. 'Goldfinch' 145
R. GRAHAM THOMAS ('Ausmas') 45
R. 'Grandpa Dickson' 145
R. 'Gruss an Aachen' 145
R. ICEBERG ('Korbin') 145
R. 'Königin von Dänemark' 145
R. 'Madame Isaac Pereire' 145
R. MARGARET MERRIL ('Harkuly') 55, 145
R. MARY ROSE ('Ausmary') 57, 145
R. 'Moonlight' 145
R. 'Mrs Oakley Fisher' 145
R. 'Nevada' 145i
R. 'Nuits de Young' 69, 145
R. nutkana 'Plena' 50
R. × *odorata:* 'Mutabilis' 145; *R.* × *o.* 'Viridiflora' 42i
R. 'Président de Sèze' 145i
R. 'Raubritter' 50i
R. 'Reine des Violettes' 69
R. 'Roseraie de l'Haÿ' 69i, 135i, 145i, 182i
R. rugosa 165b
R. 'Seagull' 145
R. sericea f. *pteracantha* 175b
R. TESS OF THE D'URBERVILLES'('Ausmove') 145i
R. 'The Fairy' 145
R. 'Tuscany Superb' 69, 145
R. 'William Lobb' 49, 69
R. WINCHESTER CATHEDRAL ('Auscat') 79
R. 'Zigeunerknabe' 145
recommended selection 50, 145
roses
for dramatic schemes 69
recommended selections 50, 145
Royal Horticultural Society
AGM (Award of Garden Merit) 7
colour chart 22
Wisley, Garden 30i
Rubus
R. cockburnianus 'Goldenvale' 36i, 176i, 183i
R. thibetanus 176
Rudbeckia
R. fulgida 153i; *R.f.* var. *sullivantii* 'Goldsturm' 45, 67, 153
R. laciniata: R.l. 'Goldquelle' 67, 153; *R.l.* 'Herbstsonne' 153
rural gardens 86–91
Ruta 90

S
Sackville-West, Vita 17, 26
Salix
S. alba 181; *S.a.* subsp. *vitellina* 181i; *S.a.s.v.* 'Britzensis' 48i, 49, 181
S. babylonica var. *pekinensis* 'Tortuosa' 175b
S. lanata 125
S. repens 125
Salvia 63, 90
plant profile 158–9
S. argentea 56, 57, 159
S. cardinalis 159
S. farinacea 'Victoria' 159i
S. fulgens 49, 159
S. guaranitica 'Blue Enigma' 159
S. involucrata 'Bethellii' 159
S. × *jamensis* 49; *S.* × *j.* 'La Luna' 158
S. lavandulifolia 53i, 159i
S. microphylla var. *microphylla* 159
S. nemorosa 'Ostfriesland' 159i
S. patens 21, 40, 63, 70, 155, 159, 165; *S.p.* 'Cambridge Blue' 159
S. pratensis Haematodes Group 159
S. sclarea var. *turkestanica* white-bracted 55i, 158i
S. splendens 15, 158
S. × *sylvestris* 'Mainacht' 140i, 159i
S. uliginosa 40, 41, 155, 159, 165, 167b
S. viridis 158
Sambucus
S. nigra 39, 148i; *S.n.* f. *porphyrophylla: S.n.f.p.* 'Eva' 38i, 39; *S.n.f.p.* 'Gerda' 33, 39; *S.n.* f. *porphyrophylla: S.n.* 'Black Beauty' 39; *S.n.* 'Black Lace' 39
S. racemosa 'Plumosa Aurea' 97i; *S.r.* 'Sutherland Gold' 67i,
Sanguisorba
S. canadensis 157
S. officinalis 75i
Santolina 93
S. chamaecyparissus 'Lambrook Silver' 78
Saponaria ocymoides 141b
Sarcococca 97, 173
S. confusa 97, 173
S. hookeriana 183i; *S.h.* var. *digyna* 61i, 173; *S.h.v.d.* 'Purple Stem' 97, 173i; *S.h.* var. *humilis* 173
Sasaella masamuneana 'Albostriata' 77
Saxifraga × *urbium* 141b
Scabiosa 87, 141
S. atropurpurea 'Ace of Spades' 79
S. caucasica 141i; *S.c.* Perfecta Series 'Perfecta Alba' 79i
scale and distance 32–5
scarlet, origin of 23
Schizostylis 149
S. coccinea 23; *S.c.* f. *alba* 54; *S.c.* 'Major' 149i, 167b
S. 'Sunrise' 149
S. 'Viscountess Byng' 149
Scilla
S. mischtschenkoana 115i
S. siberica 41, 115
Scots pine see *Pinus sylvestris*
sea buckthorn see *Hippophae rhamnoides*
sea kale see *Crambe maritima*
sea lavender see *Limonium latifolium*
seaside gardens 92–3
Sedum
S. 'Herbstfreude' 181b
S. spectabile 162
S. telephium subsp. *maximum* 'Atropurpureum' 162i
seedheads, decorative 180–1b
shade
creating, plants for 61
damp 85
dry 85, 96
improving conditions in 96
planting partners for 62–3, 90, 125, 182, 183
in urban gardens 85
white plants for 54
yellow plants for 45

see also woodland gardens
Shibataea kumasasa 77
shrubberies, history of 14
shrubs
for dramatic schemes 69
variegated 174
white-flowered 55, 122–3
for woodland gardens 97
yellow-flowered 154
see also under individual species
silver/grey plants 56–7, 79, 175
silver/white bark 175–6
single-colour borders 28–9
Sir Harold Hillier Gardens, Hampshire 95i
Sissinghurst Castle, Kent 17, 28
Skimmia japonica 'Rubella' 179
skunk cabbage see *Lysichiton americanus*
small gardens 32–4, 84, 173
Smilacina racemosa 124i, 125
smoke-bush see *Cotinus*
snakeshead fritillary see *Fritillaria meleagris*
snowberry see *Symphoricarpos albus*
snowdrop see *Galanthus*
Solanum
S. crispum 93; *S.c.* 'Glasnevin' 127b
S. laxum 'Album' 79
Soleirolia soleirolii 85
Solomon's seal see *Polygonatum*
Sorbus
S. aria 93, 95; *S.a.* 'Lutescens' 137i
S. aucuparia 161
S. cashmiriana 54, 55, 166i
S. commixta 161i; *S.c.*'Embley' 165b
S. hupehensis var. *obtusa* 95i
S. 'Joseph Rock' 163b
S. prattii 166
S. sargentiana 46, 163i
Spetchley Park, Worcestershire 91
Spiraea 'Arguta' 123
spring
borders, vibrant 64–6
bulbs 91, 92, 112–13
colour 112–21, 122–33
favourite planting groups 182
spurge see *Euphorbia*
spurge laurel see *Daphne laureola*
Stachys
S. byzantina 56i; *S.b.* 'Big Ears' 88, 138i; *S.b.* 'Silver Carpet' 57
S. macrantha 'Superba' 141i
Stachyurus 113, 178
S. chinensis 178
S. 'Magpie' 113
S. praecox 113, 178i
Staphylea
S. holocarpa 'Rosea' 129
S. pinnata 129
stems, ornamental 181
see also bark
Sternbergia lutea 45, 164–5
Stewartia pseudocamellia 137i
Sticky Wicket, Dorset 17
Stipa
S. gigantea 47, 65, 67i, 151i, 183i
S. tenuissima 43i, 171i, 183i
Strong, Roy 33
Stuart-Smith, Tom 87
subtropical plants 30–1
summer
early colour 134–47
favourite planting groups 182–3
late colour 148–59
vibrant combinations 66–7
summer snowflake see *Leucojum aestivum*
sunflower see *Helianthus*
sunny positions
favourite planting groups for 182–3
formal planting for 79
sweet cicely see *Myrrhis odorata*
sweet gum see *Liquidambar*
sweet rocket see *Hesperis matronalis*
sweet woodruff see *Galium odoratum*
Symphoricarpos albus 54, 166, 166i
Symphytum caucasicum 96, 127i
Syringa
S. meyeri 'Palibin' 84
S. vulgaris 'Katherine Havemeyer' 52i, 53

T
Tanacetum parthenium (feverfew) 138i
Taxus baccata 43, 61, 77
teasels 87
Teucrium fruticans 57, 78
Thalictrum
T. aquilegiifolium 53i; *T.a.* var. *album* 139
T. flavum 'Illuminator' 34i
T. lucidum 144
T. rochebruneanum 62–3i
Thermopsis rhombifolia 144
Thomson, George 16
Thoughts on Garden Design 103
Thymus × citriodorus 'Silver Queen' 57
Tiarella wherryi 125b
Tilia cordata 'Winter Orange' 46
Tithonia rotundifolia 'Torch' 67
topiary 77, 84
town gardens 82–5, 103
Tradescant, John 12
Tradescantia 141
T. Andersoniana Group 'Concord Grape' 141i
tree poppy see *Romneya coulteri*
trees
autumn colour 162–3b
conifers, specimen 174
espalier 84
pleached 77
white-flowered 55, 122–3
for woodland gardens 95
see also under individual species
trellis 61, 103i, 105
Trifolium
T. ochroleucon 140i
T. repens 'Purpurascens Quadrifolium' 39
Trillium
T. cernuum 124
T. chloropetalum 124
T. erectum f. *luteum* 125b
T. grandiflorum 55, 96i, 124i
T. ovatum 124
Tritonia disticha subsp. *rubrolucens* 157b
Trollius
T. chinensis 100i, 126i, 127
T.× cultorum: T.× c. 'Alabaster' 126; *T.× c.* 'Cheddar' 100; *T.× c.* 'Earliest of All' 126 *T.× c.* 'Lemon Queen' 53
Tropaeolum speciosum 20i, 150i
Tudor gardens 11–12
Tulbaghia violacea 157b
Tulipa 12i, 46, 117, 130–1
early-flowering 46, 117
plant profile 130–1
T. 'Angélique' 131i
T. 'Apeldoorn' 131
T. 'Apricot Beauty' 66, 131
T. 'Arabian Mystery' 131
T. 'Attila' 130i, 131, 173i
T. 'Ballerina' 46
T. 'Berlioz' 113
T. biflora 117
T. 'Black Hero' 52, 79i
T. 'Blue Diamond' 130i, 131
T. 'Blue Parrot' 131
T. 'Blueberry Ripple' 131i
T. 'Cape Cod' 131
T. 'China Pink' 51, 131
T. clusiana 117
T. 'Daydream' 46
T. 'Generaal de Wet' 46, 66
T. 'Golden Apeldoorn' 66
T. 'Groenland' 131
T. humilis 'Eastern Star' 117
T. kaufmanniana 113
T. linifolia Batalinii Group 'Bronze Charm' 46
T. 'Orange Emperor' 46, 130i
T. 'Orange Favourite' 46
T. 'Oranje Nassau' 46
T. orphanidea Whittallii Group 91
T. 'Pink Impression' 130i
T. polychroma 117
T. praestans 'Fusilier' 66, 131
T. 'Prinses Irene' 41, 46i
T. 'Purissima' 54, 125i, 131i
T. 'Queen of Night' 38i, 52, 131i
T. 'Red Impression' 66i
T. saxatalis Bakeri Group 'Lilac Wonder' 117i
T. 'Schoonoord' 131
T. 'Snow Parrot' 79
T. sprengeri 48, 91, 130
T. 'Spring Green' 43, 131
T. sylvestris 131
T. tarda 115i, 130
T. turkestanica 116i, 117
T. 'West Point' 131i
T. 'White Parrot' 54
T. 'White Triumphator' 40, 54i, 55, 182i
T. 'World's Favorite' 48i, 49
tulipomania 38, 130
Turner, J.M.W. 26–7

U
urban gardens 82–5, 103
Uvularia grandiflora 45, 125b, 126i

V
Valeriana phu 'Aurea' 66
van Sweden, James 43
variegated shrubs 174
Veratrum nigrum 38, 70
Verbascum 89, 93, 144
V. bombyciferum 144i
V. 'Gainsborough' 144
V. 'Helen Johnson' 50
V. 'Jackie in Pink' 28i
V. olympicum 45, 56
Verbena
V. bonariensis 156i
V. 'Sissinghurst' 143b
Veronica
V. gentianoides 21, 41i, 57, 135
V. peduncularis 135; *V.p.* 'Georgia Blue' 135
V. prostrata 135
V. spicata subsp. *incana* 19i, 57, 135i, 182i
Veronicastrum
V. sibiricum 74i, 75
V. virginicum 'Album' 87
Viburnum 176
V.× bodnantense: V.× b. 'Charles Lamont' 51i; *V.× b.* 'Dawn' 117, 180i
V.× burkwoodii 'Anne Russell' 61i, 117i
V.× carlcephalum 122
V. davidii 34
V. farreri 51, 176i
V. opulus 165b; *V.o.* 'Compactum' 55; *V.o.* 'Roseum' 42i; *V.o.* 'Xanthocarpum' 164
V. plicatum f. *tomentosum* 'Mariesii' 58i, 122i
V. tinus 82i, 84, 117, 176; *V.t.* 'Eve Price' 51
Vinca 97
V. major 'Variegata' 175i
V. minor 'Azurea Flore Pleno' 141b
Viola
V. 'Bowles' Black' 39, 79
V. cornuta 53

V. riviniana 116; *V.r.* Purpurea Group 53
violet, colour see purple/violet
violets 52–3, 87, 89, 90, 107, 116
Virginia creeper see *Parthenocissus quinquefolia*
Vitis
V. coignetiae 162i
V. vinifera 'Purpurea' 76i, 162

W
walls 103–4
see also boundary planting; fences/railings; trellis
water gardens 98–101
dramatic foliage for 100–1
natural schemes for 98–100
water lilies 99
water plantain see *Alisma*
Watsonia 'Stanford Scarlet' 49
Weigela
W. BRIANT RUBIDOR ('Olympiade') 69, 70i
W. 'Bristol Ruby' 49
W. 'Eva Rathke' 69, 71i
W. florida 'Foliis Purpureis' 69
W. 'Florida Variegata' 51
West Green House, Hampshire 17
Whateley, Thomas 14
white plants 54–5
autumn colour 166
with black/silver 79
dogwoods 55
rhododendrons/azaleas 132
roses, recommended 145
for shady areas 54
shrubs/trees, spring 122–3
spring-flowering 114, 122–5
summer-flowering 137–40, 157
tulips 131
winter-flowering 176–7
woodland perennials 124–5
white/silver bark 175–6
White Windows, Hampshire 32i, 35i, 88i
whitebeam see *Sorbus aria*
wild carrot 87
Wild Garden, The 16
wildflowers
in cottage gardens 87, 89–90
meadows 30, 90–1
wind-resistant plants 92
winter
colour 25i, 172–81
favourite planting groups 183
winter aconite see *Eranthis*
winter-flowering daphnes 181
Wisley, RHS Garden 30i
Wisteria
W. floribunda 53
W. sinensis 127
witch hazel see *Hamamelis*
wood lily see *Trillium*
woodland gardens 94–7
shrubs for 97
white perennials for 124–5

Y
yarrow see *Achillea*
yellow plants 44–5
autumn colour 164–5
plants for shade 45
rhododendrons/azaleas 133
roses, recommended 145
spring-flowering 112–14, 125–7
summer-flowering 143–4, 153–4
tulips 131
winter-flowering 177–8
yew see *Taxus baccata*
Yucca
Y. filamentosa: Y.f. 'Bright Edge' 84; *Y.f.* 'Variegata' 79
Y. flaccida 'Ivory' 157
Y. gloriosa 157
Y. whipplei 157

Z
Zantedeschia aethiopica 55, 55i
Zelkova serrata 163b
Zinnia 'Envy' 43

AUTHOR'S ACKNOWLEDGEMENTS
I would like to thank Andy McIndoe, Sue Gordon, Polly Boyd and Robin Whitecross for their great patience and skill in helping me to write and complete this book. It has been a pleasure to work with them all.

PICTURE CREDITS
The publishers would like to acknowledge with thanks all those whose gardens are pictured in this book.

All photographs were taken by Andrew McIndoe, Kevin Hobbs, John Hillier or Tim Mason with the exception of:

Bridgeman Art Library: 10/Private Collection, Accademia Italiana, London, 14–15/Private Collection, The Stapleton Collection
Patricia Elkington: 89a
Garden Picture Library:
Front cover: top/Chris Burrows, bottom left/Richard Bloom, centre/Steven Knights, right/Mark Bolton; 52b/Howard Rice, 92–93/Sunniva Harte, 93(3)/David Murray, 128a/Neil Holmes, 128b/John Glover
Simple Pleasures Nursery: 114c, 115d, 121c, 131(1), 131(3)
Jane Sterndale-Bennett: 21a, 32, 33a, 34, 35, 39d, 87a, 88, 127 Good Companions (1)
Terry Underhill: 122c, 122 Good Companions (2), 124b